THE

PHILOSOPHY

OF

KARL POPPER

THE
PHILOSOPHY
OF
KARL POPPER

Robert John Ackermann

UNIVERSITY OF MASSACHUSETTS PRESS   AMHERST 1976

Copyright © 1976 by
The University of Massachusetts Press
All rights reserved
Library of Congress Catalog Card Number 75-32480
ISBN 0-87023-198-7

Printed in the United States of America

Second Printing, 1977

Library of Congress Cataloging in Publication Data

Ackermann, Robert John, 1933–
  The philosophy of Karl Popper.
  Bibliography: p.
  Includes index.
    1. Popper, Karl Raimund, Sir, 1902–   I. Title.
B1649.P64A3   192   75-32480
ISBN 0-87023-198-7

CONTENTS

B
1649
P64
A3

PREFACE

Because I am interested in Popper as a contemporary, I have not documented changes in or elaboration of his viewpoints wherever I have discerned them. It is clear, for example, that the Popperian themes of falsifiability and Popperian animadversions against inductivism are basic, that they appear early, and that they remain continuously important and relatively unchanged in Popper's writings. On the other hand, Popper's conception of an evolutionary epistemology, and his insistence that objectivity is to be defined and defended by invocation of the notion of a third world, are relatively recent features of his methodology. They do not appear explicitly in *The Logic of Scientific Discovery*, for example, but they play an important role in *Objective Knowledge*. I have discussed the historical development of Popper's views only where that seemed crucial to understanding his views. In general, I have tried to follow Popper's own advice that the best discussion and criticism are based on the strongest and clearest possible statement of the theory to be criticized and are not to be based on an arbitrary reading of the theory, no matter how well it might be given documentary support. I am therefore presenting and discussing Popper's philosophy as an assembly of what I find to be the strongest Popperian positions that can be gleaned from his writings to date.

I describe my own stance toward Popper as one of great admiration for the major outlines of his achievements and the thrust of his basic insights coupled with friendly criticism of much of the detail. The crude upshot is that I am attracted to Popper's major claims about falsifiability and his arguments against inductivism although I do not agree with Popper on many less important matters. As will become clear, I think in particular that the full development of the evolutionary metaphor of science is incompatible with some other aspects of current Popperian methodology. There seems to be a place at this time for a fairly neutral exposition of and commentary on the Popperian textual material. I have tried hard in this book to indicate why I think Popper one of the philosophers of science most worth studying in detail by examining his major claims and what it is that he regards as the ramified consequences of these claims. Although scholarly apparatus has been kept to a minimum, the views I ascribe to Popper are, I think, ultimately defensible conjectural readings based on the totality of the published texts.

This book is intended not as a popular introduction but as a close examination of Popper's conception of scientific methodology from the standpoint of the present, that is, from the standpoint of seeing what is worthwhile in it for the ongoing philosophical examination of science. Fairly technical matters must consequently be discussed in the text, but I have tried to do this in a manner that will give the reader not familiar with the technical issues a chance to figure out what is going on. At times some expository background material has been included to provide context for the discussion. Because not all readers will want to work at this, and because some readers will already be familiar with the background issues, each chapter and each section within each chapter starts anew in the sense that it does not depend on technical discussion appearing earlier in the text. Readers who find themselves becoming mired will do best to skip ahead to the next section or the next chapter. Each chapter treats one of the important themes in Popper's philosophy; therefore, the reader should know something about Popper's views on the subject matter of each chapter if he is to consider himself familiar with the general structure and overall scope of Popper's philosophy. Chapter themes are emphatically not bits and pieces. They are articulated in a mutually dependent manner based on the grand structure of Popper's conception of methodology. Popper's stature in the philosophy of science is nicely reflected in the variety and importance of the chapter themes.

Popper's views have often been partially accepted by philosophers who have then proceeded to incorporate these views into a philosophical structure which they could not hold (according to Popper) if they were to properly understand the *significance* of Popper's views. A philosopher might, for example, accept some version of Popper's notion that scientific theories should be falsifiable, but yet remain an inductivist. For Popper, this amounts to not understanding falsifiability. There is an associated evangelical flavor about Popper's conjectures and refutations: his object is not only to explain his views but to explain what the views entail for action, much as a preacher may not only explain a text but also argue with people who claim to accept the text that they could not act in the way that they do if they really understood it. Since my own philosophy of science incorporates as basic some ideas which I have learned from Popper but rejects others, my treatment of Popper could be considered simply unorthodox. Its primary intention, however, is to demonstrate and to provide an introduction to the stimulation produced by measuring one's perhaps more scattered observations about methodology against the articulated monistic principles of a master.

Any discussion of Popper must inevitably encounter the views of at least some other philosophers. In order to keep references to a manageable level, I have explicitly mentioned Popper's relationships to just four other philosophers. Rudolf Carnap has been selected as the arch-positivist and has been my choice to stand in as the major target of Popper's animadversions against inductivism. Thomas Kuhn has been selected as the arch-subjectivist and has been my choice to stand in as the major target of Popper's animadversions against subjectivism in methodology. These choices are relatively straightforward in that a considerable literature exists representing Popperian exchanges with these representatives of positivism and subjectivism. Although other disputes have been known, it seems to me that the major features of Popper's positions are most easily discerned in these relationships and that the structure of other disputes is most easily understood by comparison to these. Among those philosophers who have developed neo-Popperian methodological positions, Paul Feyerabend and Imre Lakatos have been selected as representative of heterodox Popperianism for purposes of discussion. The differences between Popper, Feyerabend, and Lakatos are important to understanding the exact outline of Popper's views even if a crude typology of scientific methodologies might tend to lump them together. It has been hard for me to imagine exactly who might be most interested in reading a critical discussion of Popper. I have supposed that a formal or informal student of methodology who has some idea of the views of Carnap and Kuhn and who has at least heard of Feyerabend and Lakatos could easily understand what I have written. Although I have written in a fashion that should be intelligible to readers who do not possess this background, it should be noted that some familiarity with Carnap, Feyerabend, Kuhn, and Lakatos is essential to grasping Popper's importance and the location of his views in the total spectrum of contemporary methodological studies. The book has a bibliography with normal scholarly clues embedded in footnotes to the relevant leads.

The body of this study of Popper was written in 1973 for inclusion in a series of critical studies of modern philosophers. Agreement as to the significance of *critical* in this context was not achieved with the editor of that series, and the text was withdrawn from consideration for publication. In the interval, several important books and quite a number of articles have appeared which are relevant to assessing Popper's views, and I have tried to take these contributions into account without, however, having had an opportunity to fully revise the text. I should like to thank members of my seminar on Popper at the University of Massachusetts, and especially Jim Balmer, Tom McKay, and Greg Mellema, for changing some of my opinions as a result of valid criticism. I should also like to thank Professor D. J. O'Connor, Professor Robert P. Wolff, and Professor Mike Gardner for valuable discussions of Popper's philosophy in other contexts. Referees for the University of Massachusetts Press provided valuable guidance in the last stages of revision. Whoever they may be, they will recognize the final product as a compromise between my idiosyncrasies and the book they know I should have written.

Robert John Ackermann
Amherst, Massachusetts
January, 1975

THE

PHILOSOPHY

OF

KARL POPPER

ONE

Introduction

I Classical Conceptions of Methodology

In describing Sir Karl Raimund Popper as a *classical* philosopher of science I mean to class him with those philosophers who have felt that it was possible to abstract a nontrivial general description of methodology for scientific practice that would characterize scientific knowledge (as opposed to other areas of human interest) and help to explain its achievements.[1] Such a conception of methodology is highly *normative* in that it is not intended to be descriptive of actual scientific practice, but it is intended to describe an idealized standard of rationality that can be read into an explanation of the greatest scientific achievements in the history of the various sciences. Contemporary philosophy of science began in the 1920s and 1930s with a common assumption that some such methodology could be achieved that would enable philosophers to understand science.

The major school of philosophy of science which developed contemporary philosophical issues in connection with methodology in the 1920s and 1930s consisted of a group of philosophers usually known as the logical positivists. For the moment, we may note that the early positivists felt intuitively that scientific knowledge was the paradigm example of human knowledge, at least of human empirical knowledge, because of its greater *certainty* as compared to common-sense observations. Positivists attempted to show that the standards of rigor utilized by scientists in making and recording observations and data provided a foundation for the security, precision, and reliability of the claims made by scientists. From the beginning, Popper has eschewed any notion that preference for scientific knowledge is to be grounded in the greater certainty of scientific knowledge.

Except for a few central ideas involved in a philosophical account of methodology, Popper has assumed that a fine-grain analysis of rationality has to depend on the specific standards of scientists as worked out to suit scientific investigation in the various branches of science. More recently, many philosophers and historians have questioned whether the notion of a common scientific methodology is really useful. They have argued that instead of abstracting an idealized notion of rationality and then looking for cases of it in scientific history, we should simply describe great scientific achievements and accept the fact that they occur in diverse ways. The difficulty with this point of view is that simple and naive description is of no value in trying to understand science. Clearly not all of the activities of a scientist are relevant to understanding what he is doing as a scientist. We want to know what it is that is important about what he is doing and what it is that is relatively unimportant. Methodology is the effort to suggest a system of values that will draw this distinction. Some scientists have self-consciously adopted methodologies for research and practice and followed them carefully, but we should be prepared to find that many scientists have not designed their research to accommodate a methodology. In particular, we should be prepared to find that many innovative and creative scientists broke any particular set of specific rules that might have been projected from the details of scientific practice in their fields. If we could find a methodology that would be useful from the standpoint of understanding scientific practice, we should not be prepared to expect that it would fit all the details of actual practice. We would have to read its features into practice in order to see something illuminating about the practice. Historians may argue that *any* nontrivial generalization about scientific methodology can be counterexampled by an important scientist who violated the rules. Popper would not deny this. Historians should not argue that what is valid about a conception of scientific methodology should be induced from particular biographies. That is not possible. We need a conception of scientific methodology to understand the biographies. There is nothing in this that precludes an interplay between methodological reflection and scientific history; we should expect these activities to influence one another.

What has just been said would not have seemed so obvious forty years ago. When contemporary philosophy of science began, it was hoped that a *logic* of science could be discovered which would accurately capture the structure of sound scientific inference. There are, of course, some neopositivists in whose hearts this hope still burns. The moderate view developed above for reconciling history and methodology has the consequence of making methodology irredeemably ideological. Many true things, most of them virtually vacuous, can be said about science. Methodology wants more. Methodologists want to say true things about science that help us to understand why we do not regard science and theology, or science and art, as the same. It is premised on the supposition that science is somehow different from other known human activities. But we cannot expect that a methodology that can do this will explain everything about science. We should not expect that a person could do good science by learning methodology and then plugging in a few values for variables so as to practice a specific science. Methodology may give a scientist perspective on what he is doing, and its self-conscious application may supply a useful corrective in eliminating some activity that the scientist now feels himself is wasteful, or beside the point. Nevertheless, the detailed work of science depends primarily on detailed scientific knowledge and detailed information about the specific procedures that scientists in an area have found useful. Chance, luck, analogical insight, etc., will obviously play a role that would defeat any general methodology attempting to describe a method for making scientific discoveries and advancing scientific knowledge. The problem of methodology is then whether a useful characterization of *scientific* activity and *scientific* knowledge is possible at an appropriate level of abstraction for differentiating scientific practice from other sorts of human activity.

It is probably not worthwhile here to argue whether or not a general conception of scientific activity as captured in a methodological description of science is possible or valuable: it is a simple fact that philosophers and scientists have found it worthwhile for the reasons suggested to try and state a relatively clear and simple conception of scientific methodology. What is Popper's characterization? Put most simply, it is this:

> The method of science is the method of bold conjectures and ingenious and severe attempts to refute them.[2]

In this brief statement we may discern the outlines of the twin claims that Popper advances against positivism and against subjectivism, or historical relativism. Science advances *conjectures*, not *certain* information. Herein lies the heart of Popper's quarrel with logical positivism. The attempted refutation of scientific conjectures turns out to be a public process in which definite progress can be traced. Herein lies the heart of Popper's quarrel with subjectivism. Scientific preference is (ideally) given, not to those ideas which bring about some feeling of subjective satisfaction to scientists, but to those ideas which at any time have withstood the critical scrutiny, both intellectual and experimental, of other scientists. A key to understanding Popper is to appreciate his twin concerns to reject *certainty* as a criterion of scientific knowledge and yet to retain *objectivity* as a distinguishing feature of the growth and success of scientific knowledge.

The cornerstones of Popper's more detailed criticism of certainty in science are his positions on falsifiability and induction. Briefly, falsifiability is what distinguishes scientific conjectures as *refutable* from metaphysical claims. Metaphysical claims will include all nonfalsifiable interesting claims to knowledge or valuable opinion which we do not regard as nonsense. Metaphysics is *not* nonsense for Popper. Falsifiability (capacity for refutation) explains why science can have a high growth rate as an area of human knowledge. Falsifiability is, of course, a normative concept; it suggests that scientists (ideally) are perpetually critical and severe not only of the work of others but of their own work. Science progresses by rejecting falsified views in favor of new conjectures. Such a development of ideas is accelerated by sharp criticism and a willingness to accept the fact that one's favorite views have been refuted. Falsifiability would impose a stringent code of honor that few actual scientists can support psychologically in their day-to-day work. By way of contrast to the methodology of falsification, proponents of induction have claimed that there is a way of establishing that scientific statements are true, or at least probable. Induction and falsifiability are seen by Popper to be ultimately at odds. Scientists are not correctly seen as proving things true or probably true. They are to be seen (insofar as they are rational) as desiring to eliminate bad views and as wanting to construct new and better theories and explanations. Popper must show that induction has no important role to play in science if falsifiability is to play the methodologically central role he has laid out for it. Falsifiability and counterinductivism are thus closely related in Popper's general methodology.

Popper is primarily interested in the *growth* of scientific knowledge. Falsifiability can be extended to result in an evolutionary conception of the growth of such knowledge. Problems present themselves and are the stimulus for the growth of scientific knowledge. Explanations in the form of objective theories are proposed to provide solutions to the problems. Bad theories are eliminated when they are found to conflict with objective experimental fact. A series of new problems and new theories gradually brings about an elaboration of scientific knowledge which is gradually more and more adequate in the sense that it is explanatory of a wider and wider range of historical problems. The resulting evolutionary conception of the growth of knowledge is perhaps Popper's outstanding contribution to the philosophy of science.

If we can treat the history of science as a gradual evolution of refuted conjectures, and in this way attack certainty or probable truth as a paradigm property of scientific knowledge, there remains the problem of showing that science is distinguished from other human endeavor by the *ob-*

jectivity of its claims. The struggle against subjectivism has recently occupied a greater place in Popper's attention that it has in the past. This has undoubtedly occurred because so many philosophers have embraced some form of subjectivism in reaction to the gradual dissolution of the positivist movement. Verisimilitude and world 3 are Popper's key concepts in arguing against subjectivism and historical relativism. These ideas will be discussed in some detail later. In many ways, the struggle against subjectivism undertaken in Popper's philosophy is a more subtle strain than the struggle against certainty as a criterion in logical positivism. Against logical positivism one may use plausible arguments from the history of science, but not against historical relativism. If we try simply to look at the history of science, it may appear that there is chaos, that each scientist works almost alone in a unique conceptual world, and that although change and adaptation occur there is nothing that can reasonably be characterized as definite progress. A first line of defense against relativism and subjectivism is that it can't provide any basis for the intuition that scientific knowledge is particularly valuable. Subjectivism or relativism tells us that there is no method in science, that everyone simply does what he wants, and that various ideas, for inexplicable reasons, are more appealing to a majority of scientific practitioners in retrospect than are some others. As against this, it is always interesting to ask what would refute various scientific hypotheses (even if we can't always say), and it sometimes illuminates the purpose of experimentation to try to see what conjectures the possible data might refute. Thus methodology may enable us to bring order to scientific history even if it is difficult to fit it to all of the details of scientific history.

The themes just introduced will occupy us throughout our examination of Popper's philosophical account of methodology. In opposition to logical positivism, we will find in Popper some fairly sharp issues and resolutions of them which have, historically at least, forced an accommodation to Popper's views by the positivists. *Conjectural* knowledge is an important aspect of scientific knowledge, and Popper's views here have had wide influence. In opposition to what he calls subjectivism or historical relativism, we will find Popper's arguments less clear and considerably less overwhelming. Surely Popper is right that scientific knowledge is objective. The problem lies in considering what sense Popper can give to objectivity in combating the views that he finds inadequate. Perhaps the deepest problem in putting Popper together in a unified exposition is whether or not the evolutionary picture of conjectures invoked by Popper to explain the growth of scientific knowledge is at bottom compatible with his effort to achieve a description of science as achieving a closer and closer approximation to truth over time, a description he relies on in rejecting historical relativism.

II Verifiability and Dogmatic Falsifiability

Two cornerstones of Popper's views about scientific methodology are his conception of falsifiability as a way of distinguishing genuinely scientific statements from nonscientific statements and his related view that there is no inductive method for gaining (new) scientific knowledge or for proving scientific assertions to be true. In this section we will discuss background problems that helped to organize Popper's views about falsifiability. These problems will enable us to define a view about falsifiability that is not Popper's, is not a defensible view, but is a view widely attributed to Popper by casual philosophical historians who are familiar with positivism and tend to see Popper in the context of positivistic issues.

The major background problem for understanding falsifiability was explicitly raised by the logical positivists.[3] Positivist views of the sort we will discuss were worked out between 1917 and 1930. This is not the place to consider the history of logical positivism in detail. Our purpose here is to describe positivism sufficiently to achieve an understanding of Popper's views about falsifiability which stand in opposition to much that is in positivism, although they are quite clearly influenced by positivism. Positivism was motivated by a feeling of confusion and disgust at the mess which positivists thought they saw in the science and philosophy of their time. Science had just undergone two important conceptual revolutions as a result of the advent of quantum and relativity physics. The new physics contained many philosophical and conventional claims. In Einstein's special relativity theory, for example, it was assumed rather than proved by experimental evidence that various transmissions of light rays had equal velocity as measured in different reference frames. Physics had drifted so far from experimental and observational fact that physicists were squabbling like philosophers, and the positivists hoped to rescue objectivity in science by finding a definitive basis for resolving these scientific disputes. The usual course to take with a mess is to start by cleaning up thoroughly, and the positivists did this with a vengeance. Their intention was to sweep everything out and to reconstruct legitimate scientific knowledge on a clean platform only in terms of what could be proved true by inescapable facts according to a philosophical strategy based on incontrovertible assumptions. It's easy to see now why this couldn't have worked, but it provided a lot of excitement among the early positivists and their attempts to work out such a project have taught us a great deal about science.

The major technical tool of positivism was modern symbolic logic as it had been developed by Whitehead and Russell in *Principia Mathematica*.[4] *Principia* had itself been written to work out a reconstruction of mathematics not unlike the reconstruction positivists hoped to do to science. Russell and Whitehead hoped to achieve the development of the mathematics necessary for science by logical development from axioms stating either logical truths or manifestly true claims about the integers.[5] The purpose of this program was to insure that mathematics was free from internal contradiction. Positivists accepted the *Principia* program as a successful solution to the problem of mathematical knowledge. Using *Principia* notation, a logician would hold that a meaningful English sentence (or a sentence of any other natural language) could be translated into a symbolic expression which would reveal its true, or underlying, logical form. We will ignore sentences so meaningless or confused that they couldn't be translated into symbolic expression. Consider all of the symbolic expressions which would represent English sentences under such a system of translation. Some of these expressions could be shown by logical techniques alone to be either true or false. These expressions were thought to correspond to the *analytic* sentences of English. By the *Principia* program, mathematical statements were thought to be translated into the class of analytic sentences, as well as all other claims either logically true or false. Positivists were interested in the remaining sentences, the *synthetic* sentences expressing claims that were not necessarily true or false. Synthetic sentences would be true or false depending on the facts. Historically, there were many positivist programs for dealing with the synthetic sentences, but the basic intuition was to look for a way of including clearly scientific and meaningful sentences among the synthetic sentences and banning the (presumably meaningless) sentences of metaphysics, aesthetics, politics, and so forth. Various translation schemes were constructed to attempt this. For example, a positivist might argue that only a certain class of symbolic expressions and all logical combinations of these expressions could express meaningful sentences. Unless a sentence could be translated into some logical construction involving only these symbolic expressions, it would be regarded as meaningless. We cannot review positivist programs here. For our purposes, the point is that positivists wished to divide meaningful from meaningless sentences and to subdivide the meaningful sentences into analytic and synthetic sentences. The synthetic sentences were precisely the domain of empirical science, and hence of human empirical knowledge. All of these lines of demarcation were intended to be sharp in the sense that a given sentence would clearly fall on one side or the other. The class of synthetic sentences was regarded as the class of candidates for scientific knowledge, or at the very least as containing the candidates for scientific knowledge.

The question of which synthetic sentences were true was to be decided by a class of simple observation sentences of some kind. Whether or not these sentences were true or false could be definitely decided because they represented minimal observation claims. Some positivists used basic observation sentences corresponding to incorrigible personal impressions, and others used basic observation sentences corresponding to elementary physical measurements.[6] The hope was that some class of basic observation sentences could be found that could be used to define the truth or falsity of all synthetic sentences as logical functions of the truth or falsity of the basic observation sentences. We will content ourselves here with noting that a positivistic criterion of meaningfulness will be relative to a set of basic observation sentences that will be used to represent facts in determining the class of scientifically meaningful sentences. The simplest basic observations sentences (we will call them simple observation sentences) will in all cases correspond roughly to scientific data; their truth or falsity should be regarded as manifest to a careful observer who makes a certain kind of observation.

The next question that arises for positivism is how to use the class of simple observation sentences, no matter how it is characterized in detail, to work out an adequate criterion of meaningfulness. At first, positivism adopted an extremely tough criterion that will be paraphrased here as follows:

> An English sentence S is meaningful if and only if it is analytic or it is synthetic and is logically implied by a finite number of simple observation sentences that are consistent with one another.[7]

Here we are only concerned with the synthetic sentences. Consistency of the simple observation sentences is mentioned to insure the consistency of S. If a sentence satisfies this definition, its truth may be *verified* in the following sense: if the finite number of simple observation sentences are all verified to be true by observation, then S must be true since it is a logical consequence of these true sentences. The background program is to build up scientific knowledge on the basis of accumulating verified simple observation sentences and the sentences that they imply. Unfortunately, this first criterion proved defective. There are at least three objections to the criterion worth noting.

The first objection to the criterion of meaning worth noting is a relatively trivial formal objection that had some psychological bite because of the positivist commitment to *Principia* (Standard) logic. Positivists intended to mark off meaningful from nonmeaningful sentences and to purge the latter from consideration with the idea that the resultant true meaningful sentences would constitute science (human knowledge). Now let S be a meaningful sentence and N a nonmeaningful sentence obtained from theology, ethics, aesthetics, or whatever. The disjunction of S and N, which we can formalize as $S \vee N$ (either S or N), is also a sentence to be dealt with. Propositional logic shows us that $S \vee N$ is a logical consequence of S which in turn is a logical consequence of a consistent finite class of observation sentences (containing just $S!$). Therefore $S \vee N$ is meaningful according to the criterion. Since the meaningless sentence N is a component of $S \vee N$, this is sufficient to show that the sentences accepted as meaningful by the criterion may contain meaningless component sentences. The criterion does not enable the positivist to mark out *only* the intuitively meaningful sentences and is hence defective with respect to accomplishing the positivist goal. A reason for regarding this objection as relatively trivial is that it could be circumvented by using a (nonstandard) relevance logic in which $S \vee N$ was not a logical consequence of S, and it could also be circumvented by placing further restrictions on the translation idea, as will be noted shortly.

A second and much more important objection is obtained by noting that the original objection does not permit inclusion of scientific laws and hypotheses insofar as they are generalized statements since generalized statements are not derivable from any *finite* class of instantiations of their claims. What is at stake here is well known to logicians but can be conveyed by a simple example. Suppose we consider the generalized statement, "All crows are black."[8] The truth of this statement cannot follow from a finite number of observation statements to the effect that particular crows have been observed to be black. Therefore the general statement could be false in spite of any finite number of observations. Unless I know that the crows I have observed are all of the crows that there are to be observed, any finite number of observations is insufficient to establish the truth of the general claim. A generalized statement cannot follow from a finite class of simple observation sentences by logical inference. A generalized statement might follow from a finite class of simple observation sentences plus a sentence to the effect that the finite class exhausted all relevant data, but this latter sentence could not be a simple observation sentence. It is generally agreed that scientific theories and hypotheses essentially contain generalized statements in the form of laws. Positivism cannot accommodate generalized statements in terms of the first criterion and hence cannot account for the meaningfulness of general laws. Philosophers of science now regard scientific laws as "open-ended" in a sense which entails that scientists could never assert that they had observed all electrons or crows because of the possibility that new ones will appear later in time or in some unexplored area of the universe. There is thus no hope that the criterion could be amended so as to add the kind of clause that would enable general statements to be derivable from a finite class of simple observation sentences in conjunction with some claim about the exhaustive nature of the observation sentences. This second objection to the positivist criterion is crippling. Positivism simply cannot account for the truth of general statements involving theoretical terms since such

truth cannot be reduced to the truth of finite classes of observation sentences. This objection was noted early on by Popper and appears in *The
Logic of Scientific Discovery*. One way to avoid this objection compatibly
with positivism is to argue that general laws play no important role in
scientific explanation, and we will see a variant of this argument later in
connection with Carnap's inductive logic, but this position seems to violate strong intuitions based on the history of science.

A third objection to the positivist criterion is basically philosophical.
What is the status of the sentence announcing the positivist criterion of
meaning? It would seem not to be analytic, and it seems also not to be
synthetic in that it cannot conceivably be the logical consequence of a
finite set of observation sentences. By the positivist criterion of meaning,
therefore, the positivist criterion has to be regarded as meaningless.[9] There
is a pragmatic paradox involved in the juxtaposition of positivist claims
about meaningful language and their own use of language in arguing for
their philosophical program. The three objections just noticed seem sufficient to refute positivism as it is reflected in the first criterion of meaningfulness.

Historically, the positivist reaction to these objections was to attempt
greater sophistication in the step of translation into logical form. Various
methods of relating scientific statements to simple observation sentences
were attempted, but all of them seem to have failed.[10] A later idea was to
abandon the suggestion that sentences be translated into logical notation
one at a time and to set up an ideal meaningful language with specific
predicates and axiomatic structure and to make translation into this postulated language the criterion of meaningfulness. Such a program clearly
gives up any idea of grounding meaning in observation and instead allows
the positivist to express his prejudices in the form of stipulative
definitions regarding the syntax and semantics of the ideal language. It is
not useful here to examine the historical development in greater detail.
None of the revised positivistic criteria is free from severe difficulties. For
example, the axiomatic approach must take each different (nonequivalent)
axiom system to define a different theory. There does not seem to be a
principle which is internally suitable on positivistic grounds for explaining when two different theories by this criterion can be regarded as different formulations of the same physical theory and when they should be
regarded as formulations of two different theories.

The positivistic use of axiom systems is related to the fact that positivists hold the view that the development of science is irrational in the sense
that it cannot be predicted in detail. One cannot even predict precisely
what facts will be discovered to obtain. They draw the conclusion that the
philosophy of science cannot be concerned with the development of science over time. Even if a positivistic robot could be constructed to do the

work of a scientist, it would have to determine facts first and then adjust its theoretical weightings to conform to factual discovery. What philosophers can do according to positivism is to exhibit and assess the logical structure of science at some (reconstructed) time slice. Developing systems in science are usually studied by close examination of temporally frozen systems at selected points in their development. Positivists suppose that at a particular time slice a clear distinction between meaningful and nonmeaningful sentences and/or terms is both possible and useful and that this is the important contribution that a philosopher can make to understanding science. There is no doubt that axiomatizations useful for understanding scientific theories can be constructed in the manner suggested by positivism. What is at issue is whether their usefulness can be explained within a positivistic methodological account of science, or whether their usefulness presupposes a nonpositivistic account of scientific development. We will see later that, while Popper holds that the future of science is unpredictable in detail, he also holds that there are interesting things to say about the development of scientific knowledge at a suitably general level and that the *development* of scientific knowledge is the most important object of study for a philosopher who wishes to understand science. He is consequently not interested in the fine detail of time-slice structures, and it is not surprising that his philosophy of science will diverge sharply from positivism in many respects because it is directed primarily to understanding scientific growth and development. When Popper examines a time slice, he is interested in the related ambiguities and developing regions as well as in the areas where sharp logical relationships can plausibly be drawn. He is consequently not interested in resolving ambiguity by explication or legislation of artificially sharp distinctions.

It is perhaps worth noting that the sketch of positivistic motivation just completed fits easily with a personality in which fear of error plays an important role. The attraction of positivism seems to be partly that the reconstructed time slices cannot be repudiated by later developments in science because they entail nothing about development. If hypothesis h is much better confirmed than hypothesis i in a time slice, this is a fact quite compatible with the idea that i could be better confirmed than h in a later time slice. Given the time slice, however, one can argue that it is manifestly correct to act as though h were true and i false with respect to the given time slice. Positivism, in spite of its attempt to wipe the slate clean and start over, which gives it a revolutionary appearance, seems deeply conservative at root. The positivist believes that science grows by the accumulation of simple observation sentences discovered to be true which form an incontrovertible basis for scientific theorizing, and he thinks that philosophy of science grows by the accumulation of logical analyses of time slices of scientific theorizing tracing the logical connections between the observational base and available theory in the time slices. The past, in both cases, is enormously important and is the foundation of the present. By contrast, we will see that Popper's apparent conservatism is deeply revolutionary. He sees evolutionary theory as a guideline for scientific development in which the significance of the past can simply disappear and a comparatively new start be made if the environment changes in a sufficiently drastic manner.

Before we turn to deeper differences between Popperian philosophy of science and positivism, it is necessary to deal with the view about falsification that can be described against the positivistic backdrop as a move in the positivist game, but which is decidedly not Popperian. Let us go back to the original statement of the positivist criterion of meaning and change it to the following:

> A sentence is meaningful if and only if $\sim S$ (the negation of S) is significant and is logically implied by a finite number of simple observation sentences that are consistent with one another.

This *falsifiability* criterion has some advantages over the verifiability criterion proposed earlier. Instead of requiring that a meaningful scientific statement be verifiable because it is the logical consequence of an appropriate class of simple observation sentences, we require that a meaningful scientific statement be falsifiable because its negation is the consequence of some finite class of simple observation sentences which might be discovered to be true by careful observation. As a result, we can handle the important objection made to the verifiability criterion that it will not handle generalized statements. "All crows are black" is now meaningful because its negation, "Some crow is not black," is the consequence of any finite consistent class of simple observation sentences which together report the sighting of one or more nonblack crows. The falsifiability criterion stated here, it should be noted, is entirely compatible with positivism and might be regarded as a version of positivism. It may in fact be a version of positivism contemplated at one time by Popper before he worked out his different views about falsifiability. Just as the verifiability criterion was open to three major objections, this falsifiability criterion is open to three objections which closely parallel the objections to the verifiability criterion.

We will not spend much time on the parallel objections to the falsifiability criterion, but they may be constructed as follows. Let S and N be as before. Then if S is satisfied by the falsifiability criterion, so is $S \wedge N$ (the conjunction of S and N) since its negation $\sim(S \wedge N)$ is equivalent to the disjunction $\sim S \vee \sim N$ which is a consequence of the same consistent finite class of simple observation sentences that ~*S* is a consequence of. The second objection to the verifiability criterion is paralleled by an objection that no sentence of the form "Some *A*'s are not *B*'s" could be meaningful, since the negation of such a sentence is equivalent to "All *A*'s are *B*'s" which, as we have seen, is not the logical consequence of a consistent finite class of simple observation sentences.[11] But some sentences of this form seem to play an important role in science. The third objection requires no explicit parallel, since it applies to the falsifiability criterion as well as to the verifiability criterion.

We will call this version of positivistic falsifiability *dogmatic falsificationism*.[12] Everyone reading this book will know by now that Popper's name is associated with some kind of falsifiability doctrine. On many occasions dogmatic falsificationism has been attributed to Popper as his view of falsifiability, and then Popper has supposedly been taken care of by trotting out the objections to dogmatic falsificationism that we have just described. Having stated the outlines of dogmatic falsificationism and its origins in a formal variant of the positivistic verifiability criterion, we can now turn to examination of the conflict between its presuppositions and important doctrines held by Popper.

It seems sufficient to give two basic positivistic presuppositions of dogmatic falsificationism explicitly repudiated by Popper. Positivists assumed that the class of simple observation sentences could be determined completely independently of considerations of theory, so that accumulating true observation sentences constitutes a kind of neutral basis on which theorizing occurs. By contrast, Popper takes the *origin* of scientific knowledge to be common-sense grasp of certain problems, or problem situations: "Accordingly I assert that we do not start from observations but always from *problems*—either from practical problems or from *a theory which has run into difficulties*."[13] With acknowledgments to Kantian themes, Popper holds the view that all observations are theory laden and hence that simple observation sentences cannot be regarded as determined in advance of all considerations of theory. Popper's observational corpus, as we will see in the next chapter, depends on methodological agreement by scientists. When a problem arises that causes us to question the status of a theory, not only the theory but all observations made with that theory as background become open to question. In methodology, then, we should consider the possibility that *any* particular item of scientific information might be overthrown by the discovery of a problem and its resolution. This susceptibility to criticism allows for scientific growth which is compatible with far-reaching theoretical changes in science, growth that is difficult to reconcile with the fixed observational basis of positivism.

The second positivistic presupposition repudiated by Popper is that a

falsifiability criterion should be a criterion of *meaning*. Popper's falsifiability criterion is *not* a criterion of meaning; indeed, many nonfalsifiable
statements will have a perfectly clear meaning in Popper's view. As will
become clear in the next chapter, Popper is attacking quite a different
problem with his falsifiability criterion than the problem of meaning
attacked by the positivists.

TWO

Popper against Positivism

I The Problem of Demarcation and Methodological Falsificationism

Popper takes science to be an extension of common-sense knowledge. In this he shares an opinion with the pragmatists although his version of naive realism and his contention that theories are (potentially) true or false statements mean that Popper cannot be regarded as a variety of pragmatist. Popper's feeling that science is an extension of common-sense knowledge has the consequence that *we already have* a rough-and-ready satisfactory preliminary understanding of the difference between significant and nonsignificant sentences, and an understanding of what theories and explanations are. At various times Popper attempts clarification of the role of theories and explanations in science, but he does not suppose that relevant terms need be defined in terms of some primitive philosophical vocabulary which is thought to be antecedently clearer.

The aim of science, according to Popper, is explanation.[1] Suitable explanations enable us to solve the problems that stimulate scientific research. What makes science different is the fact that scientific explanations explain the known in terms of unknown but (purportedly) real objects that are postulated by high-level scientific theories. Popper was one of the first philosophers to propose the deductive model of scientific explanation. What is explained (the *explicandum*) in a scientific explanation must be a logical consequence of the explaining sentences (the *explicans*). Very little elaboration of this requirement appears in Popper, but the re-

15

quirement is natural in the sense that if an explicandum were shown not to follow logically from an explicans used to explain it a scientist would surely want to revise the explanation by finding a better explicans or give it up altogether. The rest of the requirements that are placed on the explicans are suggested in an effort to prevent explanations satisfying the deductive model from having certain intuitively undesirable features, such as being completely trivial. The sentences of the explicans should be known to be true in virtue of our methodological rules or, if that is not possible (as in the case of theories), they should not be falsified even after close critical examination and attempts to falsify them by experiment and observation.[2] Later we will see that what is wanted in the explicans is well-corroborated theories. A satisfactory explicans will be as falsifiable as possible in that it will make the strongest claims compatible with what is to be explained and various intuitions about the nature of satisfactory scientific hypotheses and theories. Popper's falsifiability criterion is not a criterion of meaning but a criterion designed to help us find satisfactory hypotheses and theories to use in scientific explanations within the class of intuitively meaningful sentences.

It may not be clear why the theories to be used in scientific explanations should be falsifiable in the sense that they must be incompatible with at least some possible observations. The motivation for this is explained by Popper as a reaction to astrology, Marxism, and psychoanalysis.[3] Popper felt (in 1919) that these "theories" were examples of "pseudo-science" rather than science, and he was concerned to find some explanation for their vacuity with respect to physics. The suspect theories provide plenty of explanations; what Popper noticed was that they could explain anything *after* the fact, partly because of vagueness in their crucial concepts and because of a lack of precise rules for applying these concepts to actual cases. While the fact that they could explain anything was thought by some of their adherents to be the strongest argument in their favor, it struck Popper that this was their greatest weakness. These theories were simply not related conceptually to possible situations which could show them false, or to situations that would discriminate between them and rivals. What is different about the theories of physics (or at least most of them) is that they make sharp predictions about what will happen in certain experimental circumstances and are hence easily falsified if something else happens. This capacity for decisive falsification was taken by Popper to be the hallmark of genuine scientific theories as opposed to pseudo-scientific or common-sense theories.

It might easily seem at this point that Popper's falsifiability notion has not really been described in a way that reveals a fundamental difference from the notion of dogmatic falsificationism discussed in the last chapter. The difference will become clearer with the express observation that

Popper does not regard the explicans of a typical explanation to consist simply of scientific hypotheses or theories that are individually falsifiable. Falsifiable *sentences* are not what science is after. "The world will disintegrate in exactly 1/2-second" may be easily falsified, but it is hard to see how it could be used in explanation. Actual scientific explanations will have explicata that will contain laws, hypotheses, or theories as well as simple observation sentences reporting boundary conditions, perhaps various existentially quantified sentences, and so forth. All of these kinds of sentences may be required in a particular explicans, and all of them can make sense and be significant. Popper is not accepting dogmatic falsifiability as a criterion of meaning for *each* sentence occurring in a scientific explanation. His views are consequently not threatened by the earlier arguments directed at positivism suggesting that a sharp distinction between meaningful and meaningless sentences cannot be drawn. Since many statements may appear in an explicans, an interesting situation arises if the explicandum turns out to be falsified. One or more of the statements in the explicans must then be false as a matter of logic, but logic cannot tell us which statements in particular should be regarded as falsified. Conventionalism is the view that particular laws or theories can be retained in science even though explanations involving them are found to have false explicanda. They can always be retained by blaming other statements in the explicata giving rise to putative explanations of false statements. Popper holds that scientific explanations and the methodology of science cannot be conventionalistic in this sense. Not only must the hypotheses and theories used in explanations be falsifiable, they must (each) be regarded as falsified in certain conceivable circumstances spelled out in advance (perhaps in conjunction with some other statements), even though logic does not compel us to regard them as falsified.

Logic must be supplemented by methodological discussion to see exactly under what circumstances any particular sentence would be regarded as falsified, or rejected because it is used as an auxiliary to a falsified sentence. Popper is not so much concerned to reconstruct scientific arguments in a clarified language as to argue that what actually occurs in scientific argument and experimentation is best seen from the perspective of attempting the falsification of scientific statements. It always seems helpful in discussing the significance of a hypothesis or theory to ask under what circumstances it should be regarded as falsified, and it seems to be correct to hold that scientific theories should be capable of this kind of falsification. Indeed, the power of the notion of falsifiability is precisely that its use forces a scientist to conceive a world in which his ideas are *at the mercy of facts,* and this has a tendency to suggest a healthy attitude toward criticism and to separate science from attitudes of, say, astrologers who cannot conceive of refutation but only of miscalculation.[4]

A large part of the difficulties with *dogmatic* falsifiability are circumvented by Popper's doctrine that falsifiability must be coupled with the primacy of scientific explanation and ongoing methodological discussion. The doctrine of falsifiability is not making a merely logical point.

We need to look more deeply into the detailed technical statement of Popper's position on falsifiability with respect to critics' observations if we are to achieve a considered philosophical assessment of its final value. To begin with, it is essential to distinguish between falsifiability and falsification. Falsifiability is a logical notion: a sentence or statement is falsifiable if it is incompatible with some clearly defined basic statements representing possible observations.[5] The criterion of demarcation introduced by Popper is a criterion of falsifiability. Falsification is actually deciding that a falsifiable sentence is false—and this will depend on methodological rules which we adopt and which set out the decisions to be made as to whether a sentence is falsified given that certain observations are made. Two important problems loom on the horizon. One is that we do not want to hold that a few stray reported observations incompatible with a theory lead automatically to a decision that it is falsified. Reproducible data or a lower level theory that is not falsified but has been independently tested and is incompatible with a second theory is what should cause us to regard the latter theory as falsified. The point is that falsification will depend on rules determined by context and dependent on scientific expertise and decision; it is not a simple matter of logic. A related problem looms with respect to statistical theories. Popper will argue that statistical theories are falsifiable, especially if the frequency interpretation of probability is correct, since they can conflict with lower level statistical theories, but falsification of statistical theories by particular data may depend on very sophisticated methodological decisions. We will look at the issues involved here in chapter 4.

Sometimes, a theory which has been apparently falsified by data will not be *rejected* by scientists because it is still in close enough approximation to the data to be useful in solving problems and no alternative nonfalsified theory has as yet been constructed to replace the falsified theory. These distinctions, falsifiable/nonfalsifiable, falsified/nonfalsified, rejected/not rejected, are all important and must be utilized in any full discussion of Popperian methodology. Popper has sensibly modified his early view that *falsified* and *rejected* are equivalent notions in rational methodology to allow a falsified but useful theory to be used until a suitable replacement theory is found. He does find that this occurs less often than some other methodologists have claimed, and he urges as part of methodology that alternative theories should be allowed to proliferate so as to provide alternatives should a given theory suddenly be falsified.

It should be obvious from these remarks that Popper's views offer no mechanical procedures for doing science. Positivists sometimes approach the philosophy of science as though they would ideally like to program a computer or robot to do science, at least to check out the support or confirmation for proposed theories. Popper does not abstract much from the blood and guts of scientific debate. When we examine a putative scientific explanation, we can perhaps tell whether the explicans contains falsifiable (scientific) statements in a quasi-mechanical fashion; we certainly *cannot* tell whether such an explicans contains nonfalsified and highly tested laws and theories without utilizing methodological rules, rules which in turn depend on a close familiarity with the relevant scientific history. Our job as philosophers is to *understand* science, not to change it.

If the notion of falsifiability is to have any bite, the class of basic statements to be used in falsification must be defined. There are some formal requirements implicit in what we have said that apply to basic statements. We know that laws and theories, which are universal statements of the form "All A's are B's," must contradict basic statements, and we know that basic statements must correspond to simple observations that might be made.[6] From this it follows that basic statements will have the form of singular existential statements. A singular existential statement will have a form like "There exists an A which is not a B," and clearly such a statement can correspond to an observable state of affairs if A and B are empirical scientific terms. The following is very important. Basic statements are to be determined by a *decision* or agreement among scientists (and perhaps philosophers) involved with any scientific theory as to what counts as *relevant data* for that theory. Basic statements are not simply true or false as they were for positivists. Popper's methodological rule for marking them out is an explicit form of the implicit understanding between scientists in many areas of scientific investigation as to what constitutes legitimate data obtained by good experimental design. We may treat Popper's methodological rules as an attempt to suggest to scientists the advantages of being more self-conscious about their commitments in these areas. The class of basic statements appropriate to some area of science could be revised in the light of new apparatus or better theory— thus the Kantian interplay of theory and observation is preserved in Popper's handling of basic statements.

In order to handle conventionalism of a kind that allows various theories or laws to be retained because of their simplicity, Popper must allow that scientists also decide that for certain experiments certain specific theories or laws—or a specific theory or law—are what is being tested, the remainder of the explicans constituting background information. Popper's view involves conventions in the setting of the basic statements as well as these experimental situations, but it differs from unbridled conventionalism in laying down requirements *in advance* rather than allowing ad hoc postexperimental adjustments. At times Popper seems not to state this explicitly. "Thus I differ from the conventionalist in holding that the statements decided by agreement are *not universal but singular.*"[7] This is a legitimate difference in that the conventionalist may decide to reinterpret basic statements after an experiment. But Popper is also committed to holding that a division between tested statements and background statements in an explicans set against a test is determined by methodological convention. This is compatible with the quotation in the sense that such conventions do not *decide* the statements in the sense intended but simply establish their *status* for methodological purposes.

Popper does allow an *a posteriori* evaluation of theories. After an experimental test, a theory may be falsified or it may have stood up to the test. If the test was a severe one (might easily have falsified the theory according to our *a priori* expectations), the theory is highly *corroborated* by the test. If the test was not so severe, it is less well corroborated. We will examine corroboration as an a posteriori evaluation later. What Popper insists on to avoid conventionalism is that the possible a posteriori evaluations be set in advance and that the evaluation be then simply read off the experiment. The purpose here is to prevent evaluation afterward calculated to preserve prejudice from counterexample. Although requiring that possible evaluations be set in advance seems a salutary method of obtaining honesty, Popper may be too sanguine about the possibility of obtaining suitable conventions, particularly where statistical hypotheses are involved. One cannot satisfactorily always forbid a change of mind as a result of experiment. Data may be so unexpected as to not have been foreseen clearly, or the data may cluster around the decision surface provided by the methodological rules. In such cases a postexperimental readjustment may be rational. I think it not possible to make *formal* allowance for such unexpected results and that they are perhaps best treated as exceptions and handled case by case. In spite of these possible objections, therefore, Popper's rule seems a good rule of thumb if not a true methodological generalization.

We now turn to a deeper discussion of Popper's criterion of demarcation. The first question we will explore more fully is the relationship of his criterion to the positivist criterion. For the purpose of considering this question, Rudolf Carnap will be taken as the major representative of positivist opinion. A recent exchange between Popper and Carnap has sharpened the issues here considerably.[8] It could be argued, and has been argued by Carnap, that the apparent clashes between Popperian and positivist criteria of demarcation for scientific statements are largely verbal and that perhaps both distinctions are of some use. For example, since Popper accepts the usefulness of some metaphysical statements and argues that myth and metaphysics play an important role in developing scientific theories, he claims that some metaphysical statements are both significant and important even if not falsifiable. The positivist claim that all metaphysics is worthless only *appears* to conflict with this, according to Carnap, since positivists would regard the statements Popper has in mind as low-grade scientific statements. To resolve this would require detailed consideration of the metaphysical status (in both senses) of particular sentences. Terminological differences have created the appearance of some contradictions that do not exist but are rather alternative definitions of key terms such as *metaphysical.*

Carnap has pointed out that some sentences with mixed quantification cannot be falsified, but are intuitively scientific. For example, suppose a theoretical sentence has the following form:

$$(x)(\exists y)(\ldots x \ldots y \ldots).$$

To be falsifiable, the negation of this sentence must be accepted on some basis and it will have this form:

$$(\exists x)(y)(\sim(\ldots x \ldots y \ldots)).$$

There are two methods for dealing with this according to Popper, involving either the idea that such sentences be taken as part of a total theory that can be falsified by some of its other consequences, or the idea that the latter sentence be accepted as a basic statement agreed to by convention even though it may not satisfy the requirement that it correspond to a simple observation or be a consequence of a finite number of simple observations. However the status of a particular sentence might be resolved in context and granting that Popper's remarks on this subject have never been very extensive, it should be pointed out that mixed quantification cannot be handled by Carnap's logic of confirmation either, at least as it has been so far developed. Mixed quantification is simply a source of puzzlement for all extant methodological schemes. Popper's approach contains a strategy for dealing with particular sentences which means that these sentences can be treated in context unless one supposes (as Popper does not but Carnap does) that individual sentences must always receive an evaluation with respect to their scientific status on any conceivable given evidence. Both sides in this controversy have avoided treating convincing examples in detail.

One problem completely obscured by the Carnapian attempt at suggesting consistency of the two lines of demarcation is the status of mathematical sentences. Carnap and the positivists were drawing a distinction in the class of sentences having a nonanalytical logical form. Mathematical sentences would not appear in the class to be divided on this construal. Popper takes mathematical sentences to be significant but not to be scientific. Mathematical sentences are grouped with metaphysical sentences by Popper's line of demarcation, although they may be stated and proved as world 3 objects. This touches on an important issue. For the positivists mathematical statements are tautologies or logical truths— they say nothing, so to speak. This appears to conflict with intuition, but positivists tended to regard intuition as corrupted by a Platonic tradition in which numbers and other mathematical objects were thought to have a special kind of existence. Popper's views on mathematics and logic cannot be developed here at length, but the following remarks seem to be true. Logically true sentences and mathematical sentences are not falsifiable, hence they are not scientific. The logically true sentences are compatible with all basic statements. The mathematical sentences are paradigm cases of sentences that can be saved by convention; where they do not apply we simply do not apply them. Popper takes the important part of logic not to be the study of logically true sentences but to be the study of valid inferences.[9] Some logically true sentences can be taken to represent correct inferences, but the inferences do not appear as sentences in a language without some important interpretation. Normally such sentences appear in a metalanguage describing valid inferences in some appropriate range of object languages. The differing roles of logical and mathematical sentences point to a substantive difference between Popper and positivism that cannot be papered over by suggesting that they both divide the same class of sentences in a different, but mutually consistent, fashion.

Any appearance of possible consistency between Popper and positivism will also not withstand examination of various other sentences besides those of logic and mathematics. Although "This bird is black" is conclusively verifiable for Carnap, *no* sentence is *conclusively* verifiable for Popper except relative to methodological convention. The suggestion that Popper and positivists are dividing the same set of sentences glosses over the fact that the same sentences are being regarded quite differently in the two camps even if they are grouped together into categories that can be placed into some kind of correspondence. Such sentences as "This bird is black" may or may not be part of the set of basic statements for Popper depending on the methodological conventions in force. Thus not only would Popper and the positivists be drawing different lines of demarcation through the sentences of English (ignoring those related to logic and mathematics), they would place particular sentences quite differently in practice. Even where sentences are placed into corresponding categories on some scheme of comparison, the underlying philosophical conception of the semantical functioning of these sentences is quite different.

We will call Popper's view *methodological falsificationism* because of its basic feature that what falsifies is determined in advance of crucial experiments or tests by agreement on relevant methodological rules. The depth of this view in explaining Popper's methodological opinions can be seen by sketching its connection with induction before the more definitive examination of chapter 6.[10] Demarcation between science and non-science is determined by falsifiability or refutability, and the *method* of science is one of looking for refutations or falsifying data for conjectural hypotheses or theories. Refutability is a slightly narrower technical notion because we can refute a theory by proving a contradiction in it, but we falsify either by proving contradiction or by finding falsifying data determined by the relevant methodological rules. We will treat the notions as roughly equivalent even though this distinction could be drawn and sometimes plays a role in Popper's writings. The reason scientists or philosophers might believe in induction is that they might believe that scientists *prove* their claims on the basis of data and inductive inference while common sense depends upon guesswork and a casual argumentative sense.

Where the inductivists see progress as the accumulation of established information and a growing body of inductively supported theories, Popper views progress as the result of falsifications of those theories which run into conflict with logic or with data and as the development of bold new conjectures for potential falsification. Popper's criterion of demarcation is thus meant to conflict with an inductivist or justificational epistemology. An inductivist who accepts the falsifiable nature of scientific claims but who argues that falsifiable theories can receive justification in terms of supporting data should not attribute the notion of falsifiability involved to Popper. Popper's view of the seriousness of the demarcation problem is precisely that he sees his answer to it to have such far-reaching methodological consequences.

Now that we have characterized methodological falsificationism more closely, we can return to the objections to dogmatic falsificationism to see whether analogous objections tell also against methodological falsificationism.

One thing this expository account should by now have made clear is that Popper is by no means unaware of the problem raised by existential statements, and that he has suggested some strategies for dealing with this problem in specific contexts. Existential statements, which no doubt do appear in science, are sufficient to refute dogmatic falsificationism but not methodological falsificationism. To claim that Popper simply can't handle existential statements is one way of making the attribution of dogmatic falsificationism to Popper, an attribution that it has been suggested is frequently used to dismiss Popper without discussing his actual views. From among many possible examples, the following quotation from R. Harré's *The Philosophies of Science* seems typical:

> But the conflict between Popper's theory and scientific practice is
> most acute in the matter of its classification of existential statements

. . . to deny existential statements a place in the community of scientific truths must surely be mistaken.[11]

In the discussion of Popper, Harré alleges that Popper cannot handle observational error and that he can provide no explanation for the superiority of reasoning by analogy over guesswork. Of course, Popper does not hold that, in general, analogical reasoning is superior to guesswork, and he does have an account of statistical inference that permits observational error to be brought within the scope of methodology. Matters become simpler for Popper when particular individual statements of data are considered. Although these are decided by convention (and observation), they can conflict with other such statements and be falsified by them, so they quite definitely fall into the class of scientific statements:

> Statements capable of clashing with a singular test statement . . . I described (in *The Logic of Scientific Discovery*, p. 41) as "falsifiable" or "testable . . ." The statement "It rained in Vienna on March 12, 1933" is an example of such a historical *and* empirical statement.[12]

The data themselves are thus scientific because they can clash with other data, and the determination of constants, etc., is scientific work because the determined constant clashes with other possible values for the constant. Thus it is possible to argue that both theoretical and observational sentences are falsifiable but not possible to argue easily that theoretical sentences and observational sentences are both verifiable. In this area, Popper's refutation of nascent positivism seems complete. Perhaps the fact that observational statements have a scientific role to play in Popper's scheme has been missed because he says so little about them explicitly— he is quite clearly most interested in the evolution of theories to which he thinks that philosophy has a contribution to make. The determination of the conventions for observational statements within the special sciences depends on expertise far removed from general methodological speculation.

The basic unit of meaningfulness for dogmatic falsificationism was the sentence. For methodological falsificationism, the basic unit of meaningfulness is the theory (law, hypothesis) used in solving a problem or in providing an explanation. A sentence may stand for a theory in an example, but Popper means his account to apply to scientific contexts where scientific standards and intuitions can be invoked. Theories with artificially high falsifiability or which contain metaphysical statements are not ruled out by Popperian methodological fiat. Popper allows scientific intuition to rule these out in context on the ground that scientists will not keep useless metaphysical sentences in a theory in response to criticism of their value, and they will not construct absurdly complicated theories with high falsifiability where a simple one will do. This may leave more to scientific intuition than some philosophers find excusable, but Popper seems to feel that no comprehensive philosophical theory can successfully legislate scientific standards.

To discuss a slightly more specific example, consider a generalized existential statement such as the following:

There is an element with such-and-such atomic number.[13]

Before such an element is observed, this statement may not be a basic (observation) statement. But it can't be falsified in any obvious way, so it would appear not to be a scientific statement according to the criterion of demarcation. It is a mistake to say that this statement has no empirical content, because, when added to a theory about elements, it has certain observational and theoretical consequences that it does not have by itself and which do not follow from the theory by itself. The statement can therefore have empirical content even though it is not technically scientific when considered by itself according to Popperian methodology. Discovery of a method to falsify it (if there were such an element, it would produce a certain result in this experiment) or discovery of its truth both seem possible. For one thing, a scientist might try to observe such an element. The possible existence of such an element creates a problem situation which may result in the discovery of a way to observe it and an addition to methodological rules stating when basic statements about the element are to be accepted. Popper should perhaps not say that verification of this kind of conjecture plays no part in science where science is taken as an intuitive given. He says that it plays no part in *science* in his technical sense which is governed by methodological rules. He regards such verification as of small consequence in the total history of science, regarding it as more important that methodology should condemn psychoanalysis by rigorous principle than that it should include this kind of verification as scientific before the element is actually discovered and the methodological rules changed to accommodate its observation. Unfortunately, Popper provides insufficient explicit discussion of cases of this kind. On balance, then, Popper's demarcation of scientific theories from nonscientific theories will not fit *all* of our intuitions about science. His defense must be that it *solves* the problem it is addressed to in ruling out blatantly nonscientific versions of Marxism and psychoanalysis and that the problem that it solves is of basic importance for understanding scientific knowledge. The issue of the total adequacy of Popper's views then becomes partly verbal in that what Popper calls *science* could be called *strict science* (or something) and the intuitive line between science and non-science drawn in some other way.

Popper originally seems to have held that the line of demarcation drawn in *The Logic of Scientific Discovery* is sufficient to dispose of the original problem of distinguishing between scientific and pseudo-scientific theories. But there are questions about the nature of philosophy and its relationship to science not touched by this line of demarcation which caused Popper to develop some remarks about the non-science side of this line of demarcation. Popper came to realize that a process somewhat like the growth of scientific knowledge may occur in philosophy as well. In philosophy one produces critical theories which purport to give us an insight into scientific knowledge or metaphysical insight into the behavior of human beings. These theories cannot be falsified or refuted in the way that scientific theories can be falsified or refuted, but they can be *criticized.* Criticism can result in the rational rejection of philosophical theories. Criticism is thus a general notion which is an analogical extension of refutation or falsification. Some of Popper's other views must now come into play. Realism in Popper's sense, briefly the idea that science describes a physical and objective world, plus Tarski's theory of truth are used to supplement the original line of demarcation and insist that scientific statements are criticizable sentences that are true or false because they are *about* objects in the physical world. Popper's more recent views about demarcation, since they allow analogous theoretical growth in both science and in (for example) philosophy, must use realism and truth as notions to supplement the original line of demarcation to preserve the distinction between scientific and pseudo-scientific theories. This will become clearer in our discussion of realism and verisimilitude in chapter 3, but let us return to the sentence about an (as yet unobserved) element with a certain conjectural atomic number as an example. If there is such an element, the sentence is true (by Tarski's theory, which is an elegant statement of the correspondence theory of truth). If we learn how to observe the element (by methodological agreement), the sentence is clearly known to be scientific, that is, we discover that it was scientific all along. We can thus describe a line of demarcation even though we may have to make discoveries about where certain sentences belong with respect to this line. This introduces a subtle change. The new criterion still draws a sharp theoretical line, but it will be necessary to make more tentative conjectures about the status of particular sentences in practice.

We have already seen that the pragmatic paradox of meaning does not affect methodological falsificationism since a methodological falsificationist can self-consistently regard his philosophical position as meaningful metaphysics. There is, however, another kind of paradox which may seem to threaten methodological falsificationism. It is part of Popper's anticonventionalism that all of our scientific views should be subject to falsification, and he holds also that the rational philosopher should hold all of his views open to criticism. Popper is deeply antiauthoritarian. He sees empiricism (the view that knowledge *originates* solely in experience) as yielding to the presumed authority of experience. Empiricism is a form of philosophical irrationalism because the authority of experience cannot be questioned by empiricists. Suppose a rationalist holds the following principle:

All of my views must be subject to criticism and possible rejection.

The problem of a consistent rationalism is then the following: can this principle itself be open to criticism and rejection? If not, the rationalist would seem to accept the principle irrationally. Thus it is not clear that a pragmatic paradox cannot be developed to threaten Popper's antiauthoritarian rationalism as expressed in methodological falsificationism.

The problem just introduced as a possible pragmatic paradox has been discussed by Bartley, Watkins, and others.[14] Bartley identifies several forms of rationalism. What he calls *Comprehensive Rationalism* is the view that one can hold any beliefs for which he has good reasons, or sufficiently good reasons. This is clearly justificationist, and it is not Popperian. *Critical Rationalism* is the view that one should (dogmatically) accept the principle given in the last paragraph but otherwise hold his beliefs open to criticism.[15] *Comprehensively Critical Rationalism* is the view that a person can and should hold all of his beliefs open to criticism including the principle that one should hold all of his beliefs open to criticism.

Comprehensively Critical Rationalism is described by Bartley as involving no paradox. Watkins claims that Comprehensively Critical Rationalism is in turn subject to a paradox because it cannot be successfully criticized. The objection is that the only way to criticize it is to prove that it is uncriticizable, but success in showing uncriticizability would constitute a criticism, defeating its purpose. If we succeed in criticizing Comprehensively Critical Rationalism because we can show that it is uncriticizable, then we have criticized it and in the process have shown that it *is* criticizable. Comprehensively Critical Rationalism appears to be uncriticizable in any manner that would cause us to give it up, but it holds that we should hold all of our beliefs open to criticism. This position is not paradoxical unless one also holds that a belief held open to criticism must be such that there is a criticism of it satisfying certain desiderata. But this further belief need not be defensible. It may result from exporting certain views about criticizing scientific theories into the philosophical arena, but if it is held, there is a problem for Comprehensively Critical Rationalism. A Comprehensively Critical Rationalist cannot hold any *metaphysical* beliefs that are not criticizable because *all* of his beliefs must be criticizable.

We can see that Popper cannot be a Comprehensively Critical Rationalist since it is not Popper's intent to forbid holding noncriticizable meta-physical beliefs, and there is no way of drawing a sharp line between criticizable beliefs and noncriticizable beliefs. A scientific belief which is falsifiable, of course, is clearly so and must be held up to suitable tests by the rationalist. An example of a belief which has no clear status is a belief in determinism. In Chapter 7 we will note that determinism may be held in a metaphysical fashion involving some consequences about predictability, in which formulation it is criticizable. It will also be seen that determinism may be held as a metaphysical doctrine which is not subject to any empirical check and which cannot be charged with inconsistency. Comprehensively Critical Rationalism should therefore hold something like the following in order to be interesting:

> A rationalist should hold all of his criticizable beliefs open to criticism including the criticizable belief that all of his criticizable beliefs should be held open to criticism.

In this version the doctrine is so weak as to hardly give rise to any interesting pragmatic paradox. What is required is a proof that the belief mentioned is criticizable, and here any dispute is clearly dealing with a claim in the vague area between clearly criticizable and clearly noncriticizable beliefs. We will not attempt here to sort out the detailed disputes that have arisen in this area when the dividing line is settled by some arbitrary fiat.

The pragmatic paradox involved in positivism was that certain positivistic principles were neither analytic nor synthetic and hence could not be construed as meaningful by the positivist criterion of meaning. A paradox seemed to loom for rationalists if they accepted the principle that all of their views must be held open to criticism. We now see that a rationalist need not hold this principle and that a clear statement of the principle may be impossible because of the vagueness of the borderline between criticizable and noncriticizable statements. There is no reason to feel that views not subject to clear criticism cannot be held by a rationalist. Indeed, a justificationist epistemology for various philosophical principles (defending them by holding that one principle encounters fewer difficulties than rival principles) would be quite compatible given a sharp line of demarcation of the scientific from the nonscientific and a totally non-justificationist scientific epistemology. The rationalist need only deal with what criticisms he encounters, and he should feel compelled to look for encounters with criticisms of his views. A Popperian rationalism can be defended by pointing out that it allows for more controlled potential change in theoretical viewpoint to accommodate solutions to new problems and new kinds of observational facts than any irrationalist or authoritarian alternative.

Looking ahead to the evolutionary view to be developed in the next chapter, we might note that Popper's position is improved when the institutional picture of science is taken into account. Popper shares with positivism the assumption that scientific investigation is undertaken by self-conscious individuals, at least under a rational methodological description. In his methodology, Popper charges individuals with careful self-scrutiny—with finding possible falsifying circumstances for their own theories. We have seen that this salutary advice can be defended in theory but is usually violated in practice. Scientists in pratice may obtain high reputations by becoming extremely knowledgeable in an area of investigation, doing careful and important research work in the area under prevailing standards, but only venturing publicly the most cautious of speculations. From a Popperian perspective, this profile represents the corruption of science by a positivist methodological conception. This situation does not tell against the normative value of a methodology based on falsifiability provided that criticism occurs within the community of scientists and that the community determines the fate of the individual hypothesis. Selection of theories will take place and the features of Popperian methodology will be met provided that the society of scientists is an appropriately open society. There is some evidence from sociology to indicate that science is open in this sense and that apparently wild conjectures may gain rapid ground against an array of scientists with high reputations who oppose them. The situation can be compared to that arising in linguistic change, say to that arising when new words are introduced into a language. Many new words are suggested over time, but only those fitting sufficiently common needs for expression seem to survive. The process is not in the control of a single person, and it follows some objective constraints even though its exact course is not predictable. Much of the soundness of Popperian methodology can be enhanced by taking the structure of the scientific community into consideration, and this theme will be developed further in the next section.

II   Sophisticated Falsificationism

We have now examined Popper's falsifiability criterion by comparing it to a view (dogmatic falsificationism) that Popper does not hold and by examining its relationships to various positivistic and conventionalistic antecedents. This examination has suggested that Popper's view is consistent and interesting, but of course it remains unrealistically abstract until specific methodological rules are provided to deal with particular cases. Since methodological rules are adopted as a result of decision, this means that the rules could be revised repeatedly over time. The decisional element in the adoption of such rules and their possible revision is a sub-

jective element in Popper's methodology that has simply not been sufficiently scrutinized.

Perhaps the root difficulty with Popper's account as given in *The Logic
of Scientific Discovery* is that although theory and observation are regarded as methodologically interdependent, methodological rules do fix
the basic observational statements that are then used in this fixed status
to assess theories.[16] Although in theory both the theoretical and observational background are regarded as conjectural in problem situations,
in practice the observational background is taken as relatively fixed by
methodological rules, and the result is that the account in *The Logic of
Scientific Discovery* is difficult to distinguish pragmatically from an
empiricism which employs methodological considerations to fix basic
statements permanently.

Popper himself never gives *explicit* examples of what constitutes methodological rules. What he clearly has in mind is the following. In any
well-defined area of scientific investigation, common techniques of gathering experimental data have become established because of a history of
false starts produced by data gathered in an inappropriate fashion. Part of
the job of scientific education involves learning how to gather data that
will be accepted as legitimate in a given scientific field. What marks to
take note of as significant in an X ray or photograph, what features to take
note of in a microscopic or telescopic view, and so forth, are learned in the
process of becoming a scientist. A rank outsider would simply not know
what data to gather. Methodological rules are largely *implicit* in the practice of science as it stands. Popper accepts the practice and notes the
existence of the rules implicit within the practice, but he urges some self-
consciousness about the status of these methodological rules and their
possible revision.

Recently, Popper has considerably relaxed some of the more awkward
features of falsifiability as it is characterized in methodological falsificationism. Even in *The Logic of Scientific Discovery* Popper had suggested
that a theory might be augmented with *an auxiliary hypothesis* to account for anomalous data. The observed motion of Uranus was inconsistent with the Newtonian theory of the solar system, but Newtonian
theory was saved by postulating another planet beyond Uranus in the
system. An augmented theory may have, as this theory did, *increased*
content (at least intuitively), so that although adjustments may be ad hoc
in the sense that they are made to accommodate anomalous data, they are
not ad hoc in the sense that they immunize the theory from refutation in
such cases. More recently, Popper has noted that a *dogmatic* phase may be
necessary for a new theory in which sympathizers attempt to *save* it by
tinkering with auxiliary hypotheses.[17] The background point here is that a
new theory will often formally conflict with older theories and may

conflict with older data supporting older theories. A bold synthesizing theory will not be such that older theories and data can be formally deduced from it: the new theory may *correct* older theories and cause us to see old data differently. This concession to scientific history must inevitably blur somewhat the distinction between scientific and nonscientific theories and statements.

In *The Logic of Scientific Discovery* it seemed that a falsified theory would have no use. We have just seen that a falsified theory may be rescued by adding an auxiliary hypothesis. Therefore a falsified theory need not be a *rejected* theory where this possibility seems promising. But there are further complexities. A given theory may entail facts about certain *specific* observations, and a scientist will regard only certain observations as relevant to its corroboration. All of the data of science considered together may well falsify this theory as well as other relevant theories if only because it is inconsistent, taken by itself. Therefore we need to choose between falsified theories for various purposes, or find some way of evaluating conflicting data all of which may be methodologically acceptable but some of which may have to be discarded as misleading by proponents of some theories. We may also prefer a new theory not yet readily testable to an older theory that has been successfully tested, gambling that a theory of observation will be developed and new data obtained that will show the former theory to be preferable to the latter. Popper now accepts the idea that theories need dogmatic supporters in order to prevent their succumbing too easily:

> Clearly, one can say that if you avoid falsification *at any price*, you give up empirical science in my sense. But I found that, in addition, supersensitivity with respect to refuting criticism was just as dangerous: there is a legitimate place for dogmatism, though a very limited place. He who gives up his theory too easily in the face of apparent refutations will never discover the possibilities inherent in his theory.[18]

We also have cases where a theoretical conjecture will be regarded as refuted because it clashes with a corroborated theory but not with any basic statements.[19] These kinds of historical situations force a revision in the simpler scheme of *The Logic of Scientific Discovery*, and Popper has acknowledged these pressures, but a more sophisticated falsificationism has not yet been adequately worked out.

Popper regards his methodology as a form of Darwinism in which there is an evolution of conjectures in response to falsifying facts which provide selection pressure. Darwinism has been regarded by many as a nonscientific theory because its explanations of change are not coupled with predictive power. An evolutionary change as a result of selection pressure can receive an account in terms of adaptation, but the adaptive change cannot be predicted from a description of selection pressure, background information, and a Darwinian evolutionary hypothesis. This point has been well taken with respect to Darwinism in the past. An analogy between Darwinism and Popperian methodology suggests therefore that Popperian methodology is not, strictly speaking, falsifiable. It can be retained as a meaningful normative conception no matter what the actual facts of scientific evolution. Nonetheless, we have seen that common sense has already forced some changes in Popper's conception of scientific evolution. There are also signs that Darwinism as a biological theory is becoming more predictive and more scientific in Popper's sense. Even if this is debatable, there is the general Popperian point that metaphysical theories can grow into scientific theories. All of these considerations suggest the possibility of a falsifiable Darwinism and raise implications for the possibility of a revised Popperian methodology. If Darwinism were scientific and testable, an analogous methodology might also become scientific and testable. It therefore seems reasonable to consider possible future directions for exploring modified Popperian methodologies although such consideration is not forced on us by the current state of methodological sophistication.

Perhaps the best method at this point for approaching a more sophisticated falsificationism would be to list some problems about falsifiability and the criterion of demarcation given in methodological falsificationism as a basis for discussion of possible elaborations of or changes in Popper's methodology. Some of these problems have already arisen in our discussion or can be found in the literature. As explained earlier, the context is the general problem of studying how the decisions and conventions of methodology which separate science from metaphysics and define falsification within science are to be rationally revisable in detail over time. If such revision is not possible, then methodological falsificationism is itself more dogmatic than our discussion of rationalism suggests that it should be. One could consistently hang on to methodological falsificationism as a *metaphysical* theory, but it is surely worthwhile to critically examine some possible changes in its structure. Most of the problems for methodological falsificationism center around the complexity of falsification as it is exhibited in detailed studies in the history of science:

(A) On Popper's view, a reproducible false observation should simply falsify a theory. Sometimes theories continue to be used even though falsifying observations are well known. An obvious example is the fact that Newton's theory was used long after figures for the precession of

Mercury experimentally at odds with its predictions were obtained. Let us call this phenomenon *the problem of Newton's longevity.*

(B)   One answer to (A) is that a theory is never regarded as falsified until a better theory is found to replace it. Hilary Putnam, Kuhn, and Feyerabend (among others) have suggested this. Perhaps a test is never a test of a single hypothesis but must discriminate between rival hypotheses by ruling out one if certain experimental results are obtained, otherwise ruling out the other one. Let us call this *the problem of comparative falsifiability.*

(C)   A theory may make a proposal whose consequences can't be tested by any known means. For example, 25 years elapsed between theoretical prediction of the neutrino and an experimental test of the prediction. For much of this time, the theory wasn't testable in any straightforward sense even though it was clear that it was scientific and that it was (potentially) falsifiable. Let us call this *the problem of currently unavailable experimentation.*

(D)   On Popper's view an inconsistent theory must be regarded as technically nonfalsifiable (everything is compatible with it) and hence as nonscientific. One could stipulate that inconsistent theories have been totally criticized and falsified, but there is still a problem. Bohr's early quantum theory turned out to be inconsistent but was worth developing even after the inconsistency was observed. Do inconsistent theories play an important role in the development of science? Let us call this problem *the problem of brilliantly unsuccessful theorizing.*

(E)   In order to avoid difficulties with conventionalism, Popper requires that the potentially refuting basic statements be specified *in advance.* But in at least some situations involving statistical reasoning, it seems natural to reinterpret experimental results after the experiment. What distinguishes such cases from illicit conventionalism? Let us call this *the problem of retrospective significance.*

(F)   Why can't a "nondogmatic" principle of induction play some kind of role in science? If we want to find the relationship of X to Y, for example, is it not possible to experiment in such a fashion that constraints on this relationship are established by the experimental results? Let us call this *the problem of accidental discovery.*

(G)   Popper's methodology seems incompatible with what Kuhn has called *normal science.*[20] For example, simply looking for new species, looking for new elements, or finding more accurate values for theoretical constants would seem to be (intuitively) scientific activity but not a Popperian scientific activity because it is not undertaken to explicitly test or falsify a theory. It would also seem to be a scientific activity to extend an available theory to provide an explanation for existing experimental facts. Let us call this *the problem of applied science.*

(H) Although high-level theories have been refuted, various low-level theories seem to remain as a basis for new theorizing.[21] The mechanical laws of equilibrium, the laws of electric circuits, the laws of reflection and refraction of light: these seem a secure basis for higher level physical theories. Are they now falsifiable in any significant sense? Let us call this *the problem of the relative theoretical base.*

(I) Would Popper be inclined to suggest that one not try to build a perpetual motion machine?[22] If so, on what grounds? How can we know in advance that a change in theory will not make what we currently regard as impossible a viable phenomenon? Let us call this *the problem of the restricted world view.*

(J) Popper holds that Newton's theory, while a paradigm example of a falsifiable theory, is now falsified. Einstein's theory has replaced and corrected it. Is this the judgment that we want to make about Newton's theory—that it no longer can function in scientific explanations? It is a fact that Newton's theory is *used* by scientists to solve certain relatively simple problems, and it is not treated in textbooks as a historical curiosity. Let us call this *the problem of the fatal beauty of a good theory.*

For at least three of these problems, the problem of currently unavailable experimentation (C), the problem of brilliantly unsuccessful theorizing (D), and the problem of accidental discovery (F), it is possible to argue that Popperian solutions are straightforward consequences of the falsifiability criterion. One can argue that the theories involved or the laws one is trying to guess at have an original metaphysical status. This line could also be pressed as we noted earlier against anyone whose intuition convinced him that single existential statements should be scientific. The difficulty is that our presystematic sense of what is a scientific statement is sometimes at odds with the falsifiability criterion, and Popper needs perhaps to point out that *scientific* in his sense of *suitable for use as a theory or law in a scientific explanation* is an explication or technical usage and defend its fruitfulness while yielding as much as possible to the intuitions giving rise to the problem. What is clear is that Popper's sense of *scientific* is normative in a strong sense and would not conform to the use of the term *scientific* by the scientific elite. There is a further hitch in any discussion of the problem of brilliantly unsuccessful theorizing (D). Because it is now known that consistency is not decidable (there is no mechanical process that will always decide correctly whether a formalized statement of a theory is consistent within a finite period of time), one cannot simply state that only consistent theories can be tested without encountering the difficulty that a theory thought to be consistent may turn out to be inconsistent, so that what seemed to be a scientific test was in fact mere metaphysics. This once again highlights the fact that Popper's theory is heavily normative, since it must be taken as a description of an ideal process that scientists can only try to emulate but may fail to emulate *in spite of their best efforts* because of such matters as the undecidability of consistency.

When the normative/descriptive distinction is applied to the philosophy of science, we can look at this as an attempt to discover how much one can teach a budding scientist about how to be a scientist or how to be a good scientist by referring to an abstract theory or account of scientific methodology. On a descriptive approach, one examines "great moments" in science and tries to elicit the methodology (if any) that is contained in an analysis of these moments. Reasonable as this may seem, most philosophers have rejected a descriptive approach on the grounds that the basis for locating methodology on this approach is left to an intuition or consensus about which are the "great moments." At least some scientists involved may have been lucky, or may not have been aware of what they are actually doing methodologically in the same sense that a great musician may have a false, inaccurate, or even nonexistent self-appraisal of what he is doing. A naive examination of "great moments," as has been mentioned elsewhere, is almost certain to give a misleading impression. Great scientists may actually break sound rules with impunity. In teaching science, it may be best to direct our attention to "little moments" in science in order to produce the skills useful for making solid contributions to scientific progress. Normative philosophy of science has insisted that the history of science and scientific practice can only be assessed by examining science through philosophically clarified models of scientific methodology. Descriptive philosophy of science shades off into history of science as fewer normative principles are utilized. For this reason, *philosophy* of science is always at least partly normative: philosophers are not historians and they are interested in general ideas that may be repeatedly applied to give a coherent picture of scientific achievement. A willingness to take history seriously is a symptom of the descriptive philosopher of science. As we have previously noted, it is clear that Popper is far less normative than the positivists, and it is correct that falsifiability is directed to history and is an illuminating concept to bring to bear on scientific history. It is also clear, in the light of a Popperian defense to some of the objections which have now been explicit raised, that the history of science cannot be brought into the form of a Popperian drama without a heavy reconstruction of events. For reasons already introduced, Popper's position seems secure from an attack on the right (positivism), but his willingness to take the historical growth of science seriously opens Popper to an attack on the left in which the normative features of his methodology are eaten away by the acid of historical counterexamples. The essential problem is here to decide how much philosophy should concede to history if we are to retain a normative philosophy of science worth discussing. We can't say that inconsistent theories should never be developed, because Bohr is around to show that they may be profitably developed. On the other hand, we can't say in general that inconsistent theories should be developed either. And to say that inconsistent theories should be developed when the intuition of genius is overseeing the development will not work since there may be cases when even genius might profit from a more coherent statement of theory. It is possible to argue that Bohr's theory was (largely?) metaphysical. This saves Popperian methodological dicta, but at a certain intuitive cost, since experiments were designed and carried out to test the empirical consequences of the theory. What may be required is a better account of the metaphysical and scientific aspects of a theory that will allow us to draw distinctions between theories all of which are, logically, inconsistent.

Returning to our budget of problems, we see that the problem of Newton's longevity (A) can be handled by holding that a falsified theory may be used cautiously for predictive purposes until a better theory is discovered. Popper seems now to accept some such idea. The problem of comparative falsifiability (B) suggests a principle of comparative falsifiability: Do not regard a theory as falsified and rejected unless there is a nonfalsified theory available that will explain relevant facts. It is clear that Popper is not willing to accept a principle of comparative falsifiability as stated. In *Objective Knowledge* he objects to this kind of adjustment by observing that it contends that criticism of a theory *requires* another theory, and yet we can criticize a theory without reference to other theories by showing that it has unintended or undesirable consequences.[23] Popper is no doubt correct, but I suspect that the appropriate rejoinder is simply that the logical consequences of a theory can only be evaluated as unintended or undesirable in the light of alternative theoretical speculation. Pure criticism based on logic plays such a small role in the growth of scientific methodology that it can be ignored, or treated in a footnote. Popper's reluctance to yield on this issue has seemed to some philosophers tantamount to a reluctance to accept criticism. Some of this, however, if not all, can be viewed as preferring a philosophical methodology with clear principles and a few counterexamples to a philosophical methodology too willing to accommodate counterexamples by using vague or loosely worded principles. It is quite clear that to apply the principle of comparative falsifiability in many situations one would have to stretch the meaning of an alternative theory to embrace rather vague conjectures that had not yet been explicitly formulated. For Popper, the adoption of the principle would be wrong because of such counterexamples as well as cases where logical criticism by itself seemed adequate to assess a theory. Some more sophisticated but precise answers to the problem of Newton's longevity and the problem of comparative falsifiability need to be found before changes in methodological falsificationism are required by a theory of rationality.

The problem of the fatal beauty of a good theory (J) presents a situation in which a theory that has been falsified and surpassed by another theory is nonetheless still used as a bona fide scientific theory. Popper, along with most positivists, seems to be committed to the notion that such a use of theory is a matter of convenience only and that such use is to be regarded as a rule-of-thumb approximation that could in principle be justified by use of the replacing theory should a challenge be mounted to the use of the falsified theory.

We have already touched on Popperian rejoinders to the problem of retrospective significance (E), the problem of applied science (G), and the problem of the relative theoretical base (H). The problem of retrospective significance requires some deeper discussion of the falsifiability of statistical theories. This discussion appears in chapter 4, and the upshot of that discussion will be that Popper intends his methodological conception to be consistent with generally accepted (objectivist) statistical practices. Retrospective significance is to be considered by handling special cases against that background. The problem of applied science can be treated by Popper as part of the process of changing a theory's status from a metaphysical to a scientific conjecture. This situation was discussed earlier in connection with looking for a conjectural element with an assigned atomic number. The problem of the relative theoretical base can be attacked head-on by arguing that such theories *are* still falsifiable. Every now and then very deeply entrenched scientific laws have been refuted. We may not expect this of any particular law, but we cannot show that it will not happen.

Some interesting problems are raised by the problem of the restricted world view (I). I believe Popper would argue (and argue correctly) that it is always all right to try to find refutations even for the best entrenched scientific principles. The law of parity, for example, was overthrown even though its place in physics once seemed secure. Problems (H) and (I) are related in that they can be answered in the same manner. Unfortunately, the Popperian answer seems polemical and not entirely satisfactory. The theories involved in the problem of the relative theoretical base (H) would probably not be severely tested unless a new high-level theory had consequences that justified such testing. At the same time, new high-level theories and their consequences are challenging, so we might expect scientists to be attacking them in an effort to refute them. What seems missing in Popper in his discussion of such cases is any appropriate discussion of scientific research as an institutional program. Although *some* scientists should try to refute any given theory, not *all* scientists should, or total scientific research could be clearly misdirected. Popper's answer may be correct, but it seems bizarre because we do not expect the activity it counsels to be a widespread concern of scientists. Popperian answers to (H) and (I) do not go very far toward explaining what a total rational plan for coordinated scientific research would look like even though they correctly warn against the bad consequences of too much conceptual conservatism.

While Popper can handle piecemeal the kind of objection provided by our problems so far, the total budget of problems has a weight that constitutes a problem for Popperian methodology since it must be stretched in a different direction to handle each of them. The methodological outlines of *The Logic of Scientific Discovery* require softening, and methodological falsificationism must be modified to handle more historically sophisticated views of scientific theories. Some modifications have been achieved in Popper's *Objective Knowledge*, but the outlines of the original rigorously normative approach remain. If all of the suggested revisions were to be made at once, it is not clear that the resulting methodology would have sufficient normative shape to constitute a useful touchstone in assessing scientific practice. It may be interesting to see what will happen if the force of the historical examples behind problems (A) – (J) is given greater weight and one attempts a further move from methodological falsificationism than Popper seems so far willing to accommodate, especially if this can be done within the framework of a modified normative methodology with some impact for the total range of scientific practice.

A detailed conception of a decisive move from Popper's position to a form of sophisticated falsificationism has been worked out in a series of important articles by Imre Lakatos.[24] Lakatos' basis for sophisticated falsificationism is partly a revision of an important principle of methodological falsificationism. Methodological falsificationism views a test as examining a relationship between a theory and experimental data resulting in possible falsification of the theory. When we examine the history of science, however, we see that tests typically involve experimental error, and so nearly any test will falsify nearly any theory in the sense that the experimental data will not be precisely predicted. As is well known, careless use of significance tests can result in rejection of any hypothesis on plausible grounds even where it is independently assumed that the rejected hypothesis is true.[25] The move at this point with an eye to history seems to be to view experimental results (reproducible results) as falsifying theory *h* only when there is a theory *i* equally good on general methodological grounds that is either in closer agreement with the experimental data or promises some sweeping conceptual simplification by replacing hitherto disjointed conjectures with a unified conceptual foundation and a related theory of large scope. Thus Lakatos attempts to work out the suggestion that a principle of comparative falsifiability be adopted that Popper, as we have seen, does not find satisfactory. An appeal to history suggests that (generally) we do not give up a theory until there is a replacement theory, provided that the theory can still be regarded as useful in explaining and predicting a wide range of data. This point, often noted by pragmatists, can easily be incorporated into sophisticated falsificationism by adopting the suggested falsification rule. This shift enables sophisticated falsificationism to absorb the examples giving rise to the problem of Newton's longevity (A) and the problem of comparative falsifiability (B).

The basis for the more extended positive program that Lakatos introduces is the idea that *single* theories are not to be methodologically appraised, even against rivals, but rather series of theories whose revisions may come as a result of falsifying experimental data. Methodological falsificationism can appraise a theory only in terms of whether it is falsifiable and whether it has been falsified. Sophisticated falsificationism will appraise a theory in terms of whether it belongs to a sequence of theories which is generating new facts—that is, a sequence of linked theories that gradually becomes falsifiable in new ways—or whether it belongs to a sequence which is not doing this but is gradually restricting its scope. These trends must be evaluated over a sufficiently significant length of time. The basic unit of appraisal is the *scientific research program*, and a theory is appraised in terms of its appearance within such a program. A program will have a *hard core* consisting of various laws and theories regarded as *not* falsifiable within the program. The program may have to be abandoned in the face of sufficiently recalcitrant data, but the hard core is conventionally treated as unrevisable.

A research program will also contain a *positive heuristic* (or, where there is no danger of confusion, simply *heuristic*) as well as the negative heuristic embodied in the hard core. The positive heuristic accumulates anomalies and purported counterexamples and attempts to integrate them into the scope of the research program by adding to or revising the laws and theories used in the program other than those in the hard core. Potential falsification is directed to the heuristic rather than to the hard core in the sense that needed revisions in the face of awkward data are made in the heuristic and not in the hard core. The Popperian principle that every statement should be regarded as falsified in at least some circumstances is considerably modified by this program, although some data can cause a whole research program to terminate, at least in theory. The existence of the heuristic enables a scientist to set aside various anomalies as problems to be dealt with and not as counterexamples falsifying the total research program or even important theories contained within it. The scientist views the program as cataloguing and gradually digesting the anomalies; it is his perception of the program as a historical entity that forestalls panic.

A research program is said to be *progressing* as long as each new theory in the series of theories in its history predicts new empirical data in a manner anticipated in its heuristics, and it stagnates or degenerates if its heuristics fail to lead to the required absorption of anomalies, or if it must make ad hoc adjustments to unanticipated discoveries. Rival research programs will have to be evaluated in a sophisticated fashion. A new, very progressive research program may not be eliminated by an existing and powerful rival in any very obvious way in terms of methodological principles.

The comparison of research programs is a sophisticated problem that we will not look at here. The major problem is to try to devise a notion of ad hoc theorizing that will successfully differentiate *progression* from *degeneration* in research programs. As a first approximation, one might argue that ad hoc theorizing is theorizing which fails to imply any novel or unanticipated facts. This move shifts the notion of ad-hoc-ness to the notion of *novelty* which in turn is problematic. Ad-hoc-ness is to be repudiated for Popperian reasons: we don't want a scientist to tinker with a theory just to save his favorite ideas. Problems arise because a scientist may honestly theorize without the intent of saving prejudice only to discover that what *he* takes to be novel facts have already been discovered by others while he was theorizing. There *are* novel facts implied by the theory from this scientist's perspective as he completes his theorizing, but we seem compelled by methodological considerations to argue that his theory is in fact ad hoc because there are, in fact, no novel facts. This move conflicts with intuition regarding historical cases. Elie Zahar has made an important advance by arguing that non-ad-hoc theorizing is theorizing which does not violate the *spirit* of a research program.[26] A deeper theory which is an elegant generalization of existing theories may then be seen as progressive even if no novel facts are predicted by it. It is not clear, however, that subjectivism can be banished by this device. Different scientists may *view* different segments of the research program as the hard core, and a scientist may shift his view to accommodate his theorizing (or at least we may invoke such a historical reconstruction of events). If the methodology of research programs is loosened sufficiently to accommodate all of the historical facts, it would seem that any sharp distinction between progressive and degenerating problem shifts, the distinction designed to rescue objectivity in this methodology, will disappear.

It would seem that refinement of the kind suggested, if it could be carried out, would make something like Lakatos' concept of a research program a sufficient concession to history to handle most of the budget of problems outlined above without lapsing into difficulties associated with pure conventionalism. One might note in particular that the methodology of research programs allows a kind of inductive confirmation to come into play. When one theory is replaced by another in a research program, discovery that some of the *excess* or new empirical content of the replacing theory is compatible with observational data confirms the progressive nature of the research program and leads to a positive appraisal. Piling up data compatible with the hard core, however, has nothing to do with positive appraisal because the hard core is conventionally removed from empirical falsification. Indeed it seems obvious that a program like Lakatos' can handle all of the problems except possibly the problem of the fatal beauty of a good theory (J) by suitable elaboration.

But now Popperian caution intrudes. The fact that sophisticated falsificationism can handle so many objections raises the question of what would force revision in the conception of sophisticated falsificationism. Here we could have sophisticated falsificationism hoist by its own petard. By accommodating methodology so closely to history, has Lakatos produced a conception of methodology which is nearly vacuous in the sense that it can be verbally adjusted to fit the facts of any epoch? It also seems a possible danger that by enlarging the nonfalsifiable role of the hard core of a research program sophisticated falsificationism runs the risk of conflating genuine scientific theories with the metaphysical theories that Popper had wished to distinguish them from.

Some historical studies using Lakatosian sophisticated falsificationism have now appeared.[27] What is clear is that the methodological suggestions of sophisticated falsificationism have produced some interesting history, but the jury is still out at this time on the magnitude of the advance in historical understanding. A major problem still centers around the distinction between *progression* and *degeneration* in a research program. By adjusting the notions of *anomaly* and *ad hoc rejoinder,* one can accommodate history in special areas as we know it to have led to contemporary science. But it is not clear at all that the adjustments correspond satisfactorily to naive historical chronology, and it is not clear that the evaluative term *progression* has an intrinsic meaning as opposed merely to an evaluation of what we *now know* to have been on the right track with respect to current theory. To put this another way, it seems clear that interesting history has been written by reconstructing a narrative of scientific discoveries in terms of Lakatosian research programs so as to provide an evaluation of history compatible with our retroactive assessment. It is not at all clear that an objective measure of *progression* has appeared that would enable us to assess current research programs. There is the possibility that scientific evolution sometimes depends on retroactive steps or useless mutants which free possibilities for development which are only later of value. If such possibilities are realized in scientific history, then the distinction between *progression* and *degeneration* would be nearly useless for the larger purposes to which it wants application in the methodology of research programs.

Lakatos' objections to Popper depend on a clash between history and Popperian normative methodology, with history the assumed arbiter. We have already seen the difficulty with history as an arbiter, and the difficulty does not disappear for sophisticated falsificationism. History is largely reconstructed by a reading of the past through current assumptions, and so the mere invocation of history can provide no objective arbiter. Without attempting a resolution of the question of how far Popper should adjust methodological falsificationism toward sophisticated falsificationism, it can be pointed out that the historical material does not force any adjustment at all in methodological falsificationism depending on the decision about the normative components of a philosophy of science that one may think it appropriate to keep. For example, the mere fact that scientists behaved as though a research program had a conventional hard core does not establish that they should have held this view from the standpoint of methodology. What is needed is some sort of theory which makes this view *rational* from the standpoint of methodology. Unanswered problem (J) will force a historical point that constitutes a valid attack from the left on both Lakatos' and Popper's conceptions of scientific methodology. This problem, the problem of the fatal beauty of a good theory, will be pursued further in chapter 3. In conjunction with a modified conception of evolutionary epistemology along Popperian lines, this problem will suggest a development from methodological falsificationism divergent from Lakatos' sophisticated falsificationism which will permit an explanation of the rationality of behavior not entirely consonant with methodological falsificationism.

THREE

Popper against Subjectivism

Realism is a philosophical and metaphysical position that Popper contrasts with idealism. The contrast between these positions seems to be intended by Popper to remain indeterminate so that a wide variety of opinions can be regarded as idealistic and rejected in comparison to a progressing series of detailed realist positions which can be developed to defend objectivism in science. Realism can be described simply as the common-sense view that our knowledge is about reality and not about ideas in our minds. The common-sense opinion that when we die the world will not end is an expression of the realism that forms one basis of a scientist's outlook. Popper's realism is quite clearly intended to be incompatible with a phenomenalistic basis for scientific knowledge.

Common sense is both hero and villain for Popper. The common-sense view that our knowledge is about the real world is correct and is taken by Popper to be elaborated in scientific knowledge. Popper thinks that idealism rather than realism has been accepted by philosophers and scientists as a result of bad philosophical arguments.[1] On the other hand, Popper sees common sense as also holding a justificationist theory of knowledge based on the idea that observation is the starting point and authority for knowledge.[2] This component of common sense must, of course, be abandoned in Popperian epistemology.

Popper's remarks about realism and the common-sense theory of knowledge are not consistent with much of the philosophical tradition which has directed its efforts toward locating *foundations* for human knowledge.

43

Foundational analyses have typically turned toward (certain) subjective impressions such as sense data or some kind of simple ideas as the *basis* on which some correct interpretation or theoretical postulation erects the total sum of human knowledge. In Popper's opinion, the basic task of epistemology is *not* to find foundations for human knowledge (these do not exist), and *not* to justify or define human knowledge (impossible because of its conjectural and fallibilistic nature); the basic task of epistemology is to investigate the process by which scientific theories may grow or progress.

In Popper's treatment, realism is a nontestable philosophical conjecture which is metaphysical rather than scientific. He calls his version of realism *naive realism* to indicate that alternative philosophical conjectures cannot be decisively refuted by criticism. This is at the very least refreshingly honest. A statement of the realism position is an excellent example of a significant view that is not scientific according to Popper's line of demarcation. Popper thinks that sufficient *criticism* of idealism (the alternative view) can be developed from analyzing the fact that all perception is theory laden. On this view there is no immediate experience, as idealists hold; the feeling that we have some kind of direct perception is due to the facility given by our practiced decoding of sensory information, as well as by innate genetically determined skills which have been honed by the process of evolutionary development. When we play the piano, practiced decoding turns perceived notes in the music directly into struck keys without intervening *conscious* thought. Popper takes perception to be like this, with the earliest interpretive thought processes given on a hereditary basis and with much of perception filled in on a conjectural basis by the mind. In terms of the analogy, the practiced pianist need not look at all of the notes in order to play them because of his familiarity with clusters of notes and how the music is likely to go. The mind frequently looks for clues to support a priori conjectures derived from evolutionary development and incorporated into hereditary transmission. The mind does not simply accumulate and then inductively test sense experiences. Popper calls this accumulative view originally associated with positivism the "bucket theory" of the mind.

The basic argument *for* idealism is often taken to be something other than the view that we can verify certain immediate experiences by feeling, introspection, or even certain lines of philosophical argument. Idealists may argue that our talk of interpreting or decoding experience, which even Popper uses, suggests that there must be something that is interpreted or decoded, and the problem is simply to discover what it is through philosophical analysis. Analysis reveals the foundation of our knowledge, even if we are not consciously aware of the fact that the foundation exists, or what it is like. Unless such an analysis were at least possible, our talk about knowledge would literally not make sense. Popper's negative criticism of idealism does not demolish this argument, although it is clear that Popper is not impressed by arguments from the intelligibility of what we can say. Popper's account glosses over the fact that an appeal to intuition is not the only defense for idealism. Perhaps the differences between realism and idealism trace ultimately to differing underlying intuitions about whether the language of interpreting or decoding itself makes sense. This is a matter too tangential to Popper's major interests to be developed here.

Popper's discussion of realism appeals to the intuition that realism is compatible with true common-sense knowledge (our starting point) and is also compatible with all the things we want to say about science. Idealism is not obviously compatible with science in the sense that it must place a tortured interpretation on scientific knowledge in order to account for scientific progress. The difficulty is to provide an idealistic account of foundational knowledge that can underlie the obvious upheavals in scientific theorizing over time. The upheavals often seem to demolish the total structure, and not just the theoretical superstructure. Arguing for a position which does not refute a rival may appear slightly at odds with Popper's general strictures about criticism and refutation, but it seems convincing in this case, and we have already suggested that refutation is not so clear cut for philosophical conjectures as for scientific theories.[3] As philosophical conjectures are often not falsifiable or refutable, there is no reason why arguments in their favor cannot be given which are not dependent on refuting rival views. The attractiveness of Popper's realism and his conception of scientific methodology lies in the way that it all hangs together in a robust normative structure, and Popper's realism is an important component of this structure. Without it, Popper's views on probability are not secure, and he would have no satisfactory conception of scientific truth, a conception he requires to rule out pragmatism as a philosophy of science and to make sense of the view that science approaches truth even if it cannot ever establish that it has found it. I believe that realism is best viewed as part of the overall consistency of Popper's position in that Popper could not consistently be an idealist and hold the views that he holds about probability and falsification. The challenge to idealist philosophers of science that Popper presents is to prove consistency of their views compatibly with a similar range of salient intuitions about scientific knowledge. Viewed in this way, the argument for realism is not a justification of realism as such but an argument for the viability of Popper's total methodology. This is perhaps a more satisfactory vindication of realism than simply attacking idealism because it is incompatible with one's intuitions.

Popper's realism is involved with his acceptance of Tarski's theory of truth, a theory which Popper takes to establish the viability of the position that truth is an appropriate correspondence of statements with facts. We can only express truth when we have a language sophisticated enough to express the relevant facts (technically, when we have a suitable meta-language available). Realism has as a consequence partly definitory of it that the facts exist before they are actually expressed. Popper is concerned to point out that the Tarskian or realist conception of truth must be construed as absolute. A relative conception of truth would be truth-in-a-language. Popper holds that there is always the possibility of expressing *any* truth in any language, at least in any natural language. A language may have to evolve somewhat to achieve this, but is always possible in principle. If sentence S in language L and sentence P in language L' are inter-translatable, then they must be true or false together. If truth were relative to a language, and different languages were untranslatable, then persons speaking different languages would be unable in general to work out their differences and arrive at a common agreement after testing various knowledge claims. As we will see, Popper's scientific epistemology and social theories suppose that progress is always possible and is possible only through free rational discussion.[4] Free rational discussion must therefore be possible, and to underlie the intution that progress is possible, truth must be absolute. The Myth of the Framework, namely, the notion that we must share common opinions and a common world view in order to discuss things, is set aside by Popper as an error equivalent to holding that truth is relative to a language. Popper not only holds the conditional claim about intertranslatability mentioned above but also holds that inter-translatability is always possible in principle in the sense that for any sentence S and a language L there will be a sentence P in language L' (or that could be introduced to L') that is a satisfactory translation of S. This is a very strong claim to make about languages.

Popper's rejection of relative truth and his acceptance of a notion of absolute truth are not trivial to begin with in that they encounter conflict with two widely held views about language in contemporary philosophy. One view is the view of Quine that intertranslatability of languages depends on conventions in such a fashion that it is typically not demonstrable that two sentences express the same proposition even where (provisional) translation has resulted in a decision that relevant terms in the sentences are correctly mapped into each other.[5] There is a certain amount of slippage in translation due to the fact that we can recognize assent to a sentence in our home language, but may have to conjecture assent on the part of a speaker of another language. There is also slippage introduced by the adoption of various analytical hypotheses about what to count as logical truth, as synonyms, and so forth. When we have accomplished the best translation manual we can, there is still the possibility that our translations pass all behavioral tests but are such that speakers in the two languages differ in ontology and in meaning. This difference may be a mere curiosity where behavioral matching has been achieved, enabling people to work together, but there is no independent check on its existence and hence no independent check on the accuracy of our translations. Quine is both a pragmatist and a kind of realist who gives privileged status to one's home language. The indeterminacy of translation applies to a group of English-speaking scientists, but here it can be discounted if the scientists are careful in working out common views because its extent will be too small (if it exists) to affect what we call scientific knowledge. Between more divergent linguistic groups, the problem is potentially serious, and Popper's rather casual remarks stating the total availability of intertranslatability seem from this perspective to be naive. Quine's pragmatism is in agreement with Popper's position that scientific knowledge is an extension of common-sense knowledge. Quine's realism, however, unlike Popper's, extends only to a coercive effect that facts have on certain observational truths expressed in one's home language. Theories are to be regarded as instrumental hypotheses, and revision in a language will take place in the face of sufficiently recalcitrant facts by conventionalist principles allowing one to opt for overall conceptual economy even if this entails giving up what had previously been taken to be observational fact. Quine's views have affinities to outright conventionalism, but they are also warped toward objectivity in science by closer attention to observational statements and their usual role in scientific theorizing. Popper states that it is always possible and fruitful to discuss ideas with people of divergent viewpoints. On the one hand, this is close to a triviality. We are not likely to learn much from people who *merely* agree with us. (We can, to be sure, learn a lot from people who agree with us but know a lot more than we do.) On the other hand, there is surely a point at which divergent viewpoints become so unintelligible to us that an increase in our knowledge from talking to people of divergent points of view is no more likely than an increase in knowledge due to a blow on the head. Popper seems too sanguine about the availability and fruitfulness of meaningful discourse even where good intentions can be postulated. Quine's gradualism here seems to fit somewhat better the salient facts. Popper's view that intertranslatability is always possible with accuracy is of a piece with his realism. The evolution of two different languages toward known scientific truth will eventually result in intertranslatable languages expressing the same truths. Unfortunately, Popper's argument here seems to rest solely on the evidence that observation shows that people can learn to speak two or more different languages (bilingualism), say English and Hopi, or English and Chinese. This does not, by itself, clinch anything.[6] Bilinguals often report that they cannot accurately intertranslate between languages if only because some term in one language has no counterpart in another.

This leaves it open whether such a term *could* be added to the language to complete translation. Popper's realism forces the conclusion that it is possible, but Popper's realism here is at best a metaphysical conjecture to which Quine's position is an undefeated alternative.

The other relative view worth mentioning here is Thomas Kuhn's well-known view that scientific explanation is relative to scientific paradigms and that scientists operating under sufficiently divergent paradigms will find one another unintelligible.[7] Quine's views are the expression of a pragmatic semantics as applied to theoretical issues in general linguistic theory. Kuhn's views were developed from a consideration of the history of science and are consequently somewhat more threatening to Popper's central concerns. Consider a *typical* scientific experiment, perhaps one whose description is located by a random sampling of scientific literature. Popper has urged that we should view an experiment as a *test* of a theory. Kuhn has urged that we should view such an experiment rather as a test of the experimenter, not of the theoretical background of the experiment. If the anticipated results are not found in the data, this may reflect badly on the experimental design and not on the background theory. Kuhn is arguing a description based on a discovery of his that scientists do not typically conform to Popperian (or other classical methodological) prescriptions in their typical work. The fixed framework in which an experiment makes sense and can be seen as a contribution to science is a situation in which a great deal of scientific information is *assumed to be true* and the experimenter is trying to extend scientific knowledge to cover new cases. A failure on his part is seen as reflecting, not on the theories involved, but rather on his competence as an experimenter. Scientific work done in this way is called *normal science,* a term which suggests that most scientific work is normal in this sense. There are also, however, periods of revolution in which so many normal experiments are producing anomalous results that scientists working in an area come to question the assumed scientific background. At such a time a *revolution* may occur in which one set of assumptions is *replaced* by another. When a revolution occurs, it need not mean that thousands of scientists change their minds explicitly about the background assumptions or paradigms which determine the relevance of their work. Indeed, the hold of paradigms is related at least partly to the fact that they cannot be fully articulated and discussed, so that a change of paradigm for a single scientist would involve an experience similar psychologically to religious conversion, after which the world would appear differently. A revolution need not involve such changes. It may be that new individuals with a different paradigm come to dominate an area because older individuals have been anesthetized by accumulating anomalies from making new discoveries.

On Kuhn's view the typical scientist is not necessarily interested, nor should he be (given limited resources of time), in critical or rational discussion with others in Popper's sense. The scientist is definitely *not* interested in all the objections which might be raised to the paradigmatic context in which he is working. He is engaged in a kind of guild activity, solving puzzles according to procedures that he has accepted in his training as part of an operative and fruitful paradigm.

Kuhn's description of science allows an objection to be formulated which requires some discussion. The difference between normal science and revolutionary science in Kuhn's description may suggest a chronological sequence in which a long period of normal science is followed by a period of revolutionary science. Historical surveys suggest however that normal and revolutionary activity go on at the same time. Indeed, a given scientist may be given to both activities with respect to some paradigm; and at any given point in time, surely different scientists will be pursuing both normal and revolutionary science. Neither Popper *nor* Kuhn has furnished detailed case histories to buttress any sociological generalizations about scientific history.[8] We will proceed as though Kuhn's distinction is not (at least not necessarily) chronological but rather logical. Normal science is scientific activity in which the paradigms are *not* questioned but puzzles are resolved in the context of the paradigm. Normal and revolutionary activity will typically be going on simultaneously in any important branch of science. The major battle lines can now be anticipated. Kuhn wishes to suggest that the appearance of normal science is an *essential* feature of science, and Popper wishes to suggest that normal science is lazy or inferior science. Popper will want to suggest that, even if scientists assume the truth of paradigms in order to pursue experimental design, they should always regard some possible experimental outcomes as refuting the assumed theory, and not simply as reflecting badly on their ability to design experiments. Revolution in permanence will be the normative guide of science and normal science will be regarded as a psychological lapse from this normative goal.

This direction in Popperian methodology has been developed into a position not compatible with Popperian origins by Paul Feyerabend.[9] Feyerabend argues for revolution in permanence, but he argues that scientific theorizing is a form of creative madness that eludes rational methodological description and cannot be accommodated within a realist framework because of the existence of incommensurable theories. Because of these points, Feyerabend is no Popperian, but he cannot be classed with Kuhn either since he doesn't feel that puzzle solving is the key to understanding the growth of science. On his view, science grows because of the interplay of tenaciously held private views. Because of this, in science everyone is *free to do what he wants*, and to hold any view, no matter how crazy to others, because it may one day drive more conservative entries

from the field. There is in fact no structural difference between the history of science and the history of theater, art, philosophy, or whatever. Madness prevails everywhere: periods of revolution are periods in which the madness, for some reason, is particularly noticed. Feyerabend's position, which began as a variant of orthodox Popperianism, has in fact now attained a perspective from which methodology disappears. It cannot be refuted since it is an ultimate concession to history in the sense that an attack from the perspective of some orthodox methodological position can always be blunted by pointing to the manifest curiosities of scientific history. Flattering as Feyerabend's description may be to scientists in characterizing them as creative geniuses, it doesn't seem to support the intuition underlying methodology that some differences should be discernible between scientific history and the history of some other human endeavors, differences which Feyerabend is unwilling to recognize. Further, it is not clear, given scarcity of resources and the possible conflicts between major scientific research schemes, that everyone should do just what he pleases. Such advice is simply beside the point to the participants in sufficiently large modern research teams. Feyerabend's position treats scientists as autonomous individuals and ignores the institutional structure that makes normal science possible and criticism at least sometimes more effective than personal passion can explain. Primarily because Feyerabend's current position simply involves the rejection of the possibility of rational methodology, we will not compare it directly to Kuhn and Popper in any greater detail, given the focus of this discussion on Popper's normative account of scientific growth.

Some commentators have suggested that the difference between Kuhn and Popper is best discerned by viewing Kuhn as engaged merely in the sociology of science, more or less describing the way in which scientists *do* close their minds to open debate in order to pursue narrow research goals. Too much methodology is like too much wine, inhibiting through the enervation consequent to philosophical speculation the irrational urge to produce sound scientific work. Kuhn has concentrated his attention on normal science and accentuated its differences from the picture of scientific history drawn by classic normative philosophy of science. With an eye to Kuhn's distinction between normal and revolutionary science, it can be said that Popper is interested only in revolutionary science, that is, the overthrow and replacement of theories. Popper regards this as the only scientific work worthy of serious philosophical scrutiny and holds that scientists *should* approach normal experimentation as though it had revolutionary implications. Anything less than this is merely engineering and shouldn't be regarded as science.

It is not clear that Popper's conception of the overthrow or rejection of theory is similar to Kuhn's revolutionary change. Because of Popper's

rejection of relativism, his view of scientific history bears some resem-
blances to the cumulative scientific history of the positivists when it is
assessed against the background of Kuhn's views. Popper's theoretical
position involving interdependence between theory and observation tends
to favor observation as the check on theory in practice. Since older scientific languages and theories will always be translatable into current languages and theories by Popper's intertranslatability thesis, what was good
data might be superficial or bad data at present but it will still be meaningful data. Although the positivist's neutral observational data must
always remain the same data, Popper's data can be replaced by better data
as a theory changes because the facts relevant to corroborating the theory
are taken to be given by revised methodological rules. The revision might
be brought about by the invention of better experimental equipment or
new techniques of observation. For Kuhn, older data may simply be *unintelligible* to present scientists. It seems quite clear that Kuhn and Popper
have different underlying conceptions of what a major change in theory is
like.

We have here a situation in which Kuhnian and Popperian methodological conceptions can be regarded as quite similar when viewed from a
rigorously normative justificationist perspective, but where they each
seem quite different to the other.[10] Consider the question of problem solving and the subsequent testing of hypotheses. Popper sees problems as the
starting point of investigation. An existing hypothesis is then invoked
which would solve the problem, or a hypothesis is invented which would
solve the problem, and the scientist turns to testing the hypothesis in an
effort to prove it false and replace it with a better one. Popper's attention is
on the potential overthrow of hypotheses through experimental observation. Kuhn's attention is focused on the solution of the problem by
means of the hypothesis and the further use of the hypothesis to solve
related problems. A scientist who simply accepts a theory as part of a
paradigm and solves some puzzle with its aid may have done a useful piece
of science. He does not have to *test* the hypothesis in Popper's sense. For
such a piece of work to be *scientific* in Popper's sense it must be regarded
as at least a potential test of the theory in the sense that, while solving the
puzzle corroborates the theory, failure to solve it would have undermined
if not falsified the theory. As against Popper, Kuhn merely observes that
scientists do not always consider potential falsification. Popper must
rebut this by arguing that they should be described as considering
falsification if their work is to be regarded as meaningful and that their
work would maximize scientific progress if it explicitly considered potential falsification.

A difficulty which exacerbates the difference in outlook here seems to
be the differing manner in which Popper and Kuhn regard the relationship

between the individual scientist and the institution of science. For Popper, the institution may set the conventions determining basic observation sentences, but the scientist theorizes on his own. *One* scientist may propose a new conjecture, test it, and establish its worth against rivals already in the field. The negative test is decisive. On the other hand, merely deducing some result that solves a puzzle could involve an error even though the deduction is widely accepted. (This has happened historically, and Popper is not wedded to the idea that scientists should use a formalism in which deductions can be proven.) For Kuhn, the institution of science validates various theories as acceptable at a given time and also validates various puzzles or problems as worth working on. A scientist who connects a theory with a puzzle has done a job that is of interest to other scientists. Thus institutional validation is much stronger on Kuhn's view than on Popper's. Variant theories are always to be welcomed on the Popperian evolutionary metaphor as providing possible better explanatory accounts, but they are not *welcomed* on the Kuhnian account unless they conform to generally accepted scientific desiderata. Theories produced simply as possible variants that have no known experimental divergence from accepted theories and that do not bear strong analogies to theories accepted in other areas are simply of metaphysical rather than scientific interest to working scientists.[11] For this reason, Kuhn sees puzzle solving as just as legitimate a form of scientific activity as trying to invent new theories and test then.

The truth about scientific knowledge seems to lie with some view accommodating both Kuhnian and Popperian insights. On the one hand, Kuhn's revolutionary metaphor seems too strong. Popper is right that scientists can often communicate across divergent Kuhnian paradigms, or understand in terms of divergent paradigms. A so-called revolution often leaves virtually untouched vast amounts of lower level theory. On the other hand, Popper need not be right that this implies intertranslatability since intertranslatability in principle is merely a consequence of asserting his form of realism. It is possible that scientists can be schizophrenic in the manner of reported bilinguals, switching back and forth from theoretical perspective to theoretical perspective in a kind of gestalt perception switch. These gestalt switches may cease if one viewpoint gradually proves an adequate perspective from which to solve all, or at least most, of the relevant problem situations. This kind of failure of translatability— that is, a willingness and ability to work with divergent conceptual frameworks, perhaps eventually resolving the disparity in favor of one of them— may be all that Kuhn is entitled to invoke. Revolutions could then be regarded as historical artifacts created in a relatively large-scale history of science by the compounded effect of a great many small gestalt switches in perspective over a relatively short period of time. We will return to this theme shortly.

Let us consider again Popper's contention that realism entails the view that intertranslatability between languages is always possible and that there are no mutually untranslatable frameworks whose inhabitants cannot come to understand one another. As a child may come to learn a language not related to any language previously spoken, a linguist may plunge into an alien culture and acquire a new language which he cannot totally translate back into his native language. This *apparently* suggests that two languages may not be intertranslatable, but it doesn't prove it because of the possibility of nonconscious linguistic processing, sheer ignorance of available terms in the languages involved, and so forth. A typical argument used to support the view that if the meaning of sentences in languages were determined only within the context of that language, then the concept of objective truth necessary for science could not be developed, is that it is *absurd* to argue that there are no pairs of terms between such languages which cannot be correlated. The notion of *object* is different between Newtonian and relativistic frameworks, but it would seem absurd to say that inhabitants of the two frameworks mean something totally different by the *sun*, since there is presumably only one sun, and not two, in the solar system which is described differently in the two frameworks. Here language may lead us astray. We are tempted to speak of one object under two different descriptions, but this manner of speaking may only be suitable for different descriptions of an object within the same language. Kuhn, who has repeatedly been attacked by such arguments, has recently suggested that it is common stimuli, not common objects, that may be used to relate two divergent frameworks.

> In *The Structure of Scientific Revolutions*, particularly Chapter X, I repeatedly insist that members of different scientific communities live in different worlds and that scientific revolutions change the world in which a scientist works. I would now want to say that members of different communities are presented with different data by the same stimuli. Notice, however, that that change does not make phrases like "a different world" inappropriate. The given world, whether everyday or scientific, is not a world of stimuli.[12]

This perspective seems to me to offer hope of handling the relationship between differing frameworks. Instead of saying that there is one world with different descriptions, we can say that there is a physical universe containing potential stimuli giving rise to different worlds as man interacts with the universe with different cognitive schemes and varied interests.

Feyerabend has suggested that Popper, in attacking subjectivism through the Myth of the Framework, has failed to take into explicit consideration the myth on which the attack is based, the myth (Popper's Myth) that there is potentially a totally accurate and detailed description of the world which science is aiming to develop.[13] The dependence of a world (in Kuhn's sense) on subjective mental states is not an accident. Different needs must have given rise in different communities to different ways of finding significance in the world. What is significant gets organized to solve the special needs of a language-using group. Berlin and Kay have discovered that focal senses of *red, green, blue,* and so forth, are similar in various languages, a similarity that is an objective basis of comparison in spite of the multiplicity of color-term usages actually found in various languages.[14] The focal senses may be related to physiology while the divergencies are related to local needs and locally available natural objects and colors. In other words, the basic semantical categories of a language are tied to special situations of the group for whom the language relevates the world. Now suppose that two or more divergent languages are translated into a single notational system. Under what circumstances will such a notational system be a language in turn? In some sense, it may always be possible to find a notational system in which all the known facts about a language are expressed, so the question here is really whether or not all the facts about a language can be expressed. Some have argued that language acquisition involves currently mysterious structural properties of the brain, which may or may not be capable later of being formulated and understood in a language. Others have held that language acquisition could in theory be made mechanical because there is no theoretical problem in expressing all the facts about a language in another language. *Language* will not be defined here in such a manner as to attempt resolution of these conflicts. The problem seems at present entirely open. What is important here is that Popper *and* the positivists seem committed to the alternative that the facts of a language can be (in principle) fully expressed and that it is possible therefore to translate apparently divergent languages into a common tongue in which all properties of relevance and explanatory power in the original languages are preserved.

Popper's realism and the associated view of language just adumbrated are essential to the consistency of his total methodological account of science, but they constitute elements for which there hardly seems to be independent proof. The Popperian attitudes toward language seem to have become clearer in his account of the three worlds. World 3 is designed to buttress the objectivity of science, but it can do this only if all of the facts which science utilizes in explanation can be clearly specified linguistically. World 3 does not seem so much a new contribution to Popper's methodology as it does a clearer expression of Popper's antecedent realism. The three worlds in Popper's philosophy are world 1, the physical world that science is interested in giving an explanatory account of; world 2, the subjective world of human thought and experience; and world 3, the world of objective human thought and the products of such thought. The doctrine of the three worlds makes a relatively late appearance in the Popperian corpus. Worlds 1 and 2 are similar to worlds proposed by other philosophers to distinguish between the universe conceived of as devoid of human minds and the universe including human minds. What is significant about the doctrine of the three worlds is the inclusion of the third world, world 3. This is best understood in terms of Popper's motivation for introducing world 3, which is to permit a philosophical basis for a sophisticated intellectual evolution in science bearing features analogous to normal biological evolution in world 1. The concept of intellectual evolution and of something like world 3 is not new with Popper.[15] What is important here is Popper's use of these notions to ground an objective notion of the growth of scientific knowledge.

World 3 is the world of human knowledge as expressed in public language. This distinguishes human knowledge from behavioral knowledge (how to *do* certain things) which may be shared with other creatures. The possibility of nonhuman minds which utilize languages is ignored here, as it is in Popper's work, without intended prejudice against such possibilities but for economy of statement. Stating one's ideas in language removes them from the realm of the subjective and places them into the objective arena of public discussion. This arena cannot be controlled by individuals because the logical consequences of expressed ideas are potentially infinite. In other words, the use of logical inference means that a few expressed ideas can create an enormous objective structure of related ideas that can be carefully explored in detail by the efforts of many human investigators. A thought in a scientist's mind (a world 2 object) is significant for scientific understanding if and only if it can be expressed as a world 3 object in language or if it leads to thoughts which can be so expressed. Sociologists and philosophers may be interested in thoughts (world 2 objects, as reported introspectively) and their relationships as an example of the natural history of human beings. The philosopher of science should be interested only in thoughts which can be expressed as world 3 objects.

If this characterization of world 3 objects as linguistically expressed observations, theories, hypotheses, etc., exhausted the use of the world 3 concept, it would not be of much interest. The significance for Popper is that world 3 objects as thought-experiments can play an important role in the evolution of scientific knowledge. In biological evolution, an organism of a given type may simply not be viable in a fixed environment. Evolution is connected directly with viability in that a species or individual which represents a deleterious genetic move may be decimated or even destroyed by a hostile environment. The significance of world 3 objects is that while they are objective and in the public domain they are also off line in the sense that we can examine them intellectually for viability while temporarily disengaging them as hypotheses for use in action. A bad theory or hypothesis can be examined and *discarded* without bringing about deleterious effects on human life. Human beings can experiment with world 3 ideas on a conjectural basis without jeopardizing the lives of human beings with perhaps irrecoverable genetic or behavioral changes. According to Popper, the evolution of scientific knowledge proceeds through the evolution of world 3 structures. World 3 is thus a concept which codes (for Popper) a large share of his specific observations about the growth and objectivity of scientific knowledge.

Although there are difficulties with the concept of world 3, it is quite clear that world 3 combats subjectivism by arguing that a proper scientific history is an internal history of transformations in world 3 structures, which can be objectively described. The selection pressure on world 3 allowing for the evolution of theories in world 3 is, on Popperian terms, the pressure supplied by objective arguments and refuting data. It is here that the redundancy of world 3 can be located. In biological evolution, selection pressure is or is not found in terms of organisms which attack the organism whose evolution concerns us. Selection pressure isn't operative in world 3, however, except by human *decision,* and it is at this point that the mind reintroduces itself as determining selection pressure. We can perhaps avoid the question of whether logical refutation (proof of inconsistency) is an objective matter, although it should be noted that differences of opinion about the viability of alternative logics have been widely discussed. Popper, perhaps significantly, has found Standard two-valued Logic a sufficient tool of criticism. The more important problem is exactly what constitutes relevant data to a theory, and in particular what constitutes relevant and refuting data. Popper's way with this has been to argue that logic can determine refutation for nonprobabilistic theories and that a sufficiently rigorous theory of statistical inference (Popper's theory will be discussed in chapter 4) can do the same job for probabilistic theories. Accommodation to history and the consequent distinction between falsified and refuted theories bring this simpler conception into question. Some theorists have argued that scientific education brings about an internalization of scientific values determining the perceived relevance of data which is similar to any other cultural assimilation and internalization of values. Perhaps the rules underlying languages which we speak or those underlying other cultural values, while they are internalized in the human mind (or the mind acts as though such rules were internalized), cannot be explicitly articulated. Kuhn speaks in this way about the acquisition on paradigms, but feels that the process of scientific perception may one day be understood, although it will probably not be describable in Standard Logic. On the other hand, perhaps as Popper and the positivists have argued in common, scientific knowledge can be fully and clearly articulated in some yet to be discovered methodological framework. Although we cannot resolve this issue, it should be seen that the world 3 idea is not an argument for Popper's position on this issue but an expression of his position on objectivity compatible with a description of how evolution of scientific theories could proceed compatibly with that position on objectivity.

We are now ready to state Popper's central evolutionary conception of the growth of objective scientific knowledge. Scientific knowledge progresses by the proposal, criticism, and falsification of falsifiable scientific theories in world 3 that are used to provide scientific explanations. We can never prove theories true; we eliminate more and more false theories, but increasing sophistication plus realism insure that our theories are becoming better over time. The metaphor is evolutionary. New theories are like new species. The unfit are weeded out by natural selection. But among the survivors, we have no guarantees. Any of them may be eliminated by a better adapted competitor or new mutant form at any time.

An organism is an evolutionary experiment (trial) that either does or does not live through some given experience. By Popperian analogy, a theory is a scientific experiment that either does or does not survive the results of some given observational datum. Falsifiability is the criterion used to decide if it is viable, that is, could live in the scientific environment. An organism is dead or alive. Similarly, it might seem that a theory (at any given time) is either falsified or not. This analogy seems to have had a strong grip on Popper. For example, it might explain why he opposes conventionalism on the grounds that it cannot keep theories alive by adjusting them. They are already dead, so to speak, once the experimental counterexample has been found.

Popper's evolutionary metaphor is, however, based on only one of many possible readings of evolutionary theory. The *fitness* of a particular (individual) organism is usually defined in evolutionary theory as the relative probability that an organism of that type will leave survivors compared to the probability that some competing (related) organism will leave survivors. A particular fit individual may die, and a relatively unfit individual may live. It's a matter of luck as far as individuals are concerned. Evolutionary theory simply does not predict or explain whether particular individuals will live or die. The focus of attention is rather on the fate of species and the potential individuals that may arise by genetic combinations within the gene pool associated with a species.

The following situation is of particular interest. Let two competing types of individuals (represented by different genotypes) exist within the same species. Suppose one type eats "fine grain" food and the other "coarse grain" food. Suppose the environment consists mostly of fine grain food. One type of individual may be "fitter" in this environment and may predominate in numbers. This does not preclude both types existing in some kind of equilibrium of numbers in this environment. The environment may not be as favorable to the one type as to the other, but the less favored type may continue to exist in smaller numbers in the same environment with the favored type by feeding in favorable areas and mating with the favored type. In a heterogeneous environment in nature, it is in fact very rare for one type of individual to so completely dominate a second that the second dies out completely. This fact is related to an evolutionary advantage of diversity, as we will see shortly. Note that in scientific history we often seem to have "better" and "worse" varieties of some kind of theory existing side by side. The retention of the worse need not be irrational. Just as retention of "less fit" types may be a rational strategy in evolution in the sense that the less fit may enable the species to adapt to a change in the environment because it becomes the fitter in the new environment, so retention of "worse" theories may be a rational strategy in science because worse theories may suddenly permit superior adaptation to changing data. To work this out in detail, we need to take species as the focus of our attention and realize that a species embracing fit and less fit types may itself be fitter because of potential adaptability than a species which has achieved perfect fit to one environment but which may be eliminated by a change in that environment because it contains no individuals capable of adaptation after the change. Using the analogy, we might expect scientific theories in an extended evolutionary metaphor to embrace a variety of interpretations in order to incorporate a rational hedge against the vagaries of an uncertain future.

I think the mistaken evolutionary metaphor relating scientific theories and single individuals present in Popper's approach is responsible for its strong conceptual ties to dogmatic falsificationism and to positivism. If theories were "killed" by a single datum, then maximum falsifiability as a desideratum and the death of theories would result in a uniform methodology such that two rational scientists would tend (strongly) to accept the same theories in the same area of investigation. The real evolutionary metaphor suggests that lots of theories (competing ones) ought to be present in any area of investigation—and that theories, like species, may survive the death of particular individuals that belong to them. This intuition may underlie Feyerabend's opinion that "anything goes" in science and that all options should be pursued.

Let us see whether a more sophisticated evolutionary metaphor is really possible. The first thing to note is that a species is to be defined by a wide variety of possible linked genotypes and that the current statistical distribution of the possible genotypes of a species will be a function of the dynamic interaction of the species with a changing environment. When the environment changes, fitness will quite likely change, and the statistical distribution of genotypes of the species will be different in response to the change if the species manages to survive. Were the environment never to change, then perfect adaptation to the environment would be a desideratum. A species would be best served by reproducing only the genotype (or group of genotypes) that results in maximally adapted individuals to that environment. Evolutionary theory, however, has highlighted the fact that successful (long-lived) species hedge against change in the environment by continuing to retain genotypes (through random or sexual mating) that are not optimal in the current environment but that would be optimal if the environment should change in certain ways. As an example, let genotype A result in a small body for members of some species and genotype B result in a large body for members of the same species (assuming suitable food supplies, and so on). Genotype A may be better adapted to warm weather and genotype B to cold weather. As summer changes to winter, the statistical distribution of members of the species of genotype A with respect to genotype B will typically undergo an inversion. But there must be individuals of genotype B (or individuals that can have genotype B offspring) that survive the summer months or this change-over could not take place. A successful species facing a fairly stable environment could have among its members only individuals of similar genotype well adapted to that environment. If the environment should change suddenly and drastically, such a species could simply disappear because none of its available genotypes could result in a viable individual in the new environment. On the other hand the species may hedge against modest environmental change as most species do by harboring ill-adapted individuals or the ability to produce them as a way of dealing with future change, thereby retaining the capacity to produce new individuals well adapted to the new environment when it occurs.

In order to use this more sophisticated approach to evolution, we need to discuss both the analogue of a species and the analogue of a "possibly changing" environment. The appropriate level at which to draw comparisons is to compare a theory with a species, not with an individual. We now begin to see why theories may be harder to kill off than Popper's evolutionary metaphor with falsifiability suggests. New facts may eliminate one version or interpretation of a theory only to bring it about that a relatively unpopular version should suddenly gain many adherents. I think it is clear that what we intuitively regard as theories exist in the literature with many slight variations that treat different cases differently. The special theory of relativity is an example. Theorists in this area dispute the answer to certain central questions. Should some of these questions be resolved by experimental advance, only some of the interpretations of the theory would be eliminated, and the more successful interpretations would be kept. In this way a theory will retain its identity over time even though it may change its composition in detail. This context suggests that axiomatized versions of theories should be regarded as just that, quickly falsifiable versions of theories whose total structure is more diffuse.

To what does a theory adapt? I regard the ecological niches or living space of a theory to be defined by what I have called elsewhere data domains.[16] A data domain will be defined as a range of data that can be gathered by certain methods. Popper's conventionalism regarding observation statements is welcome as a way of expressing, not what statements are regarded as true, but what means of gathering data are legitimate. Philosophers have apparently not noticed that the invention of new means of obtaining data (the light and radio telescopes, the light and electron microscopes, and so forth) have *typically* caused havoc in scientific theory. The reason for this, expressed metaphorically, is that the environment for relevant theories has undergone a violent change or extension which will either eliminate current theories, cause great changes in the statistical distribution of those holding various interpretations, or require colonization by variants of existing theories. The same sort of data domain extension may occur when totally new empirical phenomena are discovered.

Popper's basic insight about fallibilism remains valid in such an expanded evolutionary metaphor. The past success of a theory is no guarantee that it will continue to be viable or that it will not change the statistical distribution of its interpretations drastically. Induction is wrong if it is construed as an index of some *guarantee* of longevity for a theory. Just as unpredictable natural catastrophes may be tantamount to violent changes in the natural environment of a living species, so new data may completely change the data environment to which a theory is adapting. At the same time, evolutionary theory tells us something about the statistical distribution of genotypes within a species against a fixed environment. Similarly, induction may tell us that *as long as the environment remains stable* a given interpretation of a theory (or one theory in competition with another, although we have not yet introduced species competition) is probably the most well adapted and is most likely to appear in articles, books, and so forth, unless some change in the relevant data domain is observed. If we take the evolutionary metaphor seriously, we may expect that scientists will express divergent views as a hedge against unexpected environmental change as a rational practice but that, as long as the environment is relatively stable, most of them will be developing the (objective) consequences of the seemingly best-adapted interpretations of theories. In our wider perspective, Popper seems right about the ultimate significance of nonjustificationism and induction, but there is still a place for induction in the short-range future of science, particularly where allocation of funds and resources is involved. Amazing as it may seem, a sufficiently complicated evolutionary metaphor may yet reconcile viable features of positivism with viable features of subjectivism in a Popperian hybrid.

From our perspective, positivists may be taken as seeing data simply accumulating, rather as though there were a fixed environment for theories to adapt to that was gradually being enlarged but not fundamentally changed. For a fixed environment, a species or theory will thrive best that is best adapted. Sufficient exploration of a fixed environment in terms of trials might be expected ultimately to eliminate all but one theory. Popper realized that this was hopelessly wrong in a suitably large historical perspective because the assumption of a fixed environment as gauged by our data could not be proved. But because he viewed theories like individuals, as dead or alive, he thought you could only talk about what would live and what would die, and not about the relative viability of individuals that might be regarded as in competition. Corroboration was a gesture toward relative viability, but it fits uneasily with the stark outlines of the original methodology. Corroboration as a gesture toward relative viability in a stable data environment is compatible with that methodology. What is not easy to understand is why corroboration should be introduced. A more sophisticated evolutionary metaphor than Popper has presented so far may tie the ideas in his methodological picture of science into an integrated whole accommodating some of the insights of rival methodologies.

To this point we have not introduced the idea of competition *between* theories. What constitutes competition between species is an interesting question. Species can live in the same physical area but not compete because they utilize different food, have different time cycles of activity, and so forth. The whale and the shark, for example, exist in the same gross environment but do not compete directly for the same food and the same space. They exist in somewhat different ecological niches. A given physical environment may contain independent biological environments because of differences in food, behavior, and so forth, between species. We all know that species can be driven out of an area by other species. It is more interesting to consider cases where quite different theories are such that one does not drive out the other but exists with it in a different ecological niche.

Let us match our intuitions about species competition to what we want to say about theories. Popper's notion of realism is quite compatible with theoretical reduction in the sense that one organism (theory) could eliminate all others in a fixed environment since (realism) there is only one ultimate environment. A given biological species could drive out two other species in some natural environment, but this is rarer in nature than one might think. For example, it is hard to imagine a creature that might eliminate simultaneously both man and the field mouse. Expectations about the number of species are geared to our feelings about the number of available ecological niches. Similarly, where we have sharply divergent data domains, we may expect different theories to adapt to them. One of Kuhn's insights seems to be that different theories will pick out different ecological niches from the potential data to adapt to, and that consequently direct competition between theories will be infrequent. Scientists will tend to switch to theories at revolutionary periods that can colonize new data domains provided that they are viable in older domains even though they are not as well adapted as the old theories in the older domains. Kuhn's level of analysis therefore expects to locate many different theories adapted to divergent data domains and dealing with different problems; the question of reduction or of finding a master foundational theory seems uninteresting. One may accept the same diversity of forms that occurs in nature.

The evolutionary theory suggested here has the advantages of theoretical diversity as urged by Feyerabend and Kuhn while attempting to preserve objectivity in terms of theoretical fit to data domains. Data domains will not, in general, be intertranslatable in description. What is food for a large animal may be broken into components which are food for smaller animals, but the food for the large animal is not food for the smaller animals. The extent to which a data domain is successfully occupied by a theory may be regarded as inductive support, that is, its viability in that particular data domain. The objectivity of the criteria of support in a domain may be insured partly as a function of local features of the domain. As mentioned, diversity of theoretical adaptations to a given domain is a useful hedge against the situation that arises when the domain is sharply altered. This has, as a consequence, the apparent *desirability* of some features of language generally regarded as lamentable—for example, ambiguity and fuzziness of extension. In the absence of these features, agreement might be forced too quickly, with attendant disaster should the environment change suddenly. That we talk past one another to some extent preserves automatically a variety of theories. Language may therefore embody the evolutionary strategy of containing sufficient similarity to permit cooperation in important matters while hedging against the future by preserving within these constraints a variety of forms. Sufficient ambiguity results in divergence of belief, which on this view, is a desirable feature of a scientific community, even a community sufficiently in agreement to be undertaking normal science research projects as a team.

With this extended evolutionary conception in mind, it is worthwhile going back to our budget of problems (A)–(J) facing methodological falsificationism. I think it clear that these problems can easily be accommodated in this larger perspective, and I intend to discuss only (J). We can imagine Newton's theory (or theories) as well adapted to data domains defined basically by naked-eye observations assisted by the low-power light telescope and various other pieces of classical apparatus. These data domains are not expected to change and they have been explored thoroughly. Newton's theory is therefore as good a theory as one can use, provided that no data showing relativistic effects are to be encountered in some given problem situation. Rather than viewing Newton's theory as refuted and corrected by Einstein's, we may regard it as optimally adapted to this natural data domain. This makes the theory still appropriate to use and yet objective in a sense because its features match appropriately the features of the domain to which it is adapted. Both Einstein's and Newton's theories can exist in a data domain which does not exhibit marked relativistic features. A full exploration of the evolutionary analogy would require some discussion of biological economy and its relationship to competition. Some of Einstein's answers are more accurate than Newton's, but in nearly every case Newton is sufficiently accurate with an accompanying economy of calculation that, restricted to certain domains, Einstein's theory is no real competitor of Newton's. Where relativistic phenomena are involved, of course, Newton's theory isn't even viable.

What I am suggesting is that the history of science should be reviewed, not in terms of gradually changing data but as a series of new data environments opened up by new methods of investigating nature gained partly by the use of extant theories and with theories viewed in strong competition only when they are attempting adaptation to the same domain. This would seem to me to give promise of an explanation as to why not all of the older theories of science have been eliminated for use by scientists, even where "better" theories are available. The account also explains why a still viable theory like Newton's should stop developing at some point in historical time when it is well adapted to the right data domain by comparison to the rapid changes in theories proposed at the frontiers of new data and new scientific problems.

Since this is a book primarily about Popper's philosophy and not about possible elaborations of it, the account just presented seems adequate to show that Popper's evolutionary epistemology is a relatively novel philosophical conception that points in a number of fascinating directions. We will not pursue these directions any further at this point but will return to a critical examination of the detailed consequences of Popper's major methodological positions.

The basic notions and basic positions of Popper's conception of scientific methodology have now been presented: falsifiability, counterinductivism, realism, world 3, and evolutionary epistemology. In the remaining chapters we will see how our philosophical theories about science can be shaped in greater detail by an examination of particular issues in science and the methodology of science in the light of Popper's basic conception of scientific methodology.

FOUR

Popper's Theory of Probability

I The Probability Calculus

It is typical of Popper to have attacked head-on in *The Logic of Scientific Discovery* the most obvious sort of objection that might occur to someone to whom methodological falsificationism had been described. Depending on the methodological rules adopted, a scientific law like "All *A*'s are *B*'s" can be falsified by a single instance, and more complicated laws or theories by sets of basic statements because of a logical contradiction between laws and theories and basic statements. With probability statements, however, no logical contradiction exists between a probability generalization and any finite evidence. No matter how at odds the data may seem with a probability generalization, there is always some chance that the data represent "bad luck" or an atypical sample. For example, we may have a generalization in genetics stating that 3/4 of the offspring of parents, both with a certain genotype, will be pink and 1/4 will be white. Yet all of the offspring of some actual parents of that genotype in an extended test may be white—the improbable has happened! The absence of logical contradiction in the case of probability statements means that falsification will require some sophisticated methodological rules of implementation if it is to be an effective concept. In order to examine Popper's views, we will look at three topics: the probability calculus, Popper's propensity interpretation of the calculus, and Popper's falsification rules for probability statements. Popper has no particular revelations to make about falsification of probability statements. What he is concerned to do is to show that the standard practice of objectivist statisticians is compatible with Popperian methodology and can be interpreted as the practice of methodological falsificationism.

Everyone who has studied the matter has agreed that there is a probability calculus that has the structure of an abstract deductive mathematical theory. This fact involves some differences between possible axiomatizations of the theory of a kind that are not usually encountered in the systems of standard logic. All correct axiomatizations of the propositional calculus are isomorphic in the sense that, under some suitable translation of notation, the theorems of the axiomatizations map into each other in a one-to-one fashion. In probability theory, this is not so. There is a difference between probability calculi using so-called absolute probabilities as primitive and those using so-called conditional probabilities. Conditional probabilities are introduced into calculi with absolute probabilities as primitive by definition, and vice versa. The resulting complete systems are not necessarily isomorphic. Expressions which are meaningful in one system may not be meaningful in another under a reasonable notational translation, and hence one system may contain theorems for which there are not corresponding theorems in the other system. Using conditional probabilities as primitive, it is possible to make some probability assignments that cannot be made using absolute probabilities as primitive. We will have an example using Popper's system shortly. *The* probability calculus as it is often referred to is actually a collection of closely related systems. This fact considerably complicates any comparative exposition of axiomatic probability theory, and partly as a consequence no such exposition will be undertaken here.

Probability theory is regarded as distinct from statistical inference in most textbooks. Probability theory simply explains the facts about various probability *distributions* of events or statements of events given certain information about underlying probabilities. All of this information is a priori and mathematical given the background assumptions. For example, if a fair coin is tossed three times, it may be that three heads will be observed, or two, or one, or none. Probability theory explains what the probability is of obtaining any of these results given that the probability of a head or tails on any given toss is the same. The possible outcomes and the probability assigned to each is known as a probability distribution. After probability distributions are understood, inference about them and an attempt to relate them to action is studied as statistical inference. Suppose a coin has been tossed three times and it has come up heads twice. Perhaps it is also known that the coin is either fair (P(heads) = 1/2) or biased toward heads in a certain way (P(heads) = 2/3). Probability theory will tell us what the probability is of getting two heads on each of these hypotheses. Statistical inference explains that the result obtained is more likely on the hypothesis that the coin is biased toward heads. This inference could lead someone in certain circumstances to act as though the second hypothesis were true. There is one thing worth noting here. The notion that one hypothesis is *more likely* than another is a new intuitive notion that may or may not be in turn explicable in terms of probability. There are different schools of inference which explicate this notion in diverse ways. According to these schools, different answers might be returned to the question of how much more likely the second hypothesis is than the first.

Probability theory is mathematically trivial if the probability distributions involved are finite because the possible cases can be enumerated and exhaustively studied. It can become mathematically very sophisticated when the distributions involved are theoretically infinite. Most real problems in the sciences depend on distributions that are assumed to be infinite in order to take advantage of the known probability mathematics for infinite distributions. As probability theory is developed in practice, it is often started as an axiomatic system or calculus until some forms of the Binomial Theorem, the Law of Large Numbers, and Bayes' Theorem are obtained. The Binomial Theorem is a formula which enables one to calculate the probability distribution of n independent events each of which is a p (with a given probability) or a q (with a given probability) but never both. It thus shows how complicated probability distributions can be handled mathematically. Bayes' Theorem (and the Law of Large Numbers, for which similar remarks are appropriate) paves the way for statistical inference. One simple form of Bayes' Theorem says that the post-experimental (a posteriori) probability of a hypothesis is proportional to the a priori probability of the hypothesis times the *likelihood* of the experimental data given the assumption that the hypothesis is true. (The likelihood is just the conditional probability of the data given the hypothesis.) Using Bayes' Theorem twice on the coin example, it is possible to show that if the two hypotheses are equally likely before the two heads are observed, then the second hypothesis has higher probability after the experiment, because the likelihood of getting two heads is higher assuming it to be true than if we assume the other hypothesis true. Development of the probability calculus encourages the belief that the related probability theory is consistent, and it helps in understanding probability concepts. After versions of the mentioned theorems are are obtained, however, mathematical intuition and more advanced mathematical reasoning begin to operate so as to obtain results which it would be very difficult to obtain axiomatically. The Binomial Theorem is extended to the familiar Gaussian "bell-shaped curve" by techniques of analysis that the so-called probability calculus cannot accommodate. The development of a probability calculus thus plays an important role in foundational aspects of probability theory without in any way exhausting the range of topics usually covered in the whole theory.

These matters are too technical to be developed further here, but we need to say enough to explain Popper's achievements in this area. In an axiomatized probability theory, probabilities are now usually regarded as functions which assign real numbers to sets of events, sets of sets, or sets of statements (and the members thereof) according to the constraints of the probability axioms. We will deal with the set interpretation. The other approaches are all intertranslatable. $P(A)$ is the symbol used to express the value of the probability function P on the set A. It is known as the *absolute probability* of A. $P(A \mid B)$ expresses the *conditional probability* of *A given B*. This expresses the probability that a randomly chosen member of the set B will also be a member of the set A. (The formal arguments of the conditional probability function sometimes appear the other way around in the symbolism of some authors.) Both absolute and conditional probabilities are required in probability theory, but it is usual to take only one as a primitive notion and to introduce the other probabilities by definition. The rough idea is this. If conditional probabilities are primitive, and U is the set of sets over which the probability function is defined, then the absolute probability of A can be expressed as the conditional probability of A given U:

$$P(A) = P(A \mid U).$$

If absolute probabilities are taken as primitive, then conditional probabilities can be introduced as the measure of the intersection of the two sets involved divided by the measure of the given set:

$$P(A \mid B) = \frac{P(A \cap B)}{P(B)}.$$

In this definition, $P(B)$ cannot be 0, or the conditional probability would be meaningless. If conditional probabilities are primitive, then $P(A \mid B)$ could be given a value even if $P(B)$ is 0. Axiomatizations using conditional probabilities can sometimes give more probabilities assignments over certain sets, and this is one reason why probability calculi are not always isomorphic in a straightforward sense.

Most modern axiomatizations of the probability calculus depend on an axiomatization of the probability calculus in terms of sets of sets developed by Kolmogoroff.[1] These axiomatizations take probabilities to be normalized measure functions. Since the set of all subsets of a set in the infinite case may not be such that every set in it is measurable (a classic result of measure theory), probabilities are usually defined over special sets of sets (σ-fields or Borel fields) closed under properties that make them mathematically tractable and yet rich enough for applications of probability theory. Popper's axiomatizations of the probability calculus are roughly of the same period as Kolmogoroff's but were developed independently. Popper uses axiomatizations with conditional probabilities as primitive, and for good reason. We will see in chapter 5 that Popper wants to define corroboration as a function of probabilities in which $P(A|B)$, where B is a scientific law, can be greater than 0 even though $P(B) = 0$, expressing the idea that a law statement is so strong as to have 0 a priori probability of being true.[2] Intuition suggests that a law may be positively corroborated by data in spite of this fact. If absolute probabilities were taken as primitive, then $P(A|B)$ could not be introduced as positive using the standard definition for conditional probabilities cited earlier. By starting with conditional probabilities, Popper produced a probability calculus equivalent to the usual probability calculus in scientific interpretations but allowing another interpretation (corroboration) in which the possibility of making some additional conditional probability assignments was of considerable philosophical interest.

Popper's independent development of the probability calculus is historically interesting when we consider that he did most of his work before becoming acquainted with Kolmogoroff's book or other modern treatments.[3] Claims advanced by Popper that his work is a consistent generalization of other calculi because his calculus is uninterpreted are no longer interesting because modern axiomatics has extensively developed probability systems including those with unusal assignments of conditional probabilities.[4] It is true that Kolmogoroff's system was partly interpreted so that the probability function ranged over sets, but Popper's claims for superiority on the grounds that his calculus is totally uninterpreted seem weak now that the distinction between a calculus and its interpretation has been carefully worked out.[5] We can easily consider statements, events, or whatever as sets in order to use Kolmogoroff's axiomatization or similar modern treatments. The interpretation of the probability function as ranging over sets thus seems harmless. The reason for constructing axiomatizations on fields of sets is to use set-theoretic truths in the development of the probability calculus without requiring that they be proved piecemeal in the probability systems. This leads to a perspicuous and compact development of a probability system. Recently, extensive probability systems where the probability function is defined over sentences in a language have been proposed because modern developments in the semantics of formal languages can be assumed which permit perspicuous and compact development of systems using provable theorems about semantic structures.[6] There is no perspective from which it is entirely clear what should be regarded as purely formal and what should be regarded as interpretation in the development of a probability calculus.

The difficulty just mentioned about not carefully distinguishing syntactic axiomatizations from axiomatizations involving mathematical or semantical structures means that the general question concerning the relationship of structures satisfying Popper's axioms to structures satisfying other axioms, such as Kolmogoroff's, cannot result in a determinate solution. If the usual set-theoretic semantics is employed, then the product or meet of two sets is their (standard) set-theoretic intersection. As we have noticed, all normal probability systems erected on such set-theoretic structures will satisfy Popper's axioms. It is, however, possible to construct some nonstandard set-theoretic structures on which a probability system can be erected because "product" is given a nonstandard interpretation. Since Popper's *product* is undefined, it is possible to satisfy Popper's axioms by such structures although they could not satisfy axioms, like Kolmogoroff's, having an assumed set-theoretic interpretation.

The apparent greater generality of Popper's system is partly real and partly apparent. Insofar as Popper's system is an uninterpreted calculus, the greater range of interpretations appears to make it more general; but this is *apparent only* because it is perfectly possible now that axiomatics has been more fully developed to regard other systems as uninterpreted calculi similar to Popper's with an intended or normal interpretation. Popper's calculus is different from many such calculi in that he defines $P(A|B)$ in some cases where $P(B) = 0$. For example, $P(\overline{A}|A) = 0$ in many calculi, but $P(\overline{A}|A) > 0$ if $P(A|B\overline{B}) = 1$ in Popper's system.[7] Popper has in effect defined some singularities at the limits 1 and 0 of the system that are not treated as defined in some other systems. Among other consequences, this allows him to discuss the corroboration of a law. The corroboration of a law can be positive even though the law has 0 a priori probability. It is a moot point whether to say (as Popper does) that his system is more general (weaker) or whether to say that his system is stronger than the usual systems. If you start with his system, you need to add information restricting its theorems to a smaller class to get various typical interpretations; but starting with the conventional systems, you need to add information defining probabilities that are admissible in Popper's system. Generality here depends on point of view and on how the break between the syntax and semantics of various systems is viewed in detail. This discussion should make it clear that the class of structures satisfying Popper's axioms and the class satisfying Kolmogoroff's (for example) cannot be compared without invoking many technical distinctions. It should also make it clear why a precise answer to such questions of comparison is not of much general interest.

Summarizing Popper's work on the probability calculus, we can say that he provided an interesting axiomatization of the probability calculus at a time when the issue of axiomatization was still of theoretical interest, and this was a considerable achievement. Popper also clearly saw the difference between the probability calculus and an interpretation of it, in this he was ahead of his time. His remarks about the restrictedness of other axiomatizations, however, are not particularly helpful or clear since he seems not to have attempted drawing a charitable distinction between the calculus and its interpretation for other systems. With modern axiomatizations in view, many of Popper's remarks about generality have become pointless. His system nonetheless *is* an interesting extension of the usual probability calculus in which $P(A|B)$ can sometimes be defined for a special purpose such as a discussion of corroboration. In other words, Popper's system interpreted for a discussion of corroboration is a probability system worth discussion because of its special features. Where probability theory is to be applied to empirical situations, Popper's system is consistent with, or identical to, typical probability systems introduced in the literature.

II   The Frequency and Propensity Interpretations

Popper begins chapter 8 of *The Logic of Scientific Discovery* by restricting his discussion in chapters 8 and 9 to the probability of events. This means that the special features of his own calculus can be ignored, and we can consider Popper's interpretation of the probability calculus as equivalent to any standard treatments of it as a calculus of events or sets of events. With respect to this question, Popper was a frequentist in *The Logic of Scientific Discovery* but later in his career offered a revision of the frequentist interpretation that he called the *propensity* interpretation of the calculus. We will first examine the frequency interpretation and then turn to the propensity interpretation.

The classic form of the frequentist theory is usually taken as due to von Mises.[8] Originally, von Mises described random sequences which he called collectives (these can be exhaustively represented and studied as sequences of numbers), and he worked out the rules of probability (corresponding to the theorems of a probability calculus) from the intuitive properties of the collectives. Intuition was heavily involved as the correct rules were worked out from a description of the collectives which was technically inconsistent or empty. By contrast, the usual modern approach (adopted by Popper in the thirties) is to work out a probability calculus and then to define random sequences that will satisfy the calculus nontrivially in the sense that they will provide a sufficiently rich theory for statistical inference in science. I deliberately gloss over the fact that there is no consensus about foundations, that is, exactly which sequences are adequate for this job and are free from philosophical objections.

For our purposes, we will consider only infinite random sequences of 1's and 0's corresponding, for example, to heads and tails in a sequence of coin tosses with a single coin.[9] There are two trivial sequences, those consisting of all 1's and all 0's. The usual problem is to define a much larger class of sequences which are intuitively random. In particular, it would be very desirable to find a random sequence in which the probability of getting a 1 at any place in the sequence was 1/2 and which sequence might then correspond to an actual random sequence given by tossing a fair coin, at least over initial subsequences. By suitably collating this sequence with the trivial sequences, one could gradually build up sequences in which the probability of getting a 1 was 1/4 or 3/4, and so forth, gradually approximating any desired stated probability of getting a 1 at a random place in a sequence needed for scientific purposes. A description of sequences which is such that it cannot be proved that there is at least one nontrivial sequence of 1's and 0's is said in the literature to be inconsistent or empty.

The collectives of von Mises may be regarded as infinite sequences of 1's and 0's satisfying a limit axiom and a randomness axiom. An *initial segment* of a collective will be the first n terms of such a sequence. The limit axiom requires that the ratio of the number of 1's in an initial segment to the length of the initial segment (where the length is the number of places or the number of 1's and 0's) should approach a limit p as the length of the initial segment approches infinity. Clearly the limit p is the probability of finding a 1 in a randomly chosen place in the collective. The randomness axiom requires that any infinite subsequence formed by deleting some of the terms of the original subsequence—according to a rule which makes the deletion or retention of a particular term depend only on its place n in the sequence and not on whether it is a 1 or 0 plus possibly the values of places before it—should have the property that the ratio of the number of 1's in any initial segment of the subsequence to its length approaches a limit p (the same limit p as in the limit axiom applied to the original sequence) as the length of the initial segment of the selected subsequences approaches infinity. Randomness in this sense is supposed to insure that no betting sequence based on properties of the sequence can insure a profit. We can show what this means by an example. If you could make money on a fair bet by betting that 1's would appear more frequently in odd places in the sequence, or by betting on a 1 at odd places, then the sequence would clearly not be random. It would violate the randomness axiom because the subsequence obtained by choosing only the values at odd places would not have the same limit probability as the original sequence.

Frequency views of probability have encountered the difficulty that no absolutely satisfactory way of stating the randomness axiom seems available. The use of the frequency view has not suffered, since tosses with symmetric coins, and so forth, have defined collectives in practice that can be used for experimental purposes. There is, however, considerable difficulty with the philosophical foundations. A rule for deletion or retention of members of the sequence is mentioned in the randomness axiom, but this is a vague prescription. For example, we might delete or retain a member of the sequence depending on whether or not another sequence (computer printout or coin-tossing sequence) showed a 1 in its nth place. This would be a function of n (the place in the sequence) not dependent on the value at n, but the values of some such function could just happen to match those in the collective. The collective would not then be random according to the definition, but of course no collective could be random according to the definition since some rule of this kind will always single out a sequence whose limit ratio is different from that postulated for the original sequence.

Alonzo Church established that the von Mises conception was empty in a rigorous fashion along these lines.[10] Suppose the randomness axiom is expressed in terms of a mathematical function ϕ such that the value of ϕ is 0 or 1 as a function only of n and the values $\phi(1), \ldots, \phi(n-1)$. If $\phi(n) = 1$, then the member in the original sequence at place n is selected for the subsequence in using the randomness axiom. Use of a function ϕ seems to circumvent vagueness in the general notion of a *rule* for selecting subsequences, but an analogous objection holds. A function ϕ on the positive integers can always be found such that it picks out an infinite subsequence of 1's only from the collective. Another ϕ can be found that will pick out only 0's from the collective or original sequence. Church's proof establishes rigorously something that had been suspected by many authors. The randomness axiom is not adequate as formulated by von Mises, nor is any obvious repair satisfactory. Frequentists find themselves in the following situation as a result. The probability calculus can be shown consistent by an interpretation in finite classes where the frequency of A's among B's is simply the number of A's among B's, and this ratio is calculable in the finite case. The finite case will not do for science, nor will it do conceptually for foundational theory. We want to be able to discuss conceptually an infinite (arbitrarily large) number of throws of a coin, and we want to be able to match arbitrarily large data sets to an infinite probability model rather than working out a separate finite interpretation for each set of finite data of different size. The situation is reminiscent of foundational studies elsewhere. For conceptual convenience and clarity we assume that there are an infinite number of integers even though a finite number of integers will be sufficient to permit solution of each particular arithmetic problem. Thus although one could work out a complex probability theory and a theory of statistical inference based on the assumed existence of infinite collectives, one could not satisfactorily define them and some philosophers began to suspect that the notion of a random sequence is inherently contradictory. The feeling is akin to the feeling once widely held that the differential calculus is a suitable tool for research even though the explanation of its workings in terms of infinitesimals was apparently inconsistent.

Suitable conceptual foundations for a frequency theory of probability are still required, but interesting work in two directions has been done. One direction is to attack the conceptual problem by establishing a kind of existence proof for collectives satisfying certain properties given in a restricted randomness axiom. The other direction is to attempt to *construct* collectives that will form a suitable basis for practical statistical inference. These directions are obviously not diameterically opposed in that work on either can be germane to work on the other. Church made an interesting contribution in the first direction by restricting the function in the randomness axiom to an *effectively computable* function on the positive integers.[11] (The function ϕ used in his proof of inconsistency for the von Mises definition is not effectively computable.) The set of all infinite sequences of 1's and 0's among which are the collectives to be defined corresponds to the binary fractions in the interval [0, 1]. The set of effectively computable functions on the positive integers with domain [0, 1] is at most denumerable, but the set of binary fractions has the power of the continuum. If we restrict the sequences with gambling systems to those for which an effectively computable ϕ is used to gamble, then by a diagonal argument we can say that collectives without gambling systems do exist and the notion of a random sequence is not contradictory. This existence proof is due to Church in this form, but it should be pointed out that the resulting set of collectives is very messy. We cannot determine for a particular random sequence whether some gambling system for it exists unless the sequence has an obvious pattern given by its description. We have not proved by this method that a collective with $p(1) = 1/2$ (or any value other than 1 or 0) exists. It is possible that any collectives with $p(1) = 1/2$ compatible with the definition have unintuitive properties, or at least that some of them have. A collective with $p(1) = 1/2$ in the limit for both the limit and randomness axioms could be such that the defining ratios are never less than $1/2$.[12] Intuition suggests that the defining ratio should oscillate around 1/2 in a random way. These comments should indicate why the proof that the notion of a collective is non-empty leaves us with a class of sequences that is not the class of random sequences given originally by intuition as the set of random sequences.

In spite of the difficulties just mentioned, most work on frequentist foundations has tried to deal with a class of sequences in which the function ϕ is limited to a *restricted class* of effectively computable functions.

(This is my way of describing the work of various authors that would have to be *interpreted* along these lines.) Some of the objections cited in the last paragraph will obviously still apply to random sequences generated in this way, but a certain advantage is gained. The class of sequences becomes mathematically more tractable, and it is possible to show explicitly that there are sequences which satisfy the axioms of probability, are useful for scientific purposes, have certain designated probabilities associated with them, and are demonstrably *not* subject to a gambling system within the restricted class of functions. In other words, by considering just certain kinds of gambling systems instead of all possible gambling systems based on effectively computable functions, we are able to show the existence of at least some of the sequences we would like to consider random for scientific purposes. Popper's work on sequences in *The Logic of Scientific Discovery* is located here, as is the work of Reichenbach, Copeland, Wald, and others.[13]

Reichenbach's notion of a *normal sequence* is an interesting example of this approach. A *normal sequence* is an infinite sequence of 1's and 0's such that the sequence is free from aftereffect and is invariant under regular divisions. Freedom from aftereffect means that $p(1)$ is the same in every place in a sequence that follows some fixed finite sequence of 1's and 0's. For example, if $p(1) = 1/2$ in the sequence in the limit, then $p(1)$ must be 1/2 in the (infinite) subsequence obtained by choosing every member of the sequence that follows this string of 1's and 0's: 1101. A regular division of a sequence consists of picking those elements in all places given by the function $m + \lambda n$, where m and n are integers and λ ranges over 0, 1, 2, 3, ... $p(1)$ must be the same in any subsequence obtained by taking a regular division of a sequence as it is in the original sequence. This definition does not establish that normal sequences exist, and Popper objects in *The Logic of Scientific Discovery* that Reichenbach's definitions are not provably non-empty. This was later repaired by Reichenbach who proved that his normal sequences were equivalent to Copeland's admissible numbers, and Copeland has shown how to construct admissible numbers.[14]

The sequences Popper defines are called *absolutely free* sequences. An absolutely free sequence is obtained by taking the notion of n-freedom to the limit. A sequence is 1-*free* if the subsequences obtained by taking only the successors of a 1 and the subsequences obtained by taking only the successors of a 0 have the same probability ratios as the sequence. A sequence is n-*free* if all of the subsequences obtained by taking the successors of all the fixed patterns of n 1's and 0's in the sequence show the same probability ratios as the sequence. With $n = 2$, there would be four relevant subsequences consisting of 1's and 0's chosen as successors in the sequence to the following four fixed patterns of 1's and 0's: 11, 10, 01, 00. *Absolutely free* sequences are sequences which are n-free for every n.

Clearly if a sequence is absolutely free it is free from aftereffect. It is also the case that if a sequence is not invariant under regular divisons, then it will not be absolutely free. The reason is that a subsequence chosen with the right n-period would contain a biased number of 1's, and so failure of invariance under regular divisions entails failure of absolute freedom. A general proof of this would be too difficult for our purposes, but the idea can be conveyed by a simple example. Suppose $p(1) = 1/2$ in a sequence but that 1's occurred in odd places in the sequence with a greater limit probability. Correspondingly, 0's would have to occur in even places with a greater limit probability. This would mean that the sequence would not be 1-free because selection of places after a 0 would show too many 1's. By transposition, an absolutely free sequence is invariant under regular divisions. It follows that absolutely free sequences are always normal sequences.[15] In fact, Popper's absolutely free sequences appear to be equivalent to Reichenbach's normal sequences and Copeland's admissible numbers. The superiority Popper saw for his procedure in *The Logic of Scientific Discovery* was that he was able to *construct* absolutely free sequences, thus showing the concept to be non-empty. Because of the relationship between absolutely free sequences and normal sequences, it follows immediately that Reichenbach's concept is also non-empty.

Popper begins his construction by showing how one can construct a shortest n-free generating sequence such that if this sequence is simply repeated over and over the resultant sequence will be n-free.[16] To construct such a generating sequence for an n-free period, set $x = n + 1$ and write down the 2^x possible x-tuples of 1's and 0's. Order them in a table according to increasing magnitude. Start by writing down the last entry consisting of x 1's and checking this entry off the table. Then increase this finite sequence by adding a 0 if possible, otherwise a 1. A 0 is possible if adding a 0 allows one to construct a sequence in which the last x places are an x-tuple that has not been checked off the table. As x-tuples appear in the finite sequence, they are checked off the table. For a 1-free sequence, we construct these x-tuples:

00
01
10
11

Starting with 11, we can add 0 to obtain 110 and we check off 10. Now we can add a 0 to obtain 1100 and check off 00. A 1 would have to be added next, and we would have generated the 1-free sequence 11001100 . . . . *By stipulation*, 01 is a shortest 0-free generating period. To get the shortest random-like 1-free generating period, we start with 01 and look at the first repeating segment in the 1-free sequence we have already generated beginning with 01. By omitting 110 from the start of that sequence, we get the equivalent sequence 0110011001100 . . . . This is generated by the initial sequence 0110 which is the shortest random-like 1-free generating period. Similarly, a shortest random-like n-free generating period can be obtained from the shortest random-like $(n - 1)$-free generating period by finding an n-free sequence in the manner suggested using the table and then permuting it (or beginning it) with the sequence given as the shortest random-like $(n - 1)$-free generating period and taking the resulting initial repeating segment as the shortest random-like n-free generating period. This is a recursive procedure which, when taken to the limit, produces a constructed absolutely free sequence in which $p(1) = 1/2$. Sequences with other probabilities can be constructed using this sequence and the trivial sequences.

It is worthwhile summarizing Popper's contribution to classical frequency theory at this point, but from a modern perspective. We have seen that the foundational problem reduces to finding non-empty sequences of 1's and 0's that can be regarded as random for the purposes of finding models for the probability calculus. The simple fact is that *it is not possible to satisfy all of the intuitive properties of randomness* in such sequences. In order to prove their existence we select sequences according to mathematical properties which insure sufficient randomness to link the axiomatic calculus to practical applications. Copeland's admissible numbers, Popper's absolutely free sequences, and Reichenbach's normal sequences are roughly equivalent conceptions for doing this job. Using them, we can pick out non-empty sequences that show the calculus to have interesting models. Work in this area continues.[17] It is clear that these sequences are not completely random because of the objection that sequences in the Copeland-Popper-Reichenbach class may have $p(1) = 1/2$ even though the limit frequency of $p(1)$ in initial segments is never less than 1/2. It is also the case that collation of suitable sequences to produce a sequence in which $p(1) = x$ can only be achieved when x is a computable real number, as of course 1/2 is in our examples. Popper's work in this area is of minor general historical importance, partly because it was the work of Church and Copeland which was primarily noticed by researchers in the foundations of probability theory, although it is true that Popper had an influence on Abraham Wald and possibly through Wald's work an indirect influence on modern authors.[18] Retrospectively, Popper's work makes explicit the link between constructible sequences and von Mises' original notion of a collective. We can thus take him to have made an interesting contribution to an important foundational problem in probability theory which was inexplicably ignored by his contemporary philosophers who were interested in such foundational problems.

In more recent years Popper has considerably modified his version of the frequency theory in favor of a view that he has proposed, called the *propen-*

sity theory.[19] The propensity theory has become fairly popular and is one of the interpretations of probability widely discussed in constructing current probability systems.[20] Adoption of the propensity theory does not entail outright rejection of the frequency theory. Popper believes that the frequency theory does provide a coherent interpretation of the probability calculus. The propensity interpretation is regarded by Popper as a version of the frequency interpretation designed to handle several minor flaws in the classical frequency conception, not major errors.

Popper has repeatedly argued against all subjectivistic and logical interpretations of the probability calculus. His major objection to the subjectivistic interpretation is that in it probabilities are a measure of the strength of subjective states of belief, and as such cannot be a matter of scientific record because these are not independently testable. Popper also argues against subjectivists who accept some form of coherence (the idea that the probabilities assigned to beliefs should satisfy the probability calculus under a suitable interpretation) as the sole test of the consistency of a man's beliefs. If coherence is the sole test it seems to permit arbitrary change in probability distributions over time. One may switch from one current set of beliefs to another without reason. Popper's realism and his view of objective knowledge have apparently caused him to reject subjectivistic interpretations on philosophical grounds without a careful look at recent major work on subjectivism and personalism.[21] Apparently Popper feels that a statement of personal probability is not the kind of world 3 statement appropriate to scientific knowledge. His realism demands that probability statements be linked to a definite fact. This point will be important in realizing why the propensity theory seems an improvement on the frequency theory. Popper's dismissal of modern subjectivism is too abrupt. Subjectivists probability estimates coincide with objectivist estimates in many of the cases that Popper cites about probability of events (although they are treated differently in terms of their interpretation). Subjectivists argue that their approach handles all objectivist situations as well as various problems about inference. They see their theory as a legitimate *extension* of objectivistic accounts, although there are some marginal disputes about the validity of stopping rules, and so forth.[22] Popper seems to have overlooked the important subjectivist arguments to the effect that opinion among reasonable men will tend to coincide under the weight of increasing evidence, whether they use Bayesian conditionalization or not. Thus subjectivists do not regard themselves as saddled with irrational, divergent, a priori probability assignments in the way that Popper suggests. It would be too complicated a task here to pit extrapolation from Popper's scanty antisubjectivist arguments against modern subjectivist or personalist interpretations. We merely point out that Popper's realism forced him to take an objectivist position opposed to subjectivism and move on.

Similar Popperian arguments are designed to refute logical interpretations of the probability calculus. Logical interpretations give probabilities as logical measures of the logical *strength* of statements or their content under some content measure. These are a priori probability assignments, and Popper points out that it is not clear how they can be used in science as *rational* estimates of empirical probabilities.[23] There is no argument, of course, that the subjective and logical interpretations will not satisfy the axioms of the probability calculus; the argument is that these interpretations do not result in testable empirical claims that can play a role in scientific knowledge.

One advantage of the propensity theory is connected to a problem in quantum theory, which will be discussed in chapter 8. Another is connected to a general problem about single events,[24] which is a classical objection to the frequency theory and has to do with the fact that the collectives or sequences used by frequency theorists to develop an interpretation of the probability calculus are not empirical entities. We often want to say that the probability of getting heads on a single toss of a coin is 1/2. Strictly, this must mean that the tosses of the coin (in this case, a single toss) can be regarded as matched to the 1's and 0's of an infinite sequence. But suppose the coin is to be tossed only once and then will not be used again. Clearly we are committed to matching the possible tosses of the coin to an infinite sequence. Our general problem is how to pick out an infinite sequence to represent the possible tosses of a coin or any other empirical random variable. The restriction to mathematical entities in working out consistency proofs of the probability calculus comes back to haunt the frequentist when he turns to applications of probability theory. Subjectivists have always been able to handle the single event since their probabilities are measures of the strength of belief and an individual might have a belief about a single coin toss that he is willing to translate into a bet. Before the propensity theory, subjectivism seemed to have the only coherent interpretation of the probability of a single event.

The notion of a propensity is introduced in analogy to that of a force in order to explain conceptually possible behavior. When we say an electron has a certain charge we *do* mean to assert that (per impossible) if it were to be tested in the same way an arbitrarily large (or conceptually infinite) number of times in a certain way the results would be uniform. This is because of a postulated property of the electron and our theory about how this property would interact with the testing apparatus. Propensity theorists regard propensities as postulated (physical) properties resulting in dispositions such that repetitions of an event will result in a sequence with certain properties. The attribution of propensities allows us to realistically ground statements about events that can be tested by experiment.

Introduction of propensities forces a significant change in viewpoint.[25] Suppose a scientist, after repeated throws of a coin, is convinced that the probability of getting heads is 1/2. What is not mentioned explicitly here is that the throws doing the *convincing* must be throws of a certain kind— call them random throws. The same coin could also be thrown by a machine that would materially increase chances of getting a head. It is not just data (as in the classical theory) that underlies our probability estimates, it is data gathered in a certain way given certain physical conjectures about the object or objects being experimented on. A sufficiently long sequence of random throws of our fair coin into which a few of the machine throws were interspersed would still lead to a probability estimate of 1/2. But the machine throws would have a higher probability even though they occurred in a sequence with empirical probability 1/2 or close to it. What a frequentist must do, therefore, is not simply talk about sequences of 1's and 0's representing heads and tails in the case of a coin but talk about the kind of sequence generated by certain conditions affecting objects with certain postulated physical properties.

Propensity interpretations of probability are thus modifications of frequency interpretations in which admissible sequences are virtual (conceptual) or actual sequences characterized as the serial outcome of a repeated conceptual or actual experiment with relevantly invariant generating conditions. A coin may now be said to have a probability on a single event because the probability is a conjecture based on postulated physical properties of the coin and generating conditions amounting to a prediction of the behavior of the coin on repeated trials.[26]

The propensity theory seems an attractive modification of the frequency theory because it does meet some of the major objections to the classical frequency theory and strengthens the conceptual ties of the theory to empirical subject matter. It is not a scientific theory but rather a metaphysical suggestion in the sense that it makes no pronouncements about how to work out probability conjectures for particular experimental arrangements or how to work out comparative probability conjectures for slightly differing experimental arrangements. All of this is left to experience. One assumes that the usual clue will be experimentally observed frequencies in the experimental arrangement or a similar arrangement that has been studied in the past.

Later we will consider at least one objection to the propensity theory in connection with Popper's views on quantum theory. It is, however, worth considering at least one general objection to the propensity theory advanced by Sklar.[27] Sklar objects to the classical frequentist view that its infinite series are an awkward ontological posit and that the theory cannot connect empirical probability assignments with the appropriate infinite sequences. His major objection to the propensity theory is that the experimental arrangement defining a propensity can be described in a variety of ways, each giving rise to a different probability conjecture. Each description is an incomplete, hence possibly misleading, account of the situation. Consider a single coin toss in a situation. A *complete* description might enable us to predict heads, so $p(\text{heads}) = 1$ on this description. An incomplete description might only enable us to make the assignment $p(\text{heads}) = 1/2$. Sklar believes that probability must be relativized, not to an arrangement, but to a *description* of an arrangement, or that some means of specifying a preferred description of the experimental arrangement in advance needs to be set out. The details of working out either case, however, reinstate the objection to the frequency theory that no satisfactory way of linking empirical probabilities to theoretically defined probability sequences is provided.

Sklar believes that the propensity theory does not define probability precisely. We cannot define a probability unless we can *state* the distribution of precise values of initial conditions in a series of trials in an experimental arrangement. It is because we don't know this distribution that we look for a probability, but that means that propensities are inherently vague.

The objections here presented to the propensity theory seem to depend on a suggestion that (at least in theory) probabilities must be sharply defined and that there is a series of precise initial conditions under a complete description which would give us the correct probability even if we cannot know what they are. It may be thought that Popper's realism requires that he accept these premises and the criticism or lapse into subjectivism of some kind. The solution to the problem seems to be that Popper's realism is compatible with indeterminism. We will look at Popper's contention that there are inherently undetermined or chance events in nature in chapter 6. Given this view, Popper does not need to accept the determinism implicit in the suggestion that there is a perfectly precise series of initial conditions (a metaphysical assumption) and so is not saddled with the view that there is such a thing as the probability 1 or 0 for some object to show some property in an experimental arrangement when all these conditions are specified. Popper treats some events as having probability 1/2 because of this indeterminism, not because of our ignorance of the conditions. Probability assignments are like other theoretical conjectures. What we require is only that data can falsify them under our methodological rules. The status of probability conjectures depends on realism and indeterminism and is consistent under the propen-

sity interpretation with these (and the other) features of Popper's methodology.

The more serious problem for Popper seems to be whether the propensity theory coupled with indeterminism is to be sharply distinguished
from modern personalism or subjectivism. In connection with chance
events of the kind studied in science, personalist theory and propensity
theory seem to differ only metaphysically if at all. The personalist puts
any vagueness into the estimate of chance, and the propensity theorist
who is not a personalist must put it into metaphysical indeterminism of
some sort. Personalists take the same kind of observation seriously in
conjecturing probabilities such as observed frequencies and theoretical
frequencies based on them that the propensity frequentist does. Nothing
in the philosophical attitudes suggests diverse answers to the same practical questions. The difference between Popper's propensity theory and
versions of personalist theory as restricted to the probability of events
seems no difference at all except in the manner in which the views are to
be integrated into a philosophical conception of scientific methodology.
Both may choose theoretical conjectures different from empirically observed frequencies in a sample, and both can live with divergent theoretical conjectures provided that discrimination between them is possible
with sufficient data.

III   Methodological Rules of Decidability

We will now suppose that a probability calculus powerful enough to
enable deduction of the normal probability distributions required for
science is available and that an interpretation of the calculus has been
provided. Here we will assume Popper's calculus and his propensity interpretation, but the problem of decidability now arises from the philosophical perspective in which it is thought that scientific hypotheses should be
capable of refutation by experimental fact no matter what calculus and
what interpretation we adopt. The basic problem has already been mentioned and is well known: general probability conjectures are logically
compatible with any finite data. A conjecture that the probability of heads
with a coin is 1/2 in a given experimental arrangement is logically compatible with getting heads on the first eight tosses because eight heads in a
row will appear at times in any infinite conceptual sequence corresponding to repeated throws in such an arrangement. Eight heads in a row is
logically compatible with $p(\text{heads}) = 1/2$ and with $p(\text{heads}) = 3/4$ by the
same reasoning. Therefore we cannot use logic and finite data to *falsify*
probability statements without some methodological decisions. It might
be noted that no amount of finite data can verify probability statements
either. Logic and eight heads in a row (or any finite number of heads in a

row) are not sufficient to prove that $p(\text{heads}) = 3/4$ is true. Any complete philosophy of science must either rule the problem out by denying the foundational relevance of probability theory to science on the basis of a rigorous determinism, or it must provide some kind of methodological decision process for evaluating statistical hypotheses on experimental data. An empiricism which is not based on some rules for accepting or rejecting statistical hypotheses on data must be either incomplete or wrong. Once the importance of accepting rules is recognized here, it is easily seen that such methodological rules are required elsewhere, as Popper has insisted.

Popper's frequentist commitment means that he sees probability hypotheses as asserting both that certain sequences have a limit probability and that they exhibit certain random patterns. The limit assertion means that probability hypotheses can contradict one another and be organized into deductive relationships. Methodological rules for falsifying them depend primarily on the random pattern. In a preliminary move, Popper points out that the falsifiability doctrine suggests that nonstatistical universal hypotheses should be used for explanation wherever possible, since these are more easily falsifiable than statistical hypotheses. We need to discuss the relationship between a statistical hypothesis and data that can test it where a statistical hypothesis must be used to provide scientific explanations.

Popper intends only to establish that his views are compatible with any views found satisfactory by working frequentist statisticians. The very basic ideas are straightforward. In simple cases we define a space of possible experimental outcomes. For example, if we are considering a hypothesis to the effect that $p(\text{heads}) = 1/2$ for some coin, we may be considering an experiment in which that coin will be tossed eight times. The space of possible experimental outcomes then consists of the 2^8 possible sequences of heads and tails that might occur in eight tosses. We then decide to take part of this space as a rejection region, rejecting the hypothesis as false if the data obtained lie in that region. On a normal interpretation, for example, we would expect that the outcomes consisting of all heads or all tails would lie in any sensible rejection region. The idea is to reject if an outcome does not match very closely the expected pattern of an outcome as deduced from the assumption that the hypothesis being tested is true. Where more than one hypothesis is involved, different rejection regions would have to be provided in the space of all possible experimental outcomes for the various hypotheses. Expectation of outcomes can be measured by likelihood and by various other probability functions. Popper's statistical methodological rules are not intended to be general and abstract; he supposes that they are in each case what scientists working in some area will agree to as appropriate statistical tests.

Popper's approach could be developed so that the empirical data could be evaluated by matching some shortest n-free sequence of the kind developed above to the empirical data. The relevant parameter of evaluation would be the number of times the empirical data and the mathematical sequence had the same value under an appropriate coding. Matching could then be a parameter in deciding whether to reject the hypothesis under consideration. In eight tosses of a coin with $p(\text{heads}) = 1/2$, for example, we would expect more matches with the shortest random-like 3-free generating period than with a string of eight 1's. This matching procedure ties acceptance of frequentist views on statistical inference to the appropriate frequentist views on foundations and could be worked out in detail to provide a frequentist theory of statistical inference. Although such an approach is barely sketched out in Popper, it is very close in spirit to some current efforts to use computers to evaluate statistical inference in scientific problems.[28]

Although Popper's theory of statistical inference amounts to a demonstration that the views of Fisher, Neyman and Pearson, Wald, and others are *compatible* with his philosophy of science and his views about foundations, it is important to note that Popper's evolutionary epistemology requires a somewhat different *interpretation* of the same mathematics.[29] Most statisticians talk freely of accepting or rejecting hypotheses on the basis of methodological rules (including decisions about the size of various parameters); Popper can only speak of statistical inference as *rejecting* hypotheses. This raises an important problem. Whether or not to reject a hypothesis (for example a null hypothesis in a test of significance) often depends in practice, in the opinion of most statisticians, on what reasonable alternative hypotheses are available. Although some statisticians (Fisher) feel that single hypotheses can be evaluated on given evidence without considering alternatives, all statisticians agree that the most pleasant situation is when one is asked to evaluate two incompatible hypotheses on the basis of data much more likely on the one hypothesis than on the other. If we have to take a choice in this situation, the rational choice is often obvious and agreed upon by statisticians with differing methodological viewpoints. The point is that if we consider a single hypothesis and data not very likely on that hypothesis, we are likely to reject the hypothesis. But if the only reasonable alternative hypothesis is such that the data is sufficiently less likely on it, then the data which was enough to cause us to reject the first hypothesis is sufficient to cause us not to reject it in the context of the second hypothesis. Popper's logic of falsifiability dwells primarily on the relationship of a single hypothesis to data. This view is too limiting to prove revealing in the context of much of statistical practice which is based on considering alternatives, but we have already seen that Popper's views require some modification to permit greater consideration of the alternative hypotheses available.

The following aspect of statistical explanation is worth mentioning. There may be, at any given time, only a single universal hypothesis available to explain some range of phenomena. When a statistical hypothesis must be introduced, there is immediately an infinite range of hypotheses to be potentially considered, namely, all of the hypotheses differing simply in the probability assigned to some situation. For example, if a coin is such that $p(\text{heads}) = 3/4$ or $p(\text{heads}) = 1/4$ and we get eight straight heads on suitable tosses, we may be inclined to reject the latter hypothesis. Without narrowing our range of alternatives in this way, we would have too many hypotheses to evaluate. The logically possible hypotheses consist of the total set of conjectures of the form $p(\text{heads}) = x$, where x is any number in the interval $[0, 1]$. A difficulty with Popper's remarks about statistical explanation is that there must perforce always remain an infinite number of possible statistical hypotheses not rejected by past data on the basis of the usual methodological rules. It is clear that some considerations of simplicity and analogy operate in addition to the postulation of propensity analogies in order to single out a restricted class of statistical hypotheses to examine, and Popper's methodology has said virtually nothing about how this process takes place. The hypotheses involved are not distinguished in a suitable fashion by a measure of their logical content, so simplicity related to logical content cannot be involved. Consider a coin made as symmetrically as possible. In a certain tossing arrangement, perhaps all statisticians would accept $p(\text{heads}) = 1/2$ as the hypothesis to be considered first, but odd conjectures close to this hypothesis could not be ruled out. Popper has objected to this kind of arbitrariness in personalist views, but it threatens his remarks about statistical falsifiability. Simply lumping the problem with the methodological rules to be determined by scientific practice seems too easy. This is not a differential criticism of Popper in the sense that philosophical methodologies have not had much to say that is satisfactory about this problem of apparent preference for simple hypotheses.[30]

Popper's views on statistical inference are *conservative* in the sense that he is merely attempting to show that normal frequentist accounts of statistical inference are compatible with his account of falsifiability, and hence that statistical inference properly viewed (as rejecting hypotheses only) is no counterexample to his theory. This fact seems not to have been fully appreciated by some critics. Harré writes that experimental error and the technique of averaging results are not compatible with falsifiability.[31] This is because all of the results of particular measurements are different from (and falsify) the value in the hypothesis in the typical case. It seems quite clear that this is plausible if and only if the role of methodological rules in deciding what counts as falsification is ignored.[32] Popper's use of methodological rules makes it clear that the usual theory of errors of measurement can not only be used but is required by realism and the notion of objective knowledge. In spite of the initial appearance of great difficulties for falsifiability in the use of statistical hypotheses, Popper has provided sufficient argument for his view that statistical inference is compatible with the general outlines of his methodology.

FIVE

Popper's Evaluation of Scientific Theories

I Verisimilitude

In this chapter we will discuss Popper's remarks about the problem of evaluating competing scientific theories. Throughout Popper's writing he has insisted that theories with high content must be sought but that high content should be evaluated with an eye to explanatory power. To put it intuitively, a scientist searches for an explanation of a given set of events or of facts that will resolve some puzzle, and to provide this explanation he searches for the theory with highest content (compatible with scientific intuition about what constitutes a *plausible* theory in the area of the problem). Such a maxim cannot be fully formalized by known techniques because of its reliance on the notion of plausibility which has so far escaped formal definition.

The notion of content has undergone a considerable change in the development of Popper's thought. *The Logic of Scientific Discovery* discusses the "goodness" of theories, which is measured by their universality, simplicity, precison, and so forth. Mention of the *truth* of theories is simply circumvented. Popper's discovery of Tarski's theory of truth enabled Popper to see a way of discussing the truth of scientific theories in a manner compatible with his insistence on the importance of metaphysical realism. A notion of relative truth-content called *verisimilitude* then began to dominate Popper's thinking about the evaluation of theories so that by later publications verisimilitude alone is treated as the major means of assessing the intrinsic worth of scientific theories:

Thus the old philosophy linked the ideal of rationality with final, demonstrable knowledge . . . while I linked it with the *growth of conjectural knowledge.* This itself I linked with the idea of a better and better approximation to truth, or of *increasing truthlikeness or verisimilitude.* According to this view, finding theories which are better approximations to truth is what the scientist aims at; the aim of science is knowing more and more. This involves *the growth of the content of our theories,* the growth of our knowledge of the world.[1]

Rather than dealing with the various evaluative notions introduced in *The Logic of Scientific Discovery,* it seems best to turn directly to Popper's notion of verisimilitude.

The key notions underlying verisimilitude are due to Tarski: the semantical notion of truth, and the notion of the (logical) content of a statement.[2] Popper's treatment assumes that there is a fixed class of logical truths L, and also (apparently) a common language for expressing all scientific truths. Consider a statement A. The deductive closure of A (the set of all logical consequences of A) will be denoted as $Cn(A)$. A could be the conjunction of a number of axioms involved in a finitely axiomatizable theory, that is, a formal theory for which a finite set of sentences constitutes a suitable set of axioms. If A is true and B is true, so that $Cn(A)$ and $Cn(B)$ are sets of true sentences, then the verisimilitude of A and B can be easily compared if A implies B but not vice versa. Since A has greater content than B in these circumstances, we take A to have greater verisimilitude. *Verisimilitude* is a word consciously adopted to capture an intuitive notion of a distance from a scientific ideal of a total true account of the world, that is, a measure of "truth-likeness." Should neither A nor B imply the other, there is no straightforward measure of comparative verisimilitude unless some sort of measure of comparative logical content of A and B is devised. Popper has indicated how such a general comparative measure of logical content can be derived, so that if A and B are both true, we can speak meaningfully of their relative verisimilitude.[3] In many cases, however, statement A or B will be false. We may not know that a statement is false even though it is false. Many scientific theories have been proposed and discussed and then have been discovered to contradict accepted data. It might therefore seem desirable to have a notion to compare the verisimilitudes of false theories, so that we can at least say that, historically, theory B had greater verisimilitude than theory A even though both proved later to be false. This must be done if general comparisons of verisimilitude are to be possible and if we are to trace scientific progress through the graveyard of falsified scientific theories of the past. To do this, Popper splits the set of statements $Cn(A)$ into two sets, the *truth content* of A (the true sentences in $Cn(A)$) and the *falsity content* of A (the false sentences in $Cn(A)$). A true statement will have no false consequences, so its falsity content will be null. In other cases, however, a statement A will have both a non-null truth content and a non-null falsity content.[4] To compare verisimilitude, the relative "sizes" of the truth and falsity contents would have to be compared. Now suppose we have two statements A and B such that either the truth content of A is included in the truth content of B while the falsity content of B is included in or equal to the falsity content of A, or the falsity content of B is included in the falsity content of A while the truth content of A is included in or equal to the truth content of B. In either case it seems intuitively obvious that A has less verisimilitude than B. On such a basis one may hope eventually to erect a calculus of verisimilitude to compare any arbitrary pair of statements (and hence any pair of axiomatizable theories) A and B.

What Popper is driving at is quite simple. With a little care in attending to details, he hopes to be able to compare the size of the truth and falsity contents of a theory. Obviously, if the falsity content is nil, the theory has relatively high verisimilitude. A good theory will always have high truth content by comparison to its falsity content. At one point Popper had proposed a general measure $vs(A)$ of the verisimilitude of a theory A ranging from -1 to $+1$ depending on the relative sizes of the falsity and truth contents of A. All theories (true or false) have all logical truths among their logical consequences. What are wanted are theories with the greatest empirical truth and absence of empirical falsehood. The logical truths and logical falsehoods can be canceled out between rival theories, leaving verisimilitude as a measure of empirical truth and falsity contents. High verisimilitude if properly worked out would be a measure of high empirical content in this sense.

Popper has observed that competing theories, such as Newton's and Einstein's, can be compared in terms of verisimilitude.[5] Clearly Einstein's theory has an answer at least as precise as that given by Newton's to every question answerable by Newton's theory, according to Popper. (The perceptive reader should note how this opinion involves the idea that there is a language in which both theories can be stated and compared.) There are also questions that can be answered by Einstein's theory but not by Newton's. Therefore it seems reasonable to hope that we can establish that Einstein's theory has greater verisimilitude. Popper says that we can conjecture that Einstein's theory has greater verisimilitude because of these facts.

Popper's early treatment of theories resulted in the observation that we want theories with high content. The trouble with high content per se is that it is compatible with falsity. Verisimilitude is better: it is a measure of the trade-off of truth content and falsity content. Perhaps we cannot construct a theory with no falsity content—then we simply use the theory with highest verisimilitude as assessed against background knowledge at present. This allows us to use falsified theories in science, but not Newton's, of course, since Einstein's theory has higher verisimilitude as assessed against background knowledge. Although verisimilitude expresses our aims better than truth or content, we need to assess whether we can say anything useful about verisimilitude. Popper says we cannot know that we have achieved truth. That is an important aspect of fallibilism. At the same time we can assess content and order theories (in principle) according to their content. Can we assess verisimilitude? The answer seems to be that we cannot because we cannot know what is true and hence we cannot measure the "size" of the truth content of a statement A. The concept of verisimilitude shows that Popperian methodology is possibly consistent, not that it can be shown to be workable in detail in practice. Should Einstein's theory be falsified, it may turn out to have less verisimilitude than Newton's theory or even incomparable verisimilitude. The point is that it may have many more false consequences than Newton's theory just because it has higher content. Any assessment we make of verisimilitude is thus no more secure than our assumption that certain facts obtain. Since this assumption is always open to doubt, we cannot be sure but that our estimates of verisimilitude point in the wrong direction. Verisimilitude is an interesting notion to pursue, because its pursuit (based on our conjectures of verisimilitude) results in a search for more testable theories. At the same time, we are never in a position to say, as Popper sometimes suggests, that we can know that we are approaching the truth because we have theories with increasing verisimilitude. This can happen only in trivial cases—for example, where we replace an inconsistent theory with a demonstrably consistent theory. In general, we can know only that we may have increased verisimilitude or have increased apparent verisimilitude, not that we have increased verisimilitude, unless we know that we have increased the range of (unshakably true) data.

So far, we have discussed verisimilitude as though it were a workable notion. Unfortunately for Popperian intuition, all of Popper's technical proposals for capturing verisimilitude are vitiated by some formal consequences of his definitions.[6] Popper has actually offered a variety of slightly different technical proposals for defining verisimilitude, but they are all subject to criticism along similar lines, which seems to lead to at least one important negative result: the verisimilitude of false theories cannot be compared utilizing the relative sizes of truth and falsity contents along the intuitive lines suggested by Popper.

Suppose we have two theories A and B. As we saw earlier, the problem of comparison is difficult where at least one theory is false. Suppose theory A to be false. Using the intuitions about verisimilitude already discussed, we can then show that theory B cannot have less verisimilitude than a (false) theory A no matter what theory B is. (We restrict ourselves to considering logically consistent theories A and B to narrow the range of possible cases.) Since A is false, it has a non-null falsity content containing at least the statement F. If B is to have less verisimilitude than A, then the truth content of A must exceed the truth content of B while the falsity content of A is included in or is identical with that of B, or the falsity content of B must exceed the falsity content of A while the truth content of B is included in or is identical with that of A. This is simply a restatement of the basic intuition underlying comparative verisimilitude. Suppose the former case to hold.[7] Then there is a statement A^* which is in the truth content of A but not of B. Now consider the false conjunctive statement $F \wedge A^*$. Since A^* and F are consequences of A, this conjunctive statement must be in the falsity content of A. B cannot imply $F \wedge A^*$ because it would then imply A^*, and that isn't possible because of the choice of A^*. Therefore $F \wedge A^*$ cannot be in the truth content of B or the falsity content of B. So if the truth content of A exceeds that of B, then the falsity content of A must exceed that of B. Now suppose the falsity content of B to exceed that of A. Then there is a false sentence B^* in the falsity content of B but not in the falsity content of A. Consider $F \supset B^*$. Since F and B^* are false, this is a true statement which is in the truth content of B but not in the truth content of A. The reason for this is that if A is logically consistent then A must imply either the negation of F or B^* in order to imply $F \supset B^*$. (It is clear from the construction that $F \supset B^*$ is not a logical truth.) But A implies F and hence cannot imply the negation of F if it is consistent, and A cannot imply B^* by the choice of B^*. Therefore $F \supset B^*$ is in the truth content of B but not in the truth content of A. If the falsity content of B exceeds the falsity content of A, then the truth content of B must exceed the truth content of A. We thus have the result that if a consistent theory A is false, no theory B can have less verisimilitude. It follows immediately that no pair of false theories A and B can be ranked in terms of comparative verisimilitude according to Popper's intuition about the basis for comparative verisimilitude.

The defects in the currently formulated versions of verisimilitude do not establish that the notion cannot be rescued by new definitions and possibly extended intuitions about verisimilitude. There are some considerations with respect to verisimilitude, however, that suggest that verisimilitude may not be a crucial notion for an evolutionary methodology. Popper's original notion that *high content* was important in his campaign against positivism seems well worked out. To combat subjectivism, on the other hand, Popperian verisimilitude suggests that science has as its goal a total true description of the universe and that verisimilitude can measure objective progress toward this goal. The goal fits into the framework of a single language for science described earlier in that the description of the universe, if achieved, would presumably take place within this language. Scientific progress through the rejection of bold conjectures requires the notion of high content but not that of verisimilitude. Progress is in fact a slippery notion in the context of an evolutionary theory save in the sense of short-range adaption to environment. As selection pressure varies, so species adapt, and new species may invade previously uninhabitable ecological niches. We have here an account of change and of adaptation but not necessarily an account of progress toward a definable goal. Involved is a notion of fitness-to-an-environment used to compare directly competing species, but this measure is not terribly useful when one compares species adapting to nonoverlapping environments. In general an evolutionary sequence does not need to be construed as directed toward a single nonmetaphysical goal. There is short-term adaptation and competition, but the direction of change is adaptation to an environment which may change in unpredictable ways.

It would seem from one perspective that Popper's use of verisimilitude allows the cumulative picture of factual accumulation to reassert itself from positivism in order to combat subjectivism. This doesn't seem to be necessary on the evolutionary account sketched earlier. In this account we see theories as adapting to various data domains. Many theories will properly be regarded as noncomparable in the same domain even if they have overlapping but divergent truth contents. Viability will be a function of the size of truth content and perhaps some factors of elegance, and this will determine how important falsity content is, not the absolute size of falsity content. In any event, until some satisfactory unified theory appears, such theories will exist side by side no matter what their comparative verisimilitude. Similarly, theories adapting to different data domains will belong to science no matter how their comparative verisimilitude might be assessed. The upshot of these considerations is that verisimilitude is a notion of restricted value when theories are taken to be adapting to different data domains. A theory will drive out another theory only when it blankets or covers the truth content of the other theory, a situation that will arise somewhat infrequently. In parallel to evolutionary sequences elsewhere, scientific theories will proliferate over time, "high types" arising as new data domains are opened up as a result of new measuring techniques. From this perspective objectivity will have to be a limited and short-range property describing the way that particular theories are linked to particular data domains. The idea that there is a grand plan for scientific progress then goes the way of the idea that a creator is guiding the direction of organic evolution.

II   Corroboration and Testing

Even if the details of verisimilitude could be worked out, this would merely show that Popperian methodology is consistent. We would know that theories could be ranked in terms of verisimilitude, but in practice we would be unable to measure truth and falsity contents so as to have an algorithm for making arbitrary comparisons of some index of verisimilitude. The older Popperian notion of corroboration thus still has considerable importance for Popperian methodology.

Corroboration is introduced by Popper to describe how well a non-falsified but falsifiable theory has stood up to tests. On Popper's current view, because of his realism, a theory is true or false or possesses some degree of verisimilitude: it is not useful or probable. In practice we must rank theories by *apparent* verisimilitude, that is, by a measure of corroboration which explains how well they have survived the tests we have brought to them. This is our only practical test of actual verisimilitude. The major difficulty with corroboration is that its introduction (like the introduction of verisimilitude) forces Popper's total system to the brink of contradiction, since corroboration seems so close to inductive support that the intuitive idea of corroboration threatens Popper's counterinductivism. One commonplace criticism of Popper's total philosophy of science is precisely that, although he outlaws inductive support, he smuggles the notion back into his system with the introduction of corroboration.[8] Exactly what is the relationship between high corroboration and hypotheses that can be accepted and relied upon in future cases? Strictly, Popper should hold that high corroboration has nothing to do with an expectation that the hypothesis will continue to prove reliable. On the evolutionary metaphor, its possible truth may be overthrown on the very next example. Popper does say this explicitly:

> Corroboration (or degree of corroboration) is thus an evaluating *report of past performance.* . . . Being a report of past performance only, it has to do with a situation which may lead to preferring some theories to others. *But it says nothing whatever about future performance, or about the "reliability" of a theory.*[9]

What we also know is that Popper holds that of two hypotheses, the more improbable or the one with less verisimilitude may be the more highly corroborated, so that corroboration does not measure some logical probability or the verisimilitude of a hypothesis. (Of two hypotheses, of course, the more logically improbable may come to have higher a posteriori probability after certain experiments.) What corroboration does is to induce a preference ordering on scientific statements at some given point in time.

One aspect of this is that any statement derivable from various theories will have the highest corroboration of any of the theories from which it can be derived.[10] By using this principle and methods of assessing the corroboration of isolated sentences we can assign an index of corroboration (at least within certain limits—the notion is not entirely formal) to the scientific statements available at a time, and we will prefer to use the most highly corroborated statements in the explanations we offer at that time. Corroboration is a guide to conjectural truth or verisimilitude—but we cannot know that we have found truth or verisimilitude. We do not *rely* on highly corroborated statements in Popper's view, and we certainly cannot know them to be true.[11] They can be discovered false more easily in many cases than poorly corroborated statements. We use them because we find that their use maximizes the chance of falsifying them and hence of increasing the rate at which knowledge progresses. We may also use them in circumstances where we must act on theory—but we do so warily, not expecting that the theories we are acting on will continue to be corroborated.

Let us look at an evolutionary analogy. Suppose a species is attempting adaptation to a stable environment. If its reproductive cycle were to be speeded up, it could find (by random search) the best adaptation more quickly than would be the case on a slower cycle. Looking at a mutant gene or a new genotype, we could not reliably predict what it would do in the environment—we would have to wait and see. Corroboration is a measure of fitness in the current environment. It would be a projected measure of fitness if we knew the environment would remain stable. But as we have previously noted, the environment may change cataclysmically at any time, and so current fitness is not a guarantee of future fitness. As we have seen, positivistic inductivists are likely to view the data environment of science merely as cumulative and expanding, with no regions disappearing or drastically changing. Under this view, inductivism is reasonable. But the view is wrong and Popper has correctly stressed that it is wrong. His evolutionary outlook enables him to escape paradox with the notion of corroboration. Corroboration would not have to be regarded as a measure of verisimilitude. It could be taken at face value as a measure of fitness in an environment. Because of this, the idea of corroboration may escape the difficulties associated with verisimilitude.

In the rest of this section, Popper's positive view of corroboration will be examined. Popper has an important negative point—namely, that corroboration cannot be a probability function—and we will discuss this in connection with the Carnap-Popper controversy in the next chapter. The positive view of corroboration consists of a definition, some desiderata about corroboration satisfied by the definition, and some informal further considerations.

Several different definitions satisfying the stated desiderata are presented by Popper.[12] The exact formal definition is not so important to
Popper as the fact that the desiderata can be satisfied by a corroboration
function. $C(x,y)$ is the formal expression, to be read "x is corroborated by
y," or "x is confirmed by y," or "x is supported by y." Popper uses *confirmation* frequently and may have originally introduced the term, but it
is avoided here to prevent confusion with the inductivist notion of confirmation that will concern us shortly.

$C(x,y)$ is in turn dependent on a notion $E(x,y)$ of explanatory power of x
with respect to y. $E(x,y)$ is a nonadditive measure (that is, it merely *orders*
relative explanatory power) with numerical bounds $+1$ and -1. We set
$P(x,y) = 1$ whenever y is inconsistent. This is compatible with the probability calculus and is a great convenience in working with corroboration.
To work out the corroboration measure we must first work out a probability measure based on content for the sentences we are interested in as
expressed in some suitable language. Assuming that $P(y) \neq 0$, then we can
define an explanatory power function as follows:

$$E(x,y) = \frac{P(y,x) - P(y)}{P(y,x) + P(y)}.$$

Notice that $E(y,x)$ and later $C(x,y)$ are functions of probabilities. When
Popper says $C(x,y)$ is *not* a probability, he means that there is no probability $P(x,y)$ that can be identified with $C(x,y)$ without contradiction or
counterintuitive results. Functions of probabilities need not, of course, be
probabilities. $E(x,y)$ is not a probability since for some arguments its value
is negative. We should also note that the probability functions given here
are given by logical probabilities defined over sentences in a language. We
are not discussing scientific theories here in the usual framework of statistical inference but are making methodological observations about the
structure of scientific knowledge. As usual, high content is associated
with low probability and vice versa. There are various well-known ways to
do this.[13] Assuming a satisfactory logical interpretation of probability and
content, we can now turn to the meaning of $E(x,y)$. To interpret $E(x,y)$,
notice that if x is a hypothesis and y is data, then if the hypothesis x makes
the data y less credible than it had been, the numerator will be negative
since $P(y) > P(y,x)$, and so $E(x,y)$ will be negative. If $P(y) = P(y,x)$, so x is
neutral with respect to y, $E(x,y) = 0$. In the remaining cases $E(x,y) > 0$.
$E(x,y)$ is a measure of the increase in probability for available data given
the hypothesis x. If x increases the probability of y when added to background knowledge, then x is said to explain y. Note that for a given hypothesis x, $E(x,y) > E(x,y')$ if $P(y) < P(y')$. The more precise and extensive the
data (hence the less antecedently probable the data), the higher the explanatory power of a hypothesis which explains it. In practice, of course,

this is somewhat vague since given data may require application of simplicity or some form of idealization to be brought into the compass of an
explanatory hypothesis. $E(x,y)$ is defined for all pairs of sentences, of
course, and not simply for pairs consisting of hypothesis and a data sentence. $E(x,y)$ may be maximized if $P(y,x) = 1$. In this case,

$$E(x,y) = \frac{1 - P(y)}{1 + P(y)},$$

and this approaches 1 as a limit when $P(y)$ approaches 0. A similar argument shows that $E(x,y)$ can be minimized with -1 as a limit when $P(y,x)$
approaches 0. The corroboration function can now be explicitly defined:

$$C(x,y) = E(x,y) (1 + P(x)P(x,y)).$$

From the definition of $E(x,y)$ we have the restriction that the function is
not defined for $P(y) = 0$.

Popper's procedure at this point is to lay down nine intuitive desiderata
for a corroboration function and to show that his corroboration function
satisfies these desiderata.[14] We will not follow the technicalities here, but
the desiderata will be informally described. The first desideratum (i) is the
obvious requirement that $C(x,y)$ be positive, zero, or negative as y supports
x, is independent of x, or undermines x. A second desideratum (ii) gives $+1$
and -1 as the (conventional) limits of $C(x,y)$. Desideratum (iii) requires
that the a priori probability of x and the content of x be such that they
range from 0 to $+1$, as they must if $P(x)$ is a probability and content is the
inverse of probability in the a priori situation. Clearly desiderata (i)–(iii)
merely insure that the values of $C(x,y)$ code what $C(x,y)$ intuitively represents in an intuitive way. If y implies x, then according to desideratum (iv)
the corroboration of x is the same as the content of x. In other words, the
corroboration of x cannot be raised by a discovery which *could not* have
undermined x. Similarly, desideratum (v) insures that, if y entails x,
$C(x,y) = -1$ since x is totally undermined or falsified by y. Desiderata (iv)
and (v) capture basic Popperian intuitions about falsifiability. Now let x
have high content (be a priori improbable). Let y support x, namely,
$E(x,y) > 0$. Desideratum (vi) says that $C(x,y)$ should increase with the
power of x to explain y. This desideratum deals with the important case
where x is a law or theory with high content that explains some supporting instance y. In these circumstances, the corroboration of x should increase with its explanatory power with respect to y. The remaining desiderata are more complicated. Suppose the content or a priori probability of
x and y to be equal. Then desideratum (vii) allows ranking of pairs $C(x,u)$
and $C(y,w)$ where $P(x,u)$ and $P(y,w)$ can be compared. If the probability
of x given u is higher than that of y given w, then $C(x,u) > C(y,w)$. A
similar situation arises when $P(x,u) > P(y,w)$ or $P(x,u) = P(y,w)$. Then

$C(x,u) < C(y,w)$ and $C(x,u) = C(y,w)$ respectively. Now suppose x implies y. The case we are primarily interested in is where x is a law or theory that explains y. Desideratum (viii) says that the law is corroborated to the greatest extent where y is antecedently improbable, and that for fixed data, that statement is most corroborated which is antecedently most probable. The former conforms to the intuition that a theory which successfully predicts a highly unlikely event is highly corroborated by the appearance of that event. The latter allows Popper a wedge for arguing that statistical laws may be highly corroborated by certain data. Desideratum (ix) revolves around a situation in which $\bar{x}$ entails y but $P(\bar{x}) \neq 0$. Then, for given x, $C(x,y)$ and $P(y)$ increase together, and for given y, $C(x,y)$ and $P(x)$ increase together. This desideratum says that x is not corroborated by anything which is entailed by the negation of x. $P(y)$ cannot be 0, but as y becomes more trivial in the logical sense, and $\bar{x}$ entails y, the corroboration of $\bar{x}$ by y and the undermining of x by y both come close to 0, that is, y is not an interesting datum with respect to the corroboration of $\bar{x}$ or x. Also, the more probable x is, the less it is undermined by y where $\bar{x}$ entails y. This is to say that we may still be tempted to regard x as highly corroborated in many situations.

It is clear that the nine desiderata capture in a formal way (when technically stated) Popper's intuitions about laws and theories and how they may be evaluated at a given time with respect to the available data. In producing the function $C(x,y)$, he has also shown that these desiderata can be satisfied by a mathematical function. $C(x,y)$ thus provides a proof that the important intuitions underlying Popper's claims about falsifiability, deductive explanation, and the importance of theories are consistent with one another. Let us look more closely at some of the desiderata. Suppose we are concerned with deductive explanations involving laws. The content of such laws is arbitrarily high, but their probability is arbitrarily low (usually 0). By (iii) the confirmability of such laws can be arbitrarily high, and by (viii) their corroboration may be arbitrarily high if they explain data with arbitrarily high content. Even if such laws are assigned 0 a priori probability, they can have high corroboration. This is permitted because of the technical features of Popper's probability calculus in which $P(x,y)$ can be greater than 0 even though $P(y) = 0$.

Now suppose we are interested in a statement u expressing some fixed range of data. Then by (viii) the most highly corroborated law or hypothesis will be one entailing u with the highest a priori probability. If laws have probability 0, this is not very helpful. However, if the fine structure of probability is brought into context by considering how fast laws or hypotheses go to 0 a priori probability as the size of the universe increases, we can regard (viii) as affording some limited protection against ad hoc restrictions on the statement of laws. Clearly, in the former case, all laws or hypotheses entailing the data are equally well corroborated. Here it will not do to simply call for the strongest law, the one that rules out the most, for either this is not a clear idea or it is subject to various kinds of counterexamples. For example, consider these possible generalizations:

(1) All maples, except perhaps those in Eagleville, are deciduous.
(2) All maples are deciduous.
(3) All maples whatsoever, and all sassafras trees in Eagleville, are deciduous.[15]

We have it that (3) entails (2) and (2) entails (1). Now clearly (3) is the strongest, most falsifiable hypothesis, the one with the greatest logical content. There are two possibilities: either that $P(1) = P(2) = P(3)$, or that $P(1) > P(2) > P(3)$, depending on the cardinality of the universe. In the former case, a preference for (2) in explanation over (3) must depend on some intuition about simplicity or natural kinds. In the latter case, (viii) allows us to choose (2) over (3), but it does not rule out (1). Perhaps (1) can be ruled out by a consideration that maples in Eagleville should also be of scientific interest if our generalizations are to be universal, but this once again depends on a further elaboration of universality, or simplicity, or natural kinds. Popper's desiderata thus leave many detailed questions unanswered by philosophical methodology; satisfying them shows only that certain key claims about corroboration can be consistently held. The remainder of a corroboration preference ranking must depend upon features that are not formalizable, or have not yet been formalized.[16] Unless the details of a preference ranking for scientific statements can be worked out, at least in context, Popper's assertion that corroboration can provide a preference ranking for such statements is not complete. In advance of research into actual preference rankings, there is no particular reason to suppose that scientists can or should agree on the features of such statements required to produce a uniform normative ranking.

Let us return for a moment to the operative intuition behind corroboration. A statement is highly corroborated (has a high value $C(x,y)$) if and only if it is both highly falsifiable and has been severely tested. A statement is also highly corroborated if it is a logical consequence of a theory t that has high corroboration. High corroboration means highly preferred for future testing as a means of advancing scientific knowledge (not accepted as true), so that if we prefer t we must prefer all of its testable consequences.[17] $C(x,y)$ is a measure of corroboration only if y is a report on the severest tests that can be designed for x.[18] This is a kind of "total evidence" requirement except that "evidence" of a justifying kind is not in question. It is remarkably difficult to fit all of these remarks together.

Consider the case where one statement A entails another statement B and both are scientific (falsifiable) and B does not entail A. Then A is more *falsifiable* than B. A can be more severely tested in that B is just one consequence of A, and A can be tested by testing consequences other than consequence B. B can, of course, be more highly corroborated than A—for example, when A has been falsified although B has not. A can be more highly corroborated than B when A has survived severer tests. But since A entails B, B must have corroboration equal to A, unless Popper does not mean this to hold when A is not a theory, in which case the notion of *theory* requires some clarification. It therefore seems to be the case that, although A entails B under these circumstances, B can be more highly corroborated than A, but not the converse.

There are some objections and replies in the literature which trade on ambiguities or vagueness in this area. Barker, for example, has argued that Popper is committed to holding that, if A entails B and neither has been falsified, then A must be better confirmed, but in fact the situation is (contrary to Popper) that B must be confirmed to at least the degree that A is.[19] There is doubtless some confusion in this criticism regarding the notion of confirmation to be clarified. Allowing for this, we have the following facts. Let e consist only of tests of B. Then if A entails B and e represents the background evidence, Barker is correct. If f consists of tests of A (some but not all of which may be tests of B), then it is clear that $C(A,f) > C(A,e)$ if A survives the tests. It is because of this fact that A may be said to be better corroborated than B. Notice that the formulas all contain expressions of the form $C(x,y)$ which express corroboration with respect to given evidence. Whether or not A is more highly corroborated than B depends on this reference evidence. Because of the rule that all consequences of A are taken to be as highly corroborated as A, we *do* have the consequence that, after full evaluation of our theories, B cannot be less well corroborated than A.[20] Barker's confirmation law seems to rely either on different intuitions or on a misreading of Popper.

Another style of argument against Popper, which has already been noted, is that corroboration is really a form of inductive inference. Salmon, in *The Foundations of Scientific Inference*, makes the following claims about Popper's corroboration: "Corroboration is a nondemonstrative form of inference. It is a way of providing for the acceptence of hypotheses even though the content of these hypotheses goes beyond the content of the basic statements."[21] Popper's response to such charges seems to be primarily that corroboration is not an *inference* of any kind and that scientists do not *accept* hypotheses (as true), they decide to promote further critical discussion of the highly corroborated ones.[22] That corroboration is not an inference seems to follow from the latitude it permits for personal preference in practice. Highly corroborated theories are to be pursued, but differing scientists may well pursue differing highly corroborated hypotheses within the limits permitted by the notion of corroboration which relies on some intuitions regarding the notion of a severe test. I believe that close attention to the underlying evolutionary epistemology is sufficient to clear Popper of any charge of smuggling inductive inference back into his conception of methodology through the use of the notion of corroboration.

A much more interesting line of criticism has been offered by Isaac Levi.[23] Levi's position is interesting in that it is not based on inductivist proclivities and is quite sympathetic to Popper. What Levi does is to accept some of Popper's intuitions, add the notion of an epistemic utility function, and then produce a nonprobabilistic (in Popper's sense) theory of confirmation or corroboration. Levi holds that Popper is forced to view corroboration as an acceptance notion; otherwise, it would be devoid of philosophical significance. We have already repudiated this line of criticism, but Levi's remarks are so interesting that we will proceed as though Levi were correct in making this charge.[24] What Levi first observes is that a function satisfying Popper's desiderata for a corroboration function does not therefore necessarily have all of the features that Popper's informal discussions of testability imply. In other words, the desiderata function as necessary conditions only, and some of them are quite trivial in the sense that they depend on the content measure adopted by Popper in his formal discussion. Satisfying the desiderata does not establish that the goals of scientific inquiry (even as conceived by Popper) are being best realized. This is not a head-on confrontation. Levi points out that fecundity, advancement, problem raising, and so forth, are just as likely to be served by false hypotheses as true ones. Popper would not deny this: falsifiable hypotheses may well be false. The point that the desiderata do not insure fecundity, and so forth, can at least be blunted by Popper's observation that the informal discussion of testability is what is important and an admission that the desiderata are merely suggestive and may require supplementation. The proposal that Levi suggests is that the desiderata be supplemented by an epistemic utility function and that the desiderata (revised slightly) be met by maximizing expected epistemic utility rather than corroboration.

Levi's objections raise an interesting point about the development of Popper's views and the relationship between corroboration and verisimilitude. Corroboration is by far the older notion, playing an important role in *The Logic of Scientific Discovery* even though verisimilitude is not mentioned. We can regard verisimilitude as an ideal notion that we would like to achieve for our theories in practice. Corroboration can then be regarded as a measure of *apparent* verisimilitude against the conjectural truth of our background knowledge.[25] Corroboration cannot measure verisimilitude (simpliciter) due to our earlier observation that we cannot be sure we have attained truth with respect to background knowledge. It is fairly easy to show that corroboration is a measure of apparent similitude in the cases that interest us. For example, if X is a universal hypothesis and Y is the conjunction of background information (including the data), then $C(X,Y)$ becomes the following since $P(X) = 0$:

$$C(X,Y) = \frac{P(Y,X) - P(Y)}{P(Y,X) + P(Y)}.$$

This is the appropriate formula for relative verisimilitude.[26] Popper has thus now met Levi's objection that corroboration is not appropriately linked to the goals of scientific inquiry provided that verisimilitude can be given a good definition. If verisimilitude is the goal of inquiry, then corroboration is the measure of apparent verisimilitude, and this is the best we can hope to achieve in practice. A comparative evaluation of Levi and Popper (which will not be attempted here) then depends on a comparative evaluation of apparent similitude and Levi's epistemic utility.

What we need to decide now is what apparent verisimilitude tells us. Popper sees inductive logics as *compelling choice* of the hypothesis or theory with the highest probability, while he merely regards his theory as measuring the severity of tests with no compelling consequences for choosing a hypothesis or theory with high corroboration to work on.[27] Let us look briefly at the problem of a committee which has the power to fund research. We can assume that resources are scarce and compel some choice as to which projects should be funded and to what extent. The problem is equivalent to that of a single scientist who is trying to decide what hypothesis or theory he should spend his limited research time on. An inductivist might suggest spending all of the funds on the hypothesis (or those hypotheses) with the highest inductive rating. A noninductivist might suggest funding randomly chosen hypotheses or theories (perhaps those chosen only from among hypotheses or theories with positive corroboration) since one cannot support the conjecture that one hypothesis is more likely to be true than another. In this case, however, it is not clear why we should bother to evaluate corroboration, except possibly to determine if it is positive. If one's intuition is that considerable funds should be spent on the most highly corroborated hypothesis or theory but that other hypotheses or theories should also receive some support on the chance that our estimate of apparent verisimilitude is misleading, then corroboration would be a guide to the rational statistical distribution of research funds. This, incidentally, is the strategy that would be abstracted from evolutionary theory. A single scientist making a decision might rationally decide to work on a neglected hypothesis *as a contribution to science* because the highly corroborated ones were receiving a great deal of attention. It is this problem of institutional effort in science that Popper seems to miss in sharing with the positivists (and many philosophers) the idea that rational activity can be determined for a single individual confronting a range of hypotheses. If that were so, all individuals (insofar as they were rational) would do the same thing. In order to use corroboration and apparent verisimilitude as an important measure, Popperian methodology should connect it to an appropriate sociology of knowledge for guiding scientific research where a community of scientists is involved.

It should also be explicitly noted that corroboration is not a form of eliminative induction as that form of induction has been understood. Eliminative induction is employed to raise the probability of the remaining noneliminated hypotheses when some hypothesis in a range of alternatives is eliminated by falsification. A form of eliminative induction is employed by contemporary subjectivist or personalist probability theorists who distribute the a priori probability 1 among a partition of the viable hypotheses or theories in some area of scientific research in order to obtain the a priori probabilities needed to use Bayes' Theorem. Corroboration leaves all probability values for universal hypotheses at 0, and it is not a probability. Popperians, however, could use comparative corroboration values in assessing hypotheses or theories in the manner suggested in the last paragraph. This means that the pragmatic difference between Popperians and Bayesians might be small in spite of a considerable difference in philosophical outlook.

There is one aspect of corroboration that we have not yet considered. Relative corroboration seems most valuable precisely where there are a number of alternative hypotheses whose corroboration can be clearly measured against fixed data. But in many historical situations of a kind Popper is most interested in, situations in which bold new conjectures were proposed at a high theoretical level, the corroboration of these bold conjectures was extremely low. It is well known from historical cases that both the Darwinian evolutionary hypothesis and the General Theory of Relativity were accepted by scientists in spite of the fact that very little testing of these theories was done when they were proposed, and very little testing could be done because no effective tests could be devised.[28] There are also examples where competing hypotheses were accepted by different groups of scientists in spite of the fact that differential tests of the hypotheses could not be devised. An example would be the disagreement between steady-state and expanding cosmologies some years ago when tests to discriminate between them quickly could not be devised.[29] Cosmology also involves hypotheses that seem to be physical and scientific without being testable.[30] Popperians can, of course, brazen these situations out by claiming that they represent cases where metaphysical theories were gradually attaining scientific status. This appears ad hoc in view of the fact that at least the cosmological hypotheses seem or did seem to make clear physical assertions in spite of their low testability.

The answer to the budget of examples of apparent scientific hypotheses with low testability must differ with cases. Clearly where bold new hypotheses are suggested along with possible new kinds of data (as in the case of General Relativity), one may argue that the lack of serious rivals allows a hypothesis of low corroboration to be accepted by scientists because of potential fit with a plausible new data domain. But why should these hypotheses be accepted at all, even in the Popperian sense? Part of the answer may lie in a notion of simplicity based on the entrenchment of certain scientific models along with formal generalization as an appropriate means of generating new theories. In other words, a new theory that is similar to previously well-corroborated theories in the sense that its intuitive formal structure is roughly isomorphic with previously well-established theories, or is a formal generalization of a well-corroborated theory, may be widely accepted even though it has not been tested. Popper's conception of simplicity in *The Logic of Scientific Discovery* was a function of logical content. This notion of simplicity cannot override corroboration because of this fact, and it can be criticized on independent grounds.[31] The notion of simplicity suggested here is not a Popperian function of logical content but a form of conservatism with respect to theoretical style that is related to the corroboration of older theories. It is not equivalent to corroboration, but it might be used to explain acceptance in the absence of corroboration in cases of the kind cited where well-corroborated theories are absent as direct rivals, or where a theory can be seen to be a generalization of a well-corroborated theory. Some such notion needs to be worked out if the Popperian notion of corroboration is not to be subject to historical counterexample and if the material provided by these historical counterexamples is to be made consonant with a methodology dependent on the notion of corroboration.

SIX

Popper and Inductive Inference

I Carnap's c-functions

We have now stated Popper's general arguments for a nonjustificationist evolutionary epistemology and we have looked at his own conception of corroboration as a consistent means of expressing his intuitive ideas about assessing competing scientific hypotheses. We have also seen that Popper's general arguments *against* induction rest on his philosophical arguments *for* falsifiability. The situation is that although we have presented and criticized Popper's positive views we have not examined his specific critical views against competing methodological theories. In the first section of this chapter we will examine Carnap's inductive system, the major classical competitor to Popperian methodology, and hence the system Popper was most interested in rebutting through critical argument.

Let's start with a historical look. Suppose we restrict ourselves to languages in which no quantifiers appear, and since the details will not matter later, suppose we illustrate how a probability measure could be assigned to such a simple language with an example. Let the language be a predicate language having the single primitive predicate H and three individual constants 1, 2, and 3. The sentences of the language can be regarded as generated by the atomic sentences H_1, H_2, and H_3, which state respectively that 1, 2, and 3 have the property H. U (the universe set) can be taken to have as its elements the eight possible worlds which can be described by sentences constructed from H_1, H_2, and H_3 by logical operations as follows:

$$u_1 = H_1 \wedge H_2 \wedge H_3.$$
$$u_2 = H_1 \wedge H_2 \wedge \bar{H}_3.$$
$$u_3 = H_1 \wedge \bar{H}_2 \wedge H_3.$$
$$u_4 = H_1 \wedge \bar{H}_2 \wedge \bar{H}_3.$$
$$u_5 = \bar{H}_1 \wedge H_2 \wedge H_3.$$
$$u_6 = \bar{H}_1 \wedge H_2 \wedge \bar{H}_3.$$
$$u_7 = \bar{H}_1 \wedge \bar{H}_2 \wedge H_3.$$
$$u_8 = \bar{H}_1 \wedge \bar{H}_2 \wedge \bar{H}_3.$$

Each of these worlds describes a possible way in which the three individuals may or may not have the predicate. $\bar{H}_1$, of course, is the negation of H_1. Let our simple language be called L'. Every sentence of L' can be obtained as a function of H_1, H_2, and H_3 using the logical operators ~(negation), $\wedge$ (conjunction), and $\vee$ (disjunction).[1] The sentences u_i are the *strongest* sentences in L' in the sense that *any* other sentence of L' which is not contradictory can be regarded as equivalent to a disjunction of some one or more of the u_i. For example, H_1 is itself equivalent to a disjunction: $u_1 \vee u_2 \vee u_3 \vee u_4$. According to the probability calculus, the probability of the union of two disjoint sets is the sum of their probabilities. We read this as saying that the probability of the disjunction of two logically incompatible statements is the sum of their probabilities. We can use this fact to assign a probability to every sentence S of L' provided that we can assign a probability to each of the u_i, since such a probability is simply the sum of the probabilities of the u_i appearing in the disjunction of the u_i which is equivalent to S. A probability axiom for absolute probabilities is that $p(U) = 1$, where U is the universe set of sets to be assigned probability values. Any probabilities assigned to the u_i which sum to 1 (where U has a finite number of elements, as in our example) will satisfy this axiom as well as the other axioms of the probability calculus. One obvious move is to adopt a symmetric measure, that is, to assign $p(u_i) = 1/8$ for all of the u_i in the language L'. This assignment gives a probability measure satisfying the probability axioms for the language of the example.

Carnap's procedure for defining probability measure over languages was slightly different in detail, even for simple languages of the kind presented in our example. Consider a conditional probability $p(S|T)$ which might be defined over pairs of sentences (S,T) from a language L. Our aim would be to treat the conditional probability as the probability of S being true when T is known to be true, or as a measure of a rational betting function setting the odds we would regard as fair for a bet that S was to be found true when T was given as true, or as the inductive support for S given T, or as the degree of confirmation of S given T. These notions have been regarded by

Carnap as intuitively equivalent. Carnap was interested in defining a conditional probability in this sense that he could regard as a confirmation function.

Carnap's procedure was as follows. One starts with a language and defines a measure function m (this measure function can be regarded as a probability function) over the sentences of the language. The measure function gives a priori probability values to the sentences of the language. Then the confirmation function defined as follows gives the degree of confirmation of S given T in terms of the a priori assignment.

$$c(S \mid T) = \frac{m(S \wedge T)}{m(T)}.$$

Formally, it is easy to see that this is quite analogous to the way in which conditional probabilities are introduced into a system of absolute probabilities. Consequently, it is easy to show that the degree of confirmation function $c(S \mid T)$ introduced in this fashion is a probability and satisfies the axioms of a conditional probability calculus.

Consider a function $c(S \mid T)$ defined over a language L' we have used as an example where $m(u_i) = 1/8$. It is interesting that this symmetric measure has counterintuitive inductive properties. Suppose we interpret H as "lands heads" and 1, 2, and 3 as referring to three tosses of a given coin. Then H_1 expresses the claim that the coin lands heads on the first toss, and so forth. A continuing thread in Carnap is that a man's inductive assessment of sentences should change with evidence. If a man begins believing a coin fair, and he observes mostly heads when he tosses it, he should change his opinion about the coin as evidence for its bias increases. The reason $c(S \mid T)$ as defined above is counterintuitive can be related to this principle as follows. Let S be H_3, which is equivalent to $u_1 \vee u_3 \vee u_5 \vee u_7$. Although the language is simple and the tosses few in number, one expects that the degree of confirmation of H_3 should be higher if the first two tosses are heads than it is if the first two tosses are tails. We represent the possible evidence statements as follows:

$$H_1 \wedge H_2 = u_1 \vee u_2.$$
$$\bar{H}_1 \wedge \bar{H}_2 = u_4 \vee u_8.$$

Since u_i and u_j are such that they cannot be true together when $i \neq j$, we have $m(H_1 \wedge H_2) = m(\bar{H}_1 \wedge \bar{H}_2) = 1/4$, and $m(H_1 \wedge H_2 \wedge H_3) = 1/8$. Therefore

$$c(H_3 \mid H_1 \wedge H_2) = \frac{m(H_1 \wedge H_2 \wedge H_3)}{m(H_1 \wedge H_2)} = \frac{1/8}{1/4} = 1/2 =$$

$$\frac{m(\bar{H}_1 \wedge \bar{H}_2 \wedge H_3)}{m(\bar{H}_1 \wedge \bar{H}_2)} = c(H_3 \mid \bar{H}_1 \wedge \bar{H}_2).$$

Thus, although we have a probability function, it fails to satisfy a necessary intuitive desideratum. We need to require *more* of $c(S|T)$ than that it be a conditional probability. Now consider these sentences:

$$U_3 = u_1.$$
$$U_2 = u_2 \lor u_3 \lor u_5.$$
$$U_1 = u_4 \lor u_6 \lor u_7.$$
$$U_0 = u_8.$$

These sentences are those saying there is exactly one head in the three tosses, and so on, as indicated by the subscripts. As the U_i are elements of L', we can define a new measure function as follows:

$$m^*(U_i) = 1/4.$$

This does not yet define $m^*(u_3)$, for example. But we set $m^*(u_i) = m^*(u_j)$ whenever u_i and u_j belong to the same U_k. m^* is symmetric within each U_k. Now we have $m^*(u_3) = 1/12$, for example, and it is easy to see that m^* makes assignments compatible with the assignments to the u_k and that m^* makes an assignment to each sentence in the language by virtue of its assignments to the u_i. c^* is the function defined as before given the measure m^*:

$$c^*(S|T) = \frac{m^*(S \land T)}{m^*(T)}.$$

Now we can show that $c^*(H_3|H_1 \land H_2) > c^*(H_3|\bar{H}_1 \land \bar{H}_2)$. c^* satisfies the intuitive desideratum that we be able to learn from experience. c^* is the confirmation function that Carnap finds adequate for a language like L'. To get c^* for any finite language without quantifiers and a set of monadic primitive predicates which partitions the individuals into disjoint sets, one assigns m^* the same value for each set of possible worlds with the same statistical distribution of individuals and then divides the value of m^* equally among the members of each such set. c^* is then given by the definition cited. Assignments for more complicated languages (where they are possible) can be determined by consulting the literature.

These are the features of the example, and by extension of Carnap's early work, worth noting:

(1) A probability is defined for every sentence in L. This completely solves the foundational problem of when probability assignments can be made at least for sufficiently simple languages. Such a feature is always attractive to philosophers who are interested in formalization.

(2) To avoid truth-value gaps, we will assume that the coin of the example is tossed and either H_3 or $\bar{H}_3$ is true. An *inductive* estimate of the statistical probability of H_3 or $\bar{H}_3$ must be restricted to the possible

values of H_3, namely, to 1 or 0. In other words, you would have to guess that the coin will land heads or tails. A *Carnapian* estimate of the statistical probability of H_3 or $\bar{H}_3$ does not (and cannot) take the value 1 or 0 unless H_3 is part of the evidence. A Carnapian estimate *tells you how to bet*, it does not solve the problem of induction, that is, it doesn't tell you how the coin will land after a sufficient number of trials. When Carnap says that probability$_1$ values (c* values) are estimates of probability$_2$ values (statistical probabilities), he means Carnapian estimates, not inductive estimates.

(3) $c^*(S|T)$ is defined relative to a language. Thus, if the foundational problem of finding the best confirmation function is to be solved, a *best* language needs to be designated by reference to which the c-function is to be defined.

(4) As the number of individuals in L increases, the measure of the sentence representing the claim that every individual in L has some non-trivial (empirical) property tends to 0. Thus, every general law will have measure 0 in any language with an arbitrarily large number of individual constants. The subset of U containing such a claim is always a single point and hence has measure 0 when the cardinality of U becomes arbitrarily large. The Carnapian estimate of the statistical probability of a general law on any evidence is always 0; that is, the Carnapian estimate leads to the conclusion that any general law will have counterexamples and is false.[2] This has produced enormous controversy. Carnap can defend this result in terms of his intuitive understanding of what he is doing as providing a rational betting function. The probability of 0 for any hypothesis corresponds to the fact (fallibilism) that one *expects* any hypothesis to be proven false sooner or later by data. Because of this one cannot win a bet on a hypothesis because there is no point at which the bet can be won because the truth of a hypothesis can never be established. What was said a moment ago is not quite correct in the Carnapian framework. A general law could be true, but there are simply no circumstances in which it is rational to bet on the truth of a general law or hypothesis. Scientific bets must therefore be construed as bets on instances of laws to be examined over the short-range future. Instance confirmation will apply to such bets, and instance confirmation of the next few cases of a hypothesis or theory may be positive. In general, therefore, Carnap's system does not enable us to assess theoretical generalizations on the basis of observational evidence except indirectly through instance confirmation.

There is no point in following Carnap's development. *The Logical Foundations of Probability*, in which one finds the c*-function defined over simple languages like L', is out of date. Carnap himself has abandoned many features of it due to a clarified conception of the intuitive concept that he was developing at that time, and also due to assorted technical difficulties. The major technical difficulty was simply that the c^* probability could not be defined by generalization on the strategy employed for simple languages when the languages became rich enough to incorporate quantificational structure. Carnap's program has also been modified so as to allow consistency with personalism. Thus, in the current program, the two concepts of probability remain, but personal probability is seen as a partial reconstruction of *rational credibility*, the concept the Carnapians are clarifying. From their point of view, the program is truly foundational in that it accepts and consistently relates the claims of the major schools of probability. Personal probability as incorporated into the notion of rational credibility becomes the Carnapian estimate of statistical probabilities in relevant cases. The program has considerable philosophical appeal for this reason, although a way must be found to circumvent the technical difficulties, which still abound.

The final views of Carnap and the development of his work by Jeffrey and others is to be found in more recent literature.[3] Here Carnap treats inductive logic as part of the theory of rational decision making. He accepts as a first step the views of Bayesian personalists about betting. A person at some time is faced with a decision among some number of possible acts. The value of an act is the sum of the utilities of the possible outcomes or consequences of the act multiplied by the probabilities of the outcome. A rational agent chooses that act for which this sum is maximized, or any for which it is maximized if there are more than one.

Carnap sees two branches of decision theory, or the theory of rational decision making: the theory of actual decisions (which involves psychology) and the theory of rational decisions (which is close to a branch of logic). Actual decision theory depends on a credence function which gives as values the degree of credence for a person at a time of some proposition on given evidence. Different persons may have different credence functions, and the same person may (as a matter of fact) have different credence functions at different times. An actual rational decision is one that maximizes utility (in the Bayesian sense), using the credence function to determine the probabilities of the outcomes involved in an act. As is well known, a person's credence function can be determined from his actual (and hypothesized) betting behavior.[4]

Rational decision theory imposes some restraints on a credence function (a generalized confirmation function) to insure that some desiderata about rationality (different desiderata are cited by different authors) are met by the function. Most personalists require that the credence function be *coherent*. We will not be able to explain coherence in detail, but the idea of coherence is that a credence function is rational if and only if there is no betting system based on the credence function such that the agent must lose on certain fair bets based on his credence function. Coherence is achieved if the agent's credence function is a probability. Strict coherence requires further not only that the credence function be a probability but that it assign probability measure 1 to everything that the agent can prove true. The idea behind strict coherence is that a credence function is rational if and only if there is no betting system based on the credence function such that the agent might lose but at best could break even on certain fair bets based on his credence function. Personalists define rationality in such a way that a rational agent is someone who makes his decisions by maximizing utility on the basis of a coherent or strictly coherent credence function. It should be fairly clear that personalists are fairly lenient in their description of rationality in that two agents with wildly different credence functions based on completely different a priori probability assignments could both be considered rational. A credence function is strictly coherent if and only if it is *regular* in Carnap's sense.[5] Carnap requires strict coherence (which is obviously a stronger constraint than coherence), but he also requires more stringent conditions on a rational credence function. We can see the normative intention of Carnap's approach based on ignoring features of actual decisions (which may not even be coherent in the technical sense) and looking for strong constraints in the following:[6]

> Axiom systems [for strictly coherent or coherent credence functions] are extremely weak; they yield no result of the form $p(H|E) = r$ except in the trivial cases where $r = 0$ or $r = 1$. In my view, inductive logic should accomplish much more.[6]

Here we have clearly expressed the foundational drive to make probability assignments more than a matter of coherence and personal intuition.

We will not pursue here the technical developments which have come from this beginning, but it is useful to note how impoverished they are. For example, there is no treatment of languages involving relations of two or more places, and such languages are surely required for formalizing any interesting area of scientific research.[7] This fact in itself is sufficient to indicate the modest results achieved so far.

Why is the problem so difficult? Rationality requirements (in particular, strict coherence) demand that a probability measure of 0 be assigned to a molecular sentence or proposition only if it is impossible. Among the impossible propositions are those expressed by logically false sentences. When a probability structure is defined before possible data is considered, these will be the only impossible propositions along with those ruled out by the axiomatic structure of any theories imposed on the language. After evidence is accumulated certain other sentences will become impossible because of the structure of families of predicates. For example, if a is measured and found to be heavier than b, and b heavier than c, then a must be heavier than c without measurement because of the theoretical structure of weight relationships. In this case, the evidence and the relevant theory have made any sentence expressing the claim that c is heavier than a certainly false. As long as we stick to monadic predicate languages and theoremhood is decidable, the credibility function over such a language is effectively decidable and can be computed for all possible pairs of values. When we go to richer languages, this fact breaks down simply because logical truth and falsity are not decidable. Without an effectively computable confirmation function, it is hard to see how we might program a positivist robot to do scientific inference utilizing c-functions. Because of the completeness theorem for first-order logic, we can define logical truth for richer languages. We could then imagine the robot to make revisions in its credibility functions if it made discoveries about logical truth. The harder problem comes with the axiomatic structure and various inexpressibility results for the empirical statements of a richer language. Carnap has always insisted that meaning postulates giving relationships between predicates are part of the analytic apparatus of a language. The trouble comes with trying to specify all of the meaning structure that may be involved with two or more place predicates. Carnapians generally say that this is no different in principle from the monadic case. In other words, we can set down various constraints (reflexivity of a predicate, for example) and then talk about the models in which these constraints are satisfied. In view of the incompleteness results and lack of a decision procedure for theoremhood of theories involving such constraints, it is not easy to see how we can characterize a rational credence function that a robot could use within the framework of Carnapian rationality. The robot would seem forced once again to revise its credibility function *without new evidence* when it makes discoveries about theoremhood, contrary to the Carnapian conditionality requirement which insists that rational changes in credence functions must be based on new evidence.

Lest my objection be misunderstood, let me emphasize that the *theory of inductive logic* that Carnap is developing is not under attack—one can postulate that a Carnapian credence function makes the correct assignments without fear of encountering contradiction. The difficulty is to know how to proceed with it in applications of rational decision theory— that is, how to connect it with the theoretical construction of a robot mechanized to do science, or how to connect it with scientific problems the solution to which one would like to program in some fashion. The practical difficulties are enormous, even for pure theory. We have noted that no satisfactory current credence function for languages with dyadic predicates is available. The reason for the practical difficulty is partly this. For a monadic predicate, the evidence can be reduced (usually) to the number of individuals examined and the number that have had a given predicate. For a relation, we may need to keep track of all examined pairs and various patterns in the pairs (whether there are reflexive pairs, symmetric pairs, and so on). Thus the class of relevant parameters for defining a credence function (at least the class of plausible candidates which in practice will have to be exploited to represent the significance of the data) will rise very rapidly with the complexity of predicates involved with a language. I don't intend to explore Carnapian interpretations of the probability calculus as a logic of confirmation further.[8] That would take too much space to do thoroughly, and until part 2 of *A Basic System of Inductive Logic* is available, any detailed attempt may be premature.

II Carnap versus Popper

The problem now confronting us is to make some comparative evaluation of Carnap's and Popper's conceptions of scientific methodology in the area of inductive inference. Popper's most general argument (derived from Hume) against inductive systems is based on the observation that, to put it in my vocabulary, a sudden change or extension of our environment may completely scramble our assessment of available scientific theories. To say that one theory is more probably true than another is to say something that we cannot justify since odds on unexpected environmental changes simply cannot be computed. In the face of this, Carnap's system is an irritating analytic claim. Popper is opposed to *certainty* as a criterion of the scientific. Carnap's c-functions, in merely giving a priori measures on the information in a language, do not provide Popperian empirical information. The problem for Popper is to find an effective basis for criticism of Carnap. Carnap has simply calculated rational credibility functions based on certain assumptions (which Popper partly shares) about how scientific data will change over time. Attacking these assumptions cannot refute Carnap. One *can* argue that even if these assumptions are granted, or partly granted, Carnap's system violates certain intuitions. One might *also* argue that Carnap's system is simply inconsistent, assumptions and intuitions aside. Popper has pursued both lines. In this section we will examine Popper's arguments to the effect that Carnap either violates clear intuitions or is caught in an outright inconsistency.

INTUITION AND CONFIRMATION In a series of articles, Popper has attempted to show that no function satisfying the probability calculus can also satisfy clear intuitive desiderata for confirmation or corroboration.[9] The formal argument supporting this claim consists of demonstrating that various truths of the probability calculus will be false in certain cases if $p(x,y)$ is interpreted as a confirmation function, and that therefore no confirmation function can be a probability. We will consider the version of this argument provided on pp. 390–391 of *The Logic of Scientific Discovery*.

Consider the following assertion about probabilities: There exist statements x, y, and z describing events such that

(1) $p(x,z) > p(x)$ and $p(y,z) \leqslant p(y)$ and $p(x,z) < p(y,z)$.

Popper shows (1) to be true by considering an example. We will confine ourselves to a toss of a homogeneous die. Let x express the conjecture that a 6 will turn up, let y be the negation of x, and let z be the claim that an even number will turn up. We have, in terms of a priori probabilities, $p(x) = 1/6$, $p(y) = 5/6$, and $p(z) = 1/2$. We also have $p(x,z) = 1/3$ and $p(y,z) = 2/3$. Clearly (1) holds when interpreted as in this example. Now Popper claims we also have the following, letting $Co(x,z)$ stand for the fact that x is corroborated by z:

(2) $Co(x,z)$ and $\sim Co(y,z)$ and $p(x,z) < p(y,z)$.

Now if degree of confirmation and probability is identified, and $C(x,y)$ represents the degree of confirmation of x by y, we have

(**) $Co(x,z)$ and $\sim Co(y,z)$ and $C(x,z) < C(y,z)$.

Popper claims that (**) is clearly self-contradictory, so that degree of corroboration or confirmation cannot be a probability.

This is a curious refutation. To begin with, $Co(x,z)$ is identified with a probability assertion in order to get (2). The alleged fact that an even number will turn up is hardly a *test* of the claim that a 6 will turn up. Popper is sensitive to this, claiming that "degree of corroboration or confirmation" is taken here in a wider sense than usual, meaning "degree of support" rather than "degree of severity of passed tests." This clouds the picture of the intuitive notion being clarified nonetheless.[10] Further, (**) is clearly not a *formal* contradiction. To get a contradiction, some relationship between $Co(x,y)$ and $C(x,y)$ must be found.

$Co(x,y)$ is a sentential connective, and $C(x,y)$ is a function from pairs of sentences (x,y) into some interval of the real numbers. We require an r such that $Co(x,y)$ if $C(x,y) > r$, or perhaps something like $Co(x,y)$ if $p(x,y) > p(x)$. The latter reading is suggested by passages in Popper.[11] Suppose we take this reading and let $Co(x,y)$ be *Popper's* concept of corroboration. On this interpretation, (2) is not a contradiction since it is true under the reading given by the original die example. Turning to (**), (**) can be contradictory only because of a connection between $Co(x,y)$ and $C(x,y)$, as we have noted. If we identify $Co(x,y)$ and $C(x,y)$, it is fairly easy to show that the following statement which results from substitution, is false:

$Co(x,y)$ and $\sim Co(y,z)$ and $Co(x,y) < Co(y,z)$.

But although this is false, its falsity doesn't show that (**) is *contradictory*. All we have shown is that Popper's corroboration function is not a probability, which was already known.

Let us consider another way of relating $Co(x,y)$ and $C(x,y)$ so as to get a different reading of (**). We keep our definition of $Co(x,y)$ and simply identify $p(x,y)$ and $C(x,y)$. Then clearly (**) and (2) are the same after notational change, and since (2) is true in the example, neither is contradictory. The identification may give a poor definition of degree of confirmation which does not satisfy Popperian desiderata, but it is hardly contradictory. Popper has alleged that (**) shows Carnap's system (in which $C(x,y)$ is a probability) to be contradictory, but he cannot establish that. Carnap relies on differing intuitions. Kemeny seems to have put his finger on the crucial difference.[12] For Carnap, the intuitive notion of the degree of confirmation of x given y is roughly how sure we are of x when we have y as evidence. The clash of intuitions is obvious. We are never *sure* even to a degree, according to Popper, so the notion is useless. Popper's intuitive notion of the degree of confirmation of x given y is roughly how severely y tests x. Any view that careful probabilistic inductive systems can be refuted by demonstrable contradiction utilizing (**) seems incorrect once the differing intuitions are sorted out. Popper and Carnap are simply explicating different concepts. The way to relate them is to relate total philosophies of science in which they are embedded. It may then turn out that both concepts are required to develop a satisfactory philosophy of science.

THE RULE OF SUCCESSION   So far, the Popper and Carnap exchange rests on charges by Popper that Carnap's system is counterintuitive. In discussing the Rule of Succession, Popper has charged that Carnap's system was not only counterintuitive but inconsistent.

Popper's original note on this problem makes use of a probability model that we will simplify here along the lines of his later discussion of notes by Bar-Hillel and Jeffrey. Let the universe consist of a set of three boxes each containing two buttons. Box$_1$ has two amber buttons in it. Box$_2$ has one amber button and one black button, and Box$_3$ has two black buttons. We will assume $p(\text{Box}_i) = 1/3$ for $i = 1, 2, 3$ when a box is selected according to some process. Our first question is what the probability is of an unknown button in one of the boxes being amber on the assumption that the other button in the box is amber. This means we are restricting our attention to Box$_1$ and Box$_2$ and asking what the probability is that we have Box$_1$ rather than Box_2. Since they are equally likely, the relevant probability is 1/2. Now let us ask a second question which asks what the probability is of a button remaining in a box being amber when we have examined the other button and found it to be amber. This second question seems very similar to the first question.

Although the two questions seem similar, Carnap and Carnapians give a different probability in answer to the second question than they do in answer to the first. The different answer they see, not as a contradiction, but as an answer to a different question. In responding to the first question, attention was restricted to Box_1 and Box_2, but no information was available making one box more likely than another. When we have examined a button from a box and found it to be amber, we know we have examined Box_1 or Box_2 but we also know that it is more likely that we have examined Box_1 than Box_2 because we must always get an amber button from Box_1 but we might have examined the black button from Box_2 instead of the amber one.[13] The fact that we have examined an amber button thus makes it more likely that we are examining Box_1 than Box_2 and makes it more likely consequently that the next button to be examined will be amber. The relevant probability is thus greater than 1/2 and is in fact 2/3.

In view of the fact that the two probabilities represent answers to different questions, no contradiction is immediate. What Popper argues is that the different questions are conflated in Carnap's theory, so that the different answers are both answers to the same question as it is expressed in Carnap's system, and contradiction results. Suppose an umpire has Box_1, Box_2, and Box_3 and then tells us (correctly) that he is presenting us with either Box_1 or Box_2 and we are to bet on whether it is Box_1 or Box_2.[14] Popper says if the umpire announces, "There is at least one amber button in this box," we should set $p(Box_1) = p(Box_2) = 1/2$.[15] Now if we ask him to look at an amber button in the box and tell us its name, the probabilities ought not to differ. To represent this, we can imagine that the buttons are marked a and b to distinguish them and that we would describe the contents of any box in giving our hypotheses by describing the relevant possible colorations of a and b. Box_2, for example, is such that either a is black and b is amber or vice versa. Box_1 is such that both a and b are black. Names of this kind are required to formalize the problem in a Carnapian language. If the umpire tells us "a is amber in this box," then Popper argues that in Carnap's system $p(Box_1)$ is no longer 1/2 but is now 2/3. The contradiction arises because supplying the name of the observed amber button changes the probabilities even though it gives us no new information about the real world and hence should not affect the probability assignments. In other words, Popper views the Carnapian system here as a version of subjectivism, obtaining knowledge from magic, that is, assigning names to individuals. Because of this observation, Popper thinks that the root of the difficulty lies with the covert way in which names import apparent positional or order information into statements of probability problems.

Let us return to the umpire. There are at least two ways in which he may come to announce, "There is at least one amber button in this box." Suppose he starts with three indistinguishable boxes, looks into one and finds two black buttons, and then randomly selects one of the other two boxes to present to us. In this case $p(Box_1) = 1/2$. On the other hand, if he starts by looking into a box, seeing an amber button, and then presenting that box to us, $p(Box_1) = 2/3$. If he now sees that the amber button is a, the probability remains the same. What this means is that the conditional probability of Box_1 being presented to us on the information that the box presented to us has at least one amber button in it *is not well defined:* we need to know the method of selection of the box in order to determine the relevant probabilities. When Popper sees Carnap's system as changing probability assignments on no information he trades on the ambiguous significance of "There is at least one amber button in this box." In this sense many probability systems are contradictory in that we could in many cases (reasonably) formalize the same problem in conflicting ways in the same system.

We now come closer to the ultimate force of Popper's example. Suppose the umpire selects a box by the first method, that is, by rejecting Box_3 and then randomly selecting one of the others. In a Carnapian system the buttons will have names in order for us to describe the situation. Suppose the buttons in each box to have a or b written on them. We now ask the umpire to look at an amber button in the box and tell us the name written on it. (This is partly figurative, but we can *imagine* in the general case that the buttons in each box have a small a or b marked on them.) He announces that a is amber. Now the conditional probability in a Carnapian system that both buttons are amber given the evidence that a is amber is $2/3$. It looks like Popper's contradiction can be made out after all. There is, however, a subtle point still to be made. Not only do we know that the umpire found a to be amber, but we also know that he may have had to look at a because he looked at b and found b to be black. If we can express this information properly in the language we are using, $p(Box_1) = 1/2$ and not $2/3$. On the other hand, if we see the umpire draw out an amber button and look at it to make his selection, telling us that it is a, and he does not look at b, than $p(Box_1) = 2/3$ and not $1/2$. To summarize, the conditional probability that we have Box_1 given that Box_3 is excluded and a is amber is either $1/2$ or $2/3$ depending on the exact details of the way in which the information about a was acquired. Without the details, we cannot say what the probability is.

The languages used by Carnap are generally too impoverished to permit explicit statement of the various possibilities of selection of information mentioned in connection with our button problem, simple though it is. This raises a problem familiar from the use of formal systems elsewhere, namely, that great care in formalization is required in their use. The probabilities involved in the button problem that we are interested in are all 1/2 or 2/3, so care is required in using a formal language to describe the problem we are interested in, if utilizing the power of the formalism to solve the problem correctly is to be possible. Sometimes a considerable intuitive understanding of what is formalized must be kept in mind if the formalization is to result in a correct solution to the original problem. Admittedly, careless or faulty formalization will enable us to obtain contradictory answers to the same problem—but careful formalization should enable us to avoid contradiction. Popper did not show Carnap's system to be contradictory; he did show that there are problems that can be reasonably formalized in two ways yielding contradictory results if fine distinctions relating to selection of information are ignored. What Popper has shown or indicated is the extensive amount of intuition required to apply a system like Carnap's, suggesting that the system may offer no improvement on intuition and the judicious use of the ordinary formulas for statistical inference.

Another aspect of this exchange deserves comment. It would appear that, since $p(\text{Box}_1) > p(\text{Box}_2)$ in the right circumstances, probabilistic induction is a success and the success is presupposed by Popper's discussion. The rational man will bet on Box_1. Popper's indeterminism prevents him from accepting such a conclusion except in connection with trivial games of chance. The existence of the boxes with fixed contents, and so on, is simply a device for discussing Carnap's system based on accepting Carnapian assumptions. It is not meant to describe a realistic situation with important methodological overtones, and one cannot generalize from it to the use of induction in science. In studying nature, the content of the boxes (on an analogy to larger issues) would never be known, nor would it be fixed in advance. We could not bet rationally on the relevant conjectures because of the uncertainty of the future.

MILLER'S PARADOX OF INFORMATION   We now turn to an interesting puzzle introduced to the literature by Miller.[16] Let $P(A,B) = r$ be the logical probability of A given B and let $p(a) = r$ be an empirical probability given by some experimental result. Suppose, for example, that a is a fair die landing heads on some experimental arrangement such that $p(a) = 1/6$. Notice that a is an event of a certain kind. Let A be the statement "a

occurs" and let E_r^a stand for the statement $p(a) = r$. Given the right sort of background information, the following may seem intuitively necessary:

(1) $P(A, E_r^a) = r.$

We can use (1) to derive a contradiction as follows. First, we have the following from the probability calculus:

(2) $p(a) = 1/2$ if and only if $p(a) = p(-a)$.

Using our earlier abbreviation, this gives us

(3) $E_{1/2}^a \equiv E_{p(-a)}^a.$

Extensionality holds for probability functions in the sense that, if $\vdash A \equiv B$, then A may be substituted for B in any probability context and vice versa. Using this fact, we can derive the following from (3):

(4) $P(A, E_{1/2}^a) = P(A, E_{p(-a)}^a).$

Substituting 1/2 for r in (1) yields

(5) $P(A, E_{1/2}^a) = 1/2.$

Another substitution, $p(-a)$ for r, yields

(6) $P(A, E_{p(-a)}^a) = p(-a).$

Given (4), we can use (5) and (6) to get

(7) $p(-a) = 1/2.$

By probability theory, we then have

(8) $p(a) = 1/2.$

Our original assumption that $p(a) = 1/6$ is clearly contradictory with (8). Popper has endorsed Miller's paradox as showing an inconsistency in Carnap's preferred inductive system since the derivation given above is licensed by theorems of the system.[17]

The first point to notice is that (1) is quite vague as a statement of the straight rule. To work out the significance of $p(a)$ and $p(A,B)$, some relationship between a and A is required. A natural reading is to let a be the event that, say, a die X has been tossed n times and that $p(\text{heads}) = r$ on the n tosses. Let A be a statement to the effect that the die turns up heads on the $n + 1$ toss. Then $P(A, p(a) = r)$ amounts to a conditional assertion of a probability. It says that the best estimate of the probability of A (being true) when the truth of $p(a) = r$ is asserted is r. This gives (1) in the derivation a form something like the following:

If $p(a) = r$, then $P(A) = r$.

Some authors have accepted the straight rule in some such formulation. Of course, we need a treatment of $P(A,B)$ when B is not $p(a) = r$, and we can take this to be undefined unless the truth value of B is the same as the truth value of $p(a) = r$ under varying conditions. With this reading, (1), (5), and (6) are disguised conditionals, and (5) and (6) do not assert identities except conditionally in a form that cannot be used to obtain (7). The paradox can be set aside on the grounds that the derivation is invalid because (1) is a disguised conditional and this fact is overlooked in the derivation because of the coercive effect of the (misleading) symbolism.

Other methods for rejecting the paradox have been utilized. Some authors have contended that probabilities cannot be assigned to probability statements without skirting self-referential paradoxes. The derivation can be blocked by saying that (1) is simply not well formed because it takes one probability sentence within the scope of another. This "solution" seems ad hoc. We *can* construct a probability measure P taking sentences from an appropriate set of sentences as arguments, and it cannot matter in theory that some of these sentences are probability sentences. We take P as mapping pairs of sentences into the interval [0,1]. Without worrying about all such assignments, we will have a rule that, if $\vdash A \equiv B$ in the set of sentences, then $P(A) = P(B)$, and so forth, for various conditional contexts. Equation (1) now gives the rule for such assignments; (4) says that the number assigned by P to the pair $(A, E^a_{1/2})$ is the same as the number assigned by P to the pair $(A, E^a_{p(-a)})$; (5) says that the number assigned to the pair $(A, E^a_{1/2})$ is 1/2. Continuing this reading, (6) says something peculiar— that the number assigned to the pair $(A, E^a_{p(-a)})$ is $p(-a)$. This does not assign a number to the pair $(A, E^a_{p(-a)})$ unless we can discover what number $p(a)$ or $p(-a)$ actually is. Suppose $p(a) = p(-a)$ is true. Then $p(a) = p(-a) = 1/2$, and (1) and (6) produce no contradiction. Now suppose $p(a) \neq p(-a)$, *as is true in the actual case.* $p(a) = 7/8$ is also false, but $P(A, E^a_{7/8}) = 7/8$ produces no contradiction. The difference is that, even though $p(a) = 7/8$ is false, it determines a definite value for $p(a)$ and $p(-a)$. When $p(a) \neq p(-a)$, no value for $p(a)$ or $p(-a)$ has been determined. $P(A, E^a_{p(-a)})$ is thus *undefined* because no way of determining the value in the functional range [0,1] is available. Looking back, (1) is completely satisfactory if r is in the interval [0,1], that is, if r is an *explicit* real number that can be assigned as a probability. We also have this:

(9)   If $p(-a) = p(a)$, then $P(A, E^a_{p(-a)}) = p(-a)$.

Using (9), we can deduce $p(a) = 1/2$ and substitute into (1) to get (5). We do not have (6), which is *not* a substitution instance of (1) since $p(-a)$ is not (in general) a determinate number in the interval [0,1] equal to the value of $p(a)$. If we replace (6) by (9) in the derivation, we cannot obtain (7) in view of our original assumption that $p(a) = 1/6$, and no contradiction results.

Miller's paradox is not successful in its original version and cannot sustain the charge that it causes a contradiction in Carnap's system. On balance, Popper has produced no satisfactory argument that Carnap's system is inconsistent.

III Induction Evaluated

At this point we will close the discussion of corroboration or induction by discussing the ultimate success of Popper's animadversions against induction. Suppose we construe induction as a form of inference from data of some kind to the truth or probable truth of some generalization. Popper is correct, I think, that the former inference is simply invalid and that the latter inference even where possible in some technical sense is misleading because it rests on assumed probabilities assigned to possible changes in the environment which cannot be given an objective justification. Popper's general observations about induction seem correct, and similar objections have been made by others, but these objections only serve to rule out various crude views (such as old-fashioned eliminative or enumerative induction) about the nature of inductive inference.[18]

Popper's general arguments about induction do not in any sense constitute an effective criticism of so-called systems of inductive logic like Carnap's system. By an inductive inference Carnap means determining the value of a rational credibility function on given evidence, and by an inductive logic he means the characterization of a system based on such a function. But Carnap allows no inferences from rational credibility functions to truth or probable truth except in trivial cases. Therefore the general arguments against induction do not successfully criticize Carnap in spite of an (unfortunate) overlapping vocabulary between the general arguments and various statements of Carnap's systems.

There is a tendency in Popper's style of argument to go for a "quick kill" of opposing viewpoints much in the manner that he once held that scientific hypotheses could be the victims of a quick kill by certain falsifying experimental data. In criticizing a philosophical theory, the only quick kill is a proof of inconsistency. Popper's attempts at proving Carnapian systems inconsistent have not, I think, proved successful, for the reasons suggested above. The situation thus seems to be that Popperian corroboration and Carnapian confirmation can each be embedded into consistent systems, a choice between which will have to depend on the (inconclusive) normative intuitions about ideally rational scientific methodology that one chooses to abstract from historical cases.

The debate between Carnap and Popper is sometimes presented as though Carnap held that the hypothesis with the highest probability is to be accepted (if any) as a basis for action and as though Popper held that the viable hypothesis with highest content should be accepted. Neither, of course, holds any view that is this simple. Some of the confusions that can be made have been admirably elucidated by Carnap in an article titled "Probability and Content Measure."[19] A first point to notice is that probability and content stand in an inverse relationship only when a priori or initial probabilities are considered. It is not, however, generally the case that, if the relative probability (relative to the background knowledge) of a hypothesis h is greater than the relative probability of a hypothesis i, the content of i is less than that of the hypothesis h. If h implies i, but i does not imply h, then if the relative probability of h is greater than that of i, the content of i will be less than that of h. But if h and i are competing hypotheses, then h may have both greater relative probability and greater content than i. The only general rules that apply are those subject to some restriction on a comparison of the content or relative probability of h and i. For example, if the relative probability of h and of i is the same, then Carnap and Poper *agree* that the hypothesis with the greater content should be preferred. In the important case where h and i are theories, the relative probabilities of h and i are always 0, so content is the only important arbiter. A major difference between Carnap and Popper is that Carnap finds this case of relatively small methodological value because he does not believe that scientists accept theories, while Popper finds this case to be methodologically central. To take another case, if the content of h and i is equivalent, then that hypothesis with greater relative probability is to be preferred according to both Popper and Carnap. This is a theorem in Carnap's system and is equivalent to desideratum (vii) for Popper's corroboration function except for the singularity where the contents are equal because h and i are general hypotheses or theories with 0 content. The upshot of this is that Popper and Carnap agree on some basic principles, but their attention is directed to some special cases whose importance they evaluate quite differently.

Some of the points made in the preceding paragraph are illustrated by Carnap with an interesting example. Suppose that one asks for a prediction of the temperature at a place tomorrow based on background knowledge including the temperature today, past observed temperature means, and so forth. Various hypotheses about the interval within which the temperature will be found are to be entertained. Suppose only temperatures between 0° and 100° Fahrenheit are possible, so $p(0°, 100°) = 1$, and also suppose that the temperatures are equally possible a priori. We can imagine that the background knowledge e has established that the expected mean temperature tomorrow is 70° with a standard deviation of 10°. Using some information about statistical inference that we will not explicitly develop, we can imagine that Carnapians and Popperians settle on the following tabular summation of the relevant facts.[20]

	$p(h_i)$	$Ct(h_i)$	$p(h_i,e)$
$h_1 = (70°,71°)$	.01	1.00	.04
$h_2 = (69°,72°)$	.04	.33	.12
$h_3 = (86°,87°)$	.01	1.00	.01
$h_4 = (84°,89°)$	.05	.20	.05

Which hypothesis should be regarded as preferred for a basis of contemplated action? Surely not h_4, which has the highest a priori probability. Surely not h_3, which has content as high as any. Therefore the choice is between h_1 and h_2. What we need to do now is to inquire into what action is being contemplated. If we are setting a device or planning an activity and either action will result in a successful outcome provided the hypothesis we adopt is within two degrees of the correct temperature, then h_2 is clearly the hypothesis we should prefer even though it has lower content than h_1. This is an example of a problem of statistical inference. In such an inference neither content nor probability of any kind is a suitable measure. One does not maximize content in the hypothesis one prefers because that would almost always result in adopting a false hypothesis. One does not simply maximize relative probability because that would result in adopting nearly empty statements. The hypothesis $(0°,100°)$ has relative probability of 1 but it is useless. Adopting it is the same as saying that we don't care (relative to our planned action) what the temperature is. Problems of statistical inference of this kind are hence sufficient to demonstrate that neither content nor probability is to be maximized and that no simple caricature statement of the Carnap or Popper position can explain such cases, much less the full range of methodological cases.

In making a statistical inference of the kind noted, a scientist will usually set or fix some probability that he is willing to settle for given his problem and then try to find the shortest interval statement that has this relative probability.[21] Carnap's system offers a consistent way of making Carnapian probability estimates of all possible hypotheses relative to the data. The system does not solve any problem of accepting a theory or hypothesis for possible action. Such a move would have to be made relative to a particular problem and some facts about the utility of the various possible hypotheses relative to that problem. The Carnapian system simply grinds out numerical estimates that someone making such a decision might find relevant.

It is worth noting that the kind of example chosen by Carnap in the paper cited shows the enormous difference in his outlook from that of Popper's. Carnap sees this kind of (statistical) problem as the staple of scientific nondeductive inference. Popper sees it as the kind of problem which is methodologically subsidiary and belongs to that area of methodology dealing with statistical hypotheses that must be left partly to the methodological decisions made by scientists in particular cases. He is interested in preferences between hypotheses and theories, and such preference is simply not a part of the Carnapian problem.

We have now seen that the differences between Carnap and Popper can be largely resolved except in the one case of the acceptance or rational preference for general hypotheses or theories.[22] Since this is a book about Popper, we will assume that the problem is important and look at the way in which Carnap and Popper differ about the preference ranking of theories.

Both Carnap and Popper agree that the logical probability, and hence the relative probability on any evidence, of universal laws and hypotheses is 0. As we have seen earlier, Carnap is compelled to provide an a priori probability distribution in which universes of the same statistical structure receive the same a priori weight. Unless this is done, learning from experience is impossible in the sense that evidence would be irrelevant to instance predictions. Popper's view is that the only necessity of failure of independence in science is that introduced by corroborated hypotheses and theories. Our a priori expectation should be the same for each possible world. The dependence between events discovered by Carnap is partly a priori, partly the result of experience. The price Carnap pays for his a priori dependence is that he cannot always discuss various properties of the order in which individuals are observed within his system. Popper's discovery of dependence is *always* the result of a conjectured law or theory, and no part of it is a consequence of a priori distributions. In this dispute there could be no quarrel with success, but the fact remains that Carnapian confirmation systems are not yet adequate for defining confirmation in very rich languages. In view of this, the philosophical argument seems somewhat to favor Popper's outlook since it is compatible with what we know about scientific theories expressed at all levels of linguistic and mathematical complexity.

Fallibilism can be regarded as a feature of both Carnap's and Popper's views. In Carnap's system, since new evidence merely changes the probability distribution, a given hypothesis may fluctuate from high relative probability to low relative probability back to high relative probability on increasing evidence. No hypothesis, even on any plausible acceptance rule that might be added to Carnap's system, can result in establishing a hypothesis or theory as true. There is a considerable problem about acceptability. Carnap believes that scientists never accept hypotheses but mearly assign probabilities to them, at least where scientists are ideally rational. This seems a last legacy of the positivist desire to avoid mistakes. Surely scientists must act as though various hypotheses were true, and they tend to describe the world in reflective books as though various hypotheses were true and others had been discredited. Carnap sees this as a lapse from the objective scientific outlook into a practical or engineering mode where error must inevitably be encountered. As we have seen, Popper allows acceptance of any hypotheses or theories that are corroborated as a basis for action where this does not imply any belief that the hypotheses or theories are true or even likely to remain corroborated.

It seems an interesting question to discuss how lower animals may act on the basis of experience. Some philosophers have suggested that only a probabilistic, justificational approach will work. The idea here is that experience can cause an increase in strength in various neural connections corresponding to a probability weighting and that the animal will act on those neural pathways that have been most strengthened in this way. We can thus explain the behavior of lower animals by invoking a probabilistic and justificational animal physiology. Might not one expect this to be continued into human structure so that a human-type robot for doing science would operate on similar principles except that his literate brain would allow him to explicitly formulate and weight such complicated proposals as scientific hypotheses or theories? The Popperian rejoinder to this is that in animals very little learning from experience is really possible. What happens is that different behavior patterns that can be genetically coded are tried out and most of them eliminated by natural selection. Existing animals exhibit a largely precoded behavioral repertoire that can be but slightly modified by experience. With language comes the ability to augment the evolutionary process by linguistically formulating hypotheses and trying them out conceptually. If they are no good, they are discarded conceptually instead of being eliminated physically. We might say that the Popperian perspective is that behavioral change may be probabilistic when looked at in sufficiently circumscribed cases but that the major outlines of behavior and behavioral change are set by a non-justificational eliminative process captured conceptually in evolutionary theory. Here Popper's outlook seems to fit more closely the broad outlines of what is known about animal behavior.

It has been argued that some form of acceptance of hypotheses seems to best fit the phenomenology of scientific research. Kuhn and others have repeatedly pointed out that scientists make no effort to pile up confirming instances of hypotheses. The fact that thousands of freshmen find new confirmation of various laws and hypotheses utilizing the same methods as the preceding year's freshmen is hardly of scientific interest. Why should hypotheses or theories be accepted even if scientists know that they may later be discarded? One reason is that hypotheses or theories are a convenient way to store a great deal of information. Rather than compute a probability of an instance of a hypothesis or law based on the constantly changing number of past confirming instances, it is simpler to deduce the instance from appropriate boundary conditions and a stored generalization. Acceptance of hypotheses has enormous implications for conceptual and neurophysiological economy.

Perhaps one could reverse Popper's emphasis on objective knowledge and argue that, although individuals must be forced into an acceptance framework because of limitations on their neurophysiological equipment, objective scientific knowledge is properly expressed by a vast assignment of values of probability functions to all possible hypotheses expressible in a suitable language on the basis of the total available evidence. There are at least two important criticisms of this view.

It is a serious objection that the evolution of scientific concepts seems to preclude a choice of a preferred language over which a Carnapian credence function can be appropriately defined. When one language is substituted for another, credence-function values for various analogous propositions may be wildly different. On the supposition that the language of science may need occasional widespread revision, Popper's evolutionary epistemology seems more appropriate as a general methodological viewpoint since it can accommodate the existence of such changes.

The other objection is the Popperian point that the significance of evidence, particularly the severity with which it tests hypotheses, is not amenable to any known formal treatment. This kind of objection needs to be thrashed out case by case, and we will consider but one kind of case here. Confirmationists have argued that among the rules which are useful for evaluating data is a rule to the effect that a fixed number n of observations is always superior evidence if it is spatio-temporally scattered rather than spatio-temporally clustered. Apparently the intuition is that scattering will avoid any misleading local bias in the data. In spite of this intuition, clustered data can be more important than scattered data once hypotheses other than simple physical laws are being considered. Suppose we have an animal species that has been observed with a single coloration and that the species is occasionally observed in groups. The claim that the species has only that coloration may be best tested by observing n animals together rather than n scattered animals. Let us say that the animal is sensitive to the presence of human beings and that there is a coloration variant associated with reticent behavior toward humans. The unusually colored animals may only feel bold enough to present themselves in the presence of human beings in the safety of a group. Observing a group of n animals is thus a much more severe test of the hypothesis that there is a single coloration than is observing n scattered individuals.[23] But surely this could be formalized, one might suggest. The facts depend upon information known to the interested scientists. The Popperian claim is not so much that these accumulating features of relevance for evidence cannot be catalogued into a super confirmation function, but rather that the general resultant confirmation function would be too unwieldy to be methodologically illuminating. These sorts of special observations are correctly left to scientific specialists.

How can we summarize the great debate about induction? Both sides *agree* that inductive *inference* is impossible: we cannot conclude anything about the *truth* of laws or theories or hypotheses on the basis of partial information. Both sides also agree that it is possible to define mathematical functions which assign numbers to sentences expressing laws, theories, hypotheses, and other scientific claims in the light of partial information. They differ primarily as the the *significance* of the attached numbers. Carnapians take the numbers attached to sentences by their confirmation functions as a *guide* to the future in the sense that these numbers embedded in a suitable decision theory will provide the basis for rational action. Popper's arguments that confirmation functions are logically contradictory have been painstakingly examined and found wanting. Formally, confirmation functions are perfectly acceptable. A Popperian attack thus rests ultimately on a difference in intuition. One source of difference over intuitions about the importance of theory is inconclusive in the sense that Carnapian claims have not been shown to be unworkable at the level of specific problems. The important difference is between Carnapians who believe that a cumulative record of ever-widening scientific data is a reality and those Popperians (and Kuhnians) who see an interdependence of theory and observation which can at any time result in the rejection of past data as recorded in an irrelevant manner. A belief in the possibility of scientific revolution or evolution in theory with catastrophic consequences for the notion of permanently useful data would restrict the scope of an inductive logic based on a confirmation function to periods of relative calm between such changes when the data environment is not changing except in the trivial sense of getting larger. During such periods the *pragmatic* difference between confirmation and corroboration is slight, and the major facts of narrative can be accommodated by either. Popper has not won the argument about inductive logics outright, and he certainly has not lost it either. It remains to be seen whether a general philosophical inductive calculus can prove useful to science, but it is surely clear that Popper's vision of the growth of scientific knowledge has greater scope if revolution or evolution occurs. His vision will accommodate both the routine and the nonroutine in science, although it is directed primarily to the latter. And should revolution or evolution occur in an indeterministic universe, Popper is correct in saying that any inductive projections may be found totally wrong *in the short run* at any point. It is in this sense that we cannot anticipate the future and should regard inductive support for theories as a hoax.

SEVEN

Popper's Indeterminism

We have already laid the groundwork for Popper's belief in physical indeterminism in connection with his views on falsifiability and fallibilism. If determinism were true and the future of the universe were to pursue a perfectly predictable course, then a justificationist methodology might prove adequate. It is indeterminism that forces the evolutionary viewpoint and underlies the idea that our current theories may be falsified at any time no matter how well they have survived past tests. Falsifiability presupposes indeterminism if it is to be persuasive, and indeterminism requires falsifiability in our methodological outlook. Consequently Popper's indeterminism is no surprise. What is interesting is the detailed outline of his indeterminism. For example, Popper sees classical physics as essentially indeterministic, a view that is not usually held, so that he regards even the methodology of classical physics as requiring some form of indeterminism.

Any discussion of determinism and indeterminism must rest upon some clarification of the concepts involved. Many different kinds of determinism (and by contrast, indeterminism) have been proposed in the literature. At least two major kinds of determinism have been proposed, one of which holds that all details of the universe are in principle perfectly precise and that every event is caused by at least one other event or combination of events which is a sufficient condition for it. This first kind of determinism does not necessarily involve the possibility of actual prediction, but it usually supposes that a perfect intelligence of some kind could in principle predict the future course of the universe if it could have all present physical data made available to it. The other basic kind of determinism involves predictability in that it claims that human scientists can predict the future and will one day be able to accurately predict all interesting facts about the future on the basis of current information. Let us call the first *metaphysical determinism* and the second *physical determinism*.

Metaphysical determinism is not embarrassed by any actual failures of predictability. The laws required by an agent to permit his treating of the universe as determined by the present may simply be too complicated for human grasp. For one thing, the total number of events to be considered along with their descriptions may defy statement in a human language sophisticated enough to take care of the relevant detail. It is also possible that the laws involved are too complex to be grasped by human language, or that the syntactical structure of human languages renders an appropriate statement impossible. Metaphysical determinism also relies on bypassing the errors inherent in human measurement. The precise predictability of the future depends upon perfectly precise current data. Very slight and not measurable differences in the current position and velocity of particles might result in great differences later. Thus the inaccuracy of measurement may prevent accurate prediction arbitrarily far into the future even though metaphysical determinism was correct. It is easily possible to hold metaphysical determinism in some form which renders it unfalsifiable and uncriticizable, since no scientific failure can count against it. The description of the universe it would present would be meaningful but untestable. In any such form it is clearly not a view worth discussion on Popperian principles.

There are more direct ways to discuss metaphysical determinism. Some metaphysical determinists have suggested that since science is our best guide to the nature of the universe, and quantum physics is indeterministic, we should accept the meaningfulness of metaphysical determinism but judge it conjecturally false on the grounds that it is incompatible with quantum physics. This way makes metaphysical determinism an abstraction from current scientific belief which must change as those beliefs change. A deterministic reworking of quantum physics within a deeper and deterministic "hidden variable" theory would then completely change the status of metaphysical determinism. Metaphysical determinism in this form does not seem so much a component of methodology as a reflective comment on the current state of scientific knowledge.

Perhaps the most illuminating discussion of metaphysical determinism is based on the observation that it is usually stated as an abstraction from the world view of classical physics and that the world view involved is based on physical presuppositions which are quite likely to be wrong. For example, the description of a Laplacian predictor who predicts future states of the universe on total information about present states can make sense if and only if the history of the universe can be partitioned into time slices in such a manner that each pair of events is or is not in a specific time slice. At any given moment, the total set of events in the time slice of the moment is then a complete record of the past with respect to that moment and hence a sufficient basis for predicting the state at any future time slice. Newtonian space-time is well known to have this structure, and Laplace assumed that it was correct. The present moment defines a complete separation between past and future which can be used to state the deterministic doctrine. Metaphysical determinism seems dependent on this structure of space-time for its usual conceptual features, and hence the General Theory of Relativity constitutes an immediate threat to metaphysical determinism because it rejects the notions of absolute space and time on which this structure depends.[1] In the General Theory the present does not partition the past from the future in the same way that it does in Newtonian space-time. There are pairs of events which are such that neither is in the past of the other—that is, such that no light signal from one event in the past could have reached both at the present moment—but which may both influence some future event. This means that the causal consequences of each event may prove a surprise for any prediction based on the other event. Without introducing any detail, it is clear that the space-time structures of General Relativity preclude any statement of metaphysical determinism along classical lines. Any sharp statement of metaphysical determinism thus seems more embarrassed by the General Theory than by quantum physics, since quantum physics is more easily thought of as being replaced by a theory compatible with the major outlines of metaphysical determinism.

Metaphysical indeterminists need only hold that some events are determined (predictable in principle) and that some events are not determined. Popper is a metaphysical indeterminist in this sense. He believes that the indeterminism which is a feature of quantum physics is a permanent feature of physical theory. The propensity theory of probability is based partly on this assumption. It also follows from metaphysical indeterminism that one can accept some form of free-will doctrine and escape fatalism. There is an apparent difficulty here in that neither metaphysical determinism nor metaphysical indeterminism is clearly refutable. Popper's strategy is to mount the major attack on metaphysical determinism by attacking physical determinism. Physical determinism is not a logical consequence of metaphysical determinism. Someone could hold that metaphysical determinism was true and that human predictions and theories would always fail because of human limitations. In practice, however, most people who have been determinists have been determinists of both kinds, believing in predictability in principle and also that scientific progress will take place by producing theories that will allow closer and closer predictions of actual events without limitation on accuracy. A successful attack on physical determinism would seem to remove any reason for holding a version of metaphysical determinism. In view of the low empirical content of the philosophical theories involved, this strategy for attacking metaphysical determinism seems as good as any that is available.

With physical determinism we move to a claim that good physical theories are always deterministic in that they allow precise prediction of the future. It seems best to define *theories* as deterministic or indeterministic in discussing physical determinism along some such lines as the following. A typical theory will be about objects or systems of some kind which can be described as being in some theoretical state at any given time. A *state* is a description of the object or system of theoretical interest. A state is theoretically *complete* if it captures all of the information about the object or system required for prediction. Given a precise state and a time, a theory is said to be completely deterministic if, for any other time, it allows us to deduce exactly one precise state for that time. All of this, of course, is in the context of examining one object or system. Clearly we can expand details and gradually define various notions of determinism. One variation depends on the temporal aspect. A theory would be deterministic in one weaker sense, for example, if for any time there was at least one previous time and state allowing prediction of the appropriate state. We could also examine temporal structures other than the linear Newtonian time being considered, and we could also examine more closely the relevant notion of state. Many philosophers have observed, for example, that a state in classical physics always assigns a sharp numerical value to every property mentioned in the state but that in quantum physics this is not the case. By the indeterminacy principle, a precise assignment of a position to a particle at a time precludes a precise assignment of a velocity at the same time. Pairs of conjugate properties in quantum states, such as position and momentum, cannot have jointly precise values. More complicated variations on determinism will not prove germane to understanding Popper's position, and we will not explore this further.

It is usually said that classical physics was deterministic and that quantum physics is indeterministic. This apparent cliche is not true in any obvious sense and requires some careful discussion. On the one hand, the states of classical physics are different from the states of quantum physics in the way we have noted. But this does not involve indeterminism. A quantum theoretical system in an appropriate state will be deterministic in that one can use the quantum theory to predict its quantum theoretical state at later times provided that it is not disturbed by outside influences. As long as the system is isolated, it develops deterministically over time. One may say the states are not determined because they do not assign definite values to properties, but this is to mark a difference between the classical and (at least currently understood) quantum notions of state. To argue that the quantum theory is indeterministic on these grounds is to say something misleading with respect to the issues on which determinism is usually focused.

With any viable theory there will be associated a theory of measurement, including various methodological rules, explaining how the theoretical statements are to be related to certain observations. The usual difference noted between classical and quantum physics is really in this area of measurement. A measurement always involves an interaction between the system or object measured and the measuring device. The theory of measurement associated with classical physics allowed this interaction to be vanishingly small. When I observe a star on the classical theory, the star's position and other properties are not affected (in the theory) by my observation. Measurement in classical physics may involve a theoretical one-way flow of information. Quantum theory has associated with it a theory of measurement of a completely different kind. The effects of a quantum theoretical measurement on the measured or observed object or system are cataclysmic. Measurement results in a sudden and unpredictable change in state for both the measured and measuring systems. A single measurement has an unpredictable outcome even though there are statistical regularities to be observed over many quantum theoretical measurements. The usual observation that classical physics is deterministic and quantum physics is indeterministic refers to these differences in measuring or observing associated with the two theories. Popper is one of the few philosophers who have recognized the fact that this way of marking the distinction is simply wrong from a methodological point of view. There are special problems with quantum theoretical measurement which the scientists involved are fully aware of. To rest an important methodological principle on one solution (even if preferred by the majority) of a scientific problem is to risk having methodology simply reflect current opinions about scientific knowledge and lose its normative character.

Popper's approach is to argue that physical indeterminism does not depend on any peculiarities of quantum theory but is already apparent in classical physics. Some philosophers have argued that this is true on non-Popperian grounds. The usual grounds hinge on the practical impossibility of achieving one-way transmission of information in classical measurement or, to put it another way, the practical impossibility of achieving zero error of measurement. This *can* be forcibly argued. All actual measurement involves error which is, in turn, transmitted to prediction. The counterargument is that, at least in theory, errors can be arbitrarily reduced in the classical theory of measurement. There is no restriction such as the indeterminacy principle suggesting that there is a limit to the accuracy and amount of information that we can acquire through measurement. Popper's line of argument avoids this approach entirely. He argues that even if zero error of measurement is granted there are indeterministic situations in classical physics. The key example consists in situations where complicated predicting mechanisms are in two-way interaction attempting to predict one another's future states. To do this, they must predict their own future states in order to anticipate the reaction by the other predictor, but this is impossible for reasons to be given below. Therefore classical physics is already indeterministic. The key to Popper's approach is in discussing situations where a two-way flow of information is required, thus assimilating the features of classical measurement and those of quantum theoretical measurement. This argument is so important that we will examine it in some detail.

Before turning to Popper's argument that classical physics is indeterministic, we can take a moment to review the argument that indeterminism and falsifiability are linked. We have now pointed to a variety of more specific forms of determinism and indeterminism. Popper's position requires some form of physical indeterminism, but it would be possible to be a metaphysical determinist and hold some of Popper's views provided that one thought the powers of human reason to be inadequate to the task of successful prediction. Popper's views therefore require indeterminism at every level of consideration unless a fairly exotic variety of metaphysical determinism is to be retained along with a fallibilist epistemology. It seems fair to say that such a position would have little appeal. If the metaphysical view is taken to have only the practical consequence of urging scientists to look for deterministic laws, Popper would have no quarrel since he views deterministic laws as having higher content than probabilistic laws.

Popper narrows the problem to what he calls a finite version of the deterministic doctrine:

> For any specified finite prediction task, it is physically possible to construct a predictor capable of carrying out this task.[2]

A finite prediction task is the task of predicting (with some fixed degree of precision) the position and velocity of a finite number of particles in some isolated mechanical system at a future instant using precise data about the position and velocity of the particles at the present time. This position legislates away any problem caused by predictive failure based on an incapacity to formulate the problem because an infinite number of particles is involved, or due to failure of prediction because the system is interfered with. There is also a problem for such systems, not discussed by Popper, in that for any n particle system ($n \geq 3$) involving collisions of particles, there is often no known analytic solution to the predictive problem.[3] We will assume that the predictive inference is not to be defeated by an incapacity on the part of the predictive system. The predictor will be conceived of as a giant computer with access to all relevant laws and complete initial information.

Popper does not deny that the finite version of physical determinism has some solutions. If A is a finite system of particles and B is a predictor, it may be perfectly possible for B to solve the prediction problem for A provided that A itself does not contain a predictor attempting to predict B. B can then succeed if B can calculate the results of its interference with A in measuring, or if B interferes sufficiently weakly with A that in measuring it does not affect A sufficiently to change A beyond the bounds of the precision required by the prediction task. If B can amplify arbitrarily small distinctions in A, that is, can make arbitrarily precise measurements, it can succeed. All this is granted by Popper. Popper does agree that B cannot succeed by the route of calculating the effects of its interference on A because this would amount to being able to predict its own future states.

Granting the lemma that there are predictors that cannot determine the answers to all questions about their own future states, Popper argues that classical physics is indeterministic because a classical system can be described, including some of these predictors, in which not all answers about future states of the system can be determined by some predictor in the system. The whole discussion is restricted to classical mechanical systems, but this restriction is innocuous since it shows the possibility of an undetermined system within the range of classical physics.

The lemma that some predictors cannot (in general) predict their own future states is very important to Popper's argument, and we will discuss it first. Unfortunately, the lemma needs some clarification that is not achieved in Popper's article. Some predictors can clearly determine some or all of their future states barring cataclysmic encounters with powerful systems. Popper has to refute something like the following:

> Sufficiently powerful predictors can predict all of their own future states.

"Sufficiently powerful" must be included to rule out predictors that fail due to mechanical error or limited storage capacity. This kind of failure is not relevant to determinism. To refute the determinist claim about predictors, we need merely show that there is at least one sophisticated predictor that cannot determine one of its future states where the incapacity is not trivial. We will discuss this and answer it in the affirmative: there is a predictor that cannot predict all of its future states where the incapacity is not trivial.

Popper has three arguments designed to show that a predictor may fail to predict its own future states: the Tristram Shandy paradox, Gödelian sentences, and the "Oedipus Effect."

The Tristram Shandy paradox takes its name from the well-known novel in which Tristram Shandy's autobiography falls further and further behind as he attempts full description of the past. It takes Tristram Shandy longer to describe an event than it does to experience it, so his descriptive account must lag behind his experiences. As applied to predictors, the Tristram Shandy paradox depends on the fact that predictors must take some time in order to do their calculations. Suppose the predictor is to predict its state at time t_1 on the basis of its state at time t_0. Starting at time t_0, it must do some calculation that stretches over a small period of time. But the record of this calculation must be part of the predictor's state at t_1 as well as everything else that has happened before t_1. Therefore, a complete description of the predictor's state at time t_1 is not possible before t_1, and some questions about that state cannot be answered before t_1. It does not help to suppose that the predictor can complete the prediction at a time t' between t_0 and t_1, since what happened between t_0 and t' must be recorded in the state at t_1. This sets up an awkward regress. Even if the intervals become shorter, as long as the predictor is active (which we can assume for the purposes of discussion) it is the case that while it is storing information in its memory it is calculating and that when the information is stored there is residual calculation, a record of which must now be stored. Therefore a present state can never be a full record of the past. This argument is persuasive as directed against any statement of determinism depending on a predictor's having full knowledge of its present state, but there is at least one difficulty in regarding it as totally convincing. As long as the predictor can construct full knowledge of its state at t_0 by t' but before t_1 on the basis of its state at t_0, then it may achieve a prediction about its state at t_1 provided that it can code that state using part of its memory store or as a function of its state at t'. If the coding is impossible, then a limited determinism may still be possible in which full prediction of any state can be achieved at some earlier instant; at least this is possible if predictor states are stable in most respects over short periods of time. This fact is one reason why we require the predictor to remain active in a careful discussion of the problem. The existence of a coding would destroy the Tristram Shandy paradox as a logical weapon if the state at t_0 was also a code for future states so that the future states of the predictor could be read off its current state. This is, in a sense, prediction of the future, but a prediction too Pickwickian to ground the philosophical force of physical determinism.

Popper's argument about Gödelian sentences is ingenious but somewhat tortured. It seems better to replace it here by an argument from the halting problem for Turing machines to which it is apparently equivalent. Popper's arguments point in this direction and I assume he might have used the halting problem if he had been aware of it when he wrote his major paper on indeterminism. The negative solution to the halting problem is the fact which seems to establish most decisively Popper's claim that there are predictors which cannot predict all of their future states. Turing machines are abstract computers which have the advantages for purposes of argument that their memory store can be made arbitrarily large and that they can compute without error.[4] A Turing machine is deterministic and operates in discrete time as follows. From the current state of the machine and the configuration of symbols on its tape, one can compute a unique next state and next tape configuration. The number of states of the machine is finite, and the alphabet used to mark the squares of the machine tape is also finite. A Turing machine can therefore be given a finite description in terms of the finite number of computational moves it is capable of. Turing machines can compute any computable function.[5] A Turing machine can be regarded as computing some mathematical function for a numerical input expressed as a tape configuration when the machine is in the start state and the tape is inserted. Nonnumerical problems which are suitable for computation have to be expressed in some suitable numerical code. Sometimes the function computed by a given Turing machine is defined for the input and sometimes it is not. Where it is defined, the Turing machine will stop after a finite number of computations, that is, joint changes of state and tape configuration. Where it is not defined, it will compute forever, usually oscillating back and forth endlessly between two states. This leads us to the halting problem. Given a Turing machine description and a numerical input for that machine, can we tell in advance whether or not it will stop computing on that input after some finite length of time? We are asking simply whether it will find an answer, not what the answer is. As is well known, the answer to the halting problem is *negative*. We cannot always tell in advance whether a machine will halt, that is, stop computing after finding a solution to the input.[6] What this really means is that we cannot compute whether such a machine will stop in advance. Given the powers of Turing machines, this means that there is no Turing machine that will always be able to compute, for an arbitrary Turing machine and input tape, whether that machine will halt given that input. Now a Turing machine and an input can be coded as a single number, typically a very large number. Thus we can set up certain Turing machines to determine whether they themselves will stop given a fixed numerical input. The negative solution to the halting problem can be used to establish that some such Turing machines cannot compute (or predict) whether they will themselves halt on certain inputs. Therefore Turing machines cannot answer all questions about their own future states. "If I accept input x as a starting tape input, will I later halt (or have halted by t)?" is an example of a request for a prediction which cannot be fulfilled in the general case after suitable coding. The theory of Turing machines tells us that some Turing machines fail predictive tasks concerning their own future, and if this is true, actual computers with their attendant defects must sometimes also fail. From this we can conclude that Popper's lemma is correct: there are sophisticated predictors that cannot predict all of their future states. Coupled with the proof to be given shortly, this establishes that classical physics is indeterministic provided only that mechanical embodiments of Turing machines can be regarded as classical mechanical systems. Although this could be questioned, the possible moves do not seem to favor determinism. If quantum theory, for example, is thought to be required to explain the behavior of mechanical Turing machines, then this does not bolster the case *for* determinism unless a deterministic quantum theory of the "hidden variable" type can be developed. We cannot even determine in advance that such a theory would rescue an appropriate determinism for machine theory. Popper's lemma will hereafter be taken to be satisfactorily established by the negative solution to the halting problem.

The "Oedipus Effect" presents an argument for the lemma based on considerations that are not entirely distinct from the Tristram Shandy paradox. Oedipus, of course, did exactly what the oracle predicted in spite of strenuous attempts to avoid doing just that. Many have suggested that the social sciences differ from the physical sciences in that if A predicts that B will do x, then B can thwart the prediction by doing something else. As stated this simply, such an observation merely assumes that determinism is false, contrary to the lesson suggested in the tale of Oedipus. Popper argues that the introduction of human consciousness in its full perversity does not introduce a new element. The basic problem remains that an agent cannot have complete and up-to-date information about his or her current state for the same kind of reason that the predictors discussed earlier could not: a physical description of a present state must be a proper part of the present state, and in the absence of reductive coding this is an impossibility. Consequently human and nonhuman predictors are in the same position. They cannot answer all questions about their own future state.

We now turn to a rational reconstruction of the relatively vague argument proposed by Popper to prove that classical physics is indeterministic. First, for notation, let $\alpha_n = \langle A, B_1, B_2, \ldots, B_n \rangle$ be a set consisting of a predictable finite mechanical system A and n predictors $B_1, \ldots, B_n$ each of which is powerful enough to be unable to predict its own future states so that the lemma will apply to them. We regard α_n as a finite collection of particles constituting a closed system of classical physics. We let $X \Rightarrow Y$

mean that X predicts Y, that is, X can solve the problems of predicting Y's future states in the closed system α_n. X and Y are variables ranging over the set of elements of α_n. Let us set down some properties of $\Rightarrow$ in α_n:

$\Rightarrow_1$: $(X)(\sim(X \Rightarrow X))$.

This is given by Popper's lemma about predictors that cannot predict their own future states and the construction of α_n. Obviously $\sim(A \Rightarrow A)$.

$\Rightarrow_2$: $(X)(\sim(A \Rightarrow X))$.

This simply states that A is not a predictor and does not contain a predictor. We can regard this as true by the construction of α_n.

$\Rightarrow_3$: $\sim((X \Rightarrow Y) \wedge (Y \Rightarrow X))$.

If this were not negated, it would entail the negation of $\Rightarrow_1$. Of any pair of predictors in α_n, one can predict the other but not vice versa. Cases involving A are easy to establish. (Quantifiers are omitted.)

$\Rightarrow_4$: If $((X \Rightarrow Y) \wedge (Y \Rightarrow Z))$, then $(X \Rightarrow Z)$.

Clearly predicting is transitive. (Quantifiers are omitted.)

We can make a useful simplification in the construction of α_n by requiring that it contain no detached predictors. In other words, we will require that each predictor in α_n predict or be predicted by some other predictor. This assumption about the construction of α_n will be thought of as $\Rightarrow_5$. Strictly, $\Rightarrow_5$ says that the relation $\Rightarrow$ is connected in α_n.

Having constructed α_n we can now state the theorem we want to prove:

$$IN(\alpha_n) =_{df} (\exists X)(Y)(\sim Y \Rightarrow X).$$

$IN(\alpha_n)$ says that α_n is not determined because one prediction task cannot be successful. There is one predictor which cannot predict its own future states and whose future states cannot be predicted in any classical system consisting of a community of predictors for whom the Popperian lemma holds. To prove $IN(\alpha_n)$, we first established the following *chain theorem:*

For α_n, we have $X_n \Rightarrow X_{n-1} \Rightarrow \ldots \Rightarrow X_1 \Rightarrow A$.

This says that $X_i \Rightarrow X_j$ if X_i is to the left of X_j in the chain. Each X_i in the chain is identical to one of the B_i in α_n. Clearly each B_i occurs exactly once or $\Rightarrow_1$ would be violated. The chain theorem states that we can order the predictors in α_n in a chain such that each predictor in the chain predicts all of the predictors to its right. Proof is easy. By $\Rightarrow_3$ (antisymmetry), $\Rightarrow_4$ (transitivity), and $\Rightarrow_5$ (connectivity), there is a simple ordering on α_n with the chain structure.[7] Using the chain theorem notation, we can now prove $\sim(X_{n-i} \Rightarrow X_n)$ for $1 \leq i \leq n - 1$. By $\Rightarrow_1$ we have $\sim(X_n \Rightarrow X_n)$, and by $\Rightarrow_2$ we have $\sim(A \Rightarrow X_n)$. Thus $(Y)(\sim(Y \Rightarrow X_n))$. Existential generalization on this gives us $IN(\alpha_n)$.

What does this argument show? It shows that classical physics is theoretically indeterministic in that we can construct closed systems like α_n in which some predictor must always fail in a prediction task. One possible rejoinder is to argue that every set prediction task can be solved. In other words, although X_n in α_n cannot predict its own future states, another predictor X_{n+1} can be constructed to predict X_n. If it can avoid halting problem cases, this argument suggests that a potentially infinite sequence of ever more powerful predictors can be constructed. It is hard to see how such a sequence can be contained within the theoretical confines of classical mechanics. As long as only a finite number of particles is in the total system, some predictor must fail. This can be handled logically by postulating a God or other predictor with nonmechanical properties, but this move preserves physical determinism in a form not suitable for the usual conception of methodological discussion.

It seems to me that Popper has presented a very powerful and sufficient case for indeterminism that has been curiously ignored by determinists. Radner has argued that Popper has not refuted Laplacian determinism because Laplace meant some sort of metaphysical determinism and Popper has refuted a version of physical determinism.[8] In view of the care with which Popper has traced the connection between the two doctrines, this kind of objection is a non sequitur. I think Popper has established the futility of holding metaphysical determinism from the standpoint of philosophical argument about methodology, fatalism, or free will. Popper's discussion deserves an important place in the literature on determinism.

EIGHT

Popper's Interpretation of Physics and Quantum Theory

The key to Popper's approach to quantum theory is his attempt to interpret quantum theory (hereafter QT) within the framework of his philosophy of science. If QT can be so interpreted, this would constitute a strong prima facie case for the correctness of Popper's views. Popper's interpretation centers around two important components of his epistemology, realism and the objectivist propensity theory of probability. In other words, Popper wants to interpret QT as a statistical theory about real particles which always have perfectly definite states as do classical particles. Since Popper rejects determinism, he is not concerned to argue that QT as presently formulated will necessarily be replaced in the future by a micro-micro theory that is deterministic. At the same time, while accepting the outlines of QT formalism, he wants to insist that the formalism be interpreted as being about determinate (precise) physical events. He is thus concerned to attack all interpretations which allege that there is an intrinsic "fuzziness" in quantum phenomena that makes them conceptually and physically different from classical physical phenomena. Historically, his interpretation is related to the Born statistical interpretation of QT. In order to get into these matters, some review of physical theory seems to be in order.

It's a tall order to conduct a brief review of physical theory, but something needs to be said to get some perspective on Popper's views. In order to accomplish this, we will have to expand remarks made about deterministic theories in chapter 7. Classical physics (before 1900) had provided a number of mathematical models and formulas to account for various physical phenomena. From a philosophical point of view, an interesting property of all of these models was that they were about objects with perfectly definite properties. Such objects could be characterized by a vector or ordered set of numbers each of which was coded to the properties of the object. A *state vector* for an object can be thought of as any vector of minimal length from which all of the scientifically interesting properties of an object can be recovered.[1] (For example, since pressure, volume, and temperature of a perfect gas are related by a function, a state vector for a sample of the gas need contain only *two* numbers corresponding to two of these properties and the other can be recovered by calculation.) A theory is a mathematical system which can be applied to a state vector to calculate its change over time. Some theories might operate on a state vector to show a determined temporal development. For example, a state vector representing a closed system of particles at an instant under certain conditions might be a boundary condition for a theory which could calculate the value of the state vector of that system for any later instant. Other theories will operate on a state vector to show how it will change when some of its values are changed. For example, in the case of a sample of gas, the pressure, volume, and temperature need not change, but a theory will enable us to calculate the resultant pressure and temperature if the volume is changed in a certain way. Classical theories are typically deterministic in a clear way. If a state vector is given along with certain other information, the theory determines another state vector as a consequence of that information. In applying classical theories, there is a difficulty with measurement in that inexactitude of measurement enables us usually to say that the true state vector describing a system is at best in a small set of closely related state vectors. An interesting question is whether a prediction from such a set is as precise or nearly as precise as the measurements on which it is based. We might be able to take a volume of a gas into another volume of the same size. In using classical theories, our predictions are often as accurate as our original measurements, at least over short periods of time. This suggests that as we increase the precision of measurement we can increase the precision of our predictions. In practice, we sometimes guess at the state vector of the system we are observing in making a measurement, and this enables us to derive a prediction of great precision. We have now introduced the following presuppositions into our discussion of classical theories:

(1) Classical objects are described by state vectors.
(2) Classical objects have precise properties which are represented by numbers in the state vectors for the objects.
(3) Theories take state vectors into state vectors (on certain assumptions).

(4) Good theories are determinisitic.

(5) Arbitrarily precise measurements are (in principle) possible which reveal the values of the state vectors of a system of classical objects.

(6) Arbitrarily precise predictions are possible of the values of the state vectors of a system of calssical objects.

It is generally agreed that relativity theory (RT) and quantum theory (QT) are the major twentieth-century discoveries which clash with classical theories and have forced a new physics. Relativity theory will not concern us in this framework because it is more easily seen as a smooth physical and methodological generalization of classical physics. Notice that our characterization of classical physics was not complete in the sense that presuppositons (1)–(6) remain true with slight alteration in relativity theory, emphasizing the points of methodological agreement. RT clashed with classical physics because of its discovery that the classical state vectors were not adequate under certain physical assumptions. In particular, numbers were assigned in classical state vectors to show location of an object in an absolute framework of space and time. RT showed that such numbers were meaningless in certain situations and had to be replaced by numbers related to local spatio-temporal frameworks. In addition, where classical state vectors might contain numbers for the mass and energy of some object (presumed independent in classical theory), RT discovered new functional dependencies. The upshot is that the state vectors of RT are a different set than the state vectors of classical theory. RT therefore represents a break with certain physically specific presuppositions of classical theory. At the same time, however, we can turn (1)–(6) into presuppositions of RT by substituting *relativistic* for *classical*. There is a considerable basis for arguing in such a fashion that a general methodology of science can incorporate both RT and classical theory and that RT can be seen as a generalized form of various areas of classical theory.

The situation with respect to QT is considerably different. Although quantum objects are described by state vectors so that (1) remains true with notational alternation, most versions of QT conflict sharply with (2) and (5), and to some extent with (3), (4), and (6). We assume, of course, that *quantum* is substituted for *classical* throughout. QT therefore seems to represent a sharper methodological and physical break with classical theory, at least from this perspective, than does RT. Further, although there is such a thing as relativistic quantum mechanics, a theory which allows for the relativistic effects shown by micro-particles traveling at great speed, there is some evident general incompatibility between QT and RT in that their interpretations are philosophically at odds and they have not both been fitted into any sort of unified physical theory. Finding a unified theory is, of course, clearly seen as a desideratum on which many theoretical physicists are working. We can expect, therefore, to find both QT and RT somewhat changed in the compass of some future general physical theory. The current philosophical and methodological problem to which we are addressing ourselves is how to see both RT and QT as sound methodological extensions of classical physics, if that is possible.

One style is simply to deny that QT as it stands is an acceptable physical theory. In other words, we could accept (1)–(6), suitably translated, as constitutive of good scientific theory and treat QT (as currently formulated) as a preparatory step to an adequate QT based on a deeper notion of state vector and a deterministic theory to go with this notion. This is the so-called hidden-variable approach offered by David Bohm, J. P. Vigier, and others.[2] So far as I can see, there is no way to say that the hidden-variable approach is wrong. A deeper deterministic theory may one day be discovered, along with a theory of measurement with affinities to classical theories of measurement. QT could be given up and replaced by a theory with markedly different features much in the same way that theories have been drastically revised at other times in scientific history. At the moment, however, there are several lines of thought that force attention to QT as it stands. For one thing, the formalism of QT has been enormously successful in dealing with a very wide range of certain very real physical problems, and it is employed in much the same way in physical applications by physicists whose philosophical interpretations of the formalism are divergent. Thus the QT formalism is important, and we can regard the question of philosophical interpretation as similar to questions of philosophical interpretation in dealing with other widely used formal systems such as the probability calculus. Another important consideration is that two early approaches to QT which were formally divergent, wave mechanics and matrix mechanics, are now thought to be interchangeable formulations of the theory.[3] Discovery that two independently motivated formalisms are equivalent is often a sign that some system of objective importance has been discovered. A third consideration is the famous von Neumann "proof" that a hidden-variable theory is impossible, along with subsequent elaborations of this theme.[4] What this proof shows is that QT *as currently formulated* is not subject to a hidden-variable interpretation, that is, no micro-micro hidden-variable theory can approximate QT in the limit. Some important parts of the QT formalism would require revision in a more general theory. Physicists are not generally willing to consider such a more general theory until one exists which explains some range of experimental phenomena more adequately than QT does.

It is now time to look more closely at QT itself. In classical theory, many phenomena are thought of as wave phenomena (light, sound) or as particle phenomena (electrons). With respect to classical experiments, these dichotomies are supported by the experimental evidence and are seemingly satisfactory. In micro-experiments, however, light and electrons exhibit both wave-like and particle-like properties. Since the electron is assumed to be a particle in classical physics, and light propagation a wave phenomenon, we will concentrate on evidence showing that (in QT) electrons exhibit wave properties and light exhibits particle properties.

We take the latter first, since most readers will be aware that photons (light particles) are postulated to account for various phenomena. (Actually, the wave-particle duality of light makes an appearance within the limits of classical physics although it is of minor importance.) Planck's original postulation of quantized energy states to account for the spectrum of black body radiation amounts to a claim that light propagation is a corpuscular phenomenon. A decisive case is generally thought to be that offered by the photoelectric effect. When light falls on the surface of a metal, electrons may jump out from the surface resulting in an electric charge on the metal. The electrons in the metal absorb energy from incoming light and may jump out when sufficient (release) energy is obtained. Since the energy required can be calculated, we can illuminate a metal surface with a light of such low intensity that it would take one second (let us say) to trigger the first electron, assuming that light is a wave phenomenon and the energy is "spread out" over the incoming wave. What happens, however, is that an electron may be released immediately, before enough energy could have been absorbed from the incoming light in terms of the wave calculation. Overall, the average energy absorbed on the wave hypothesis equals the average energy of the released electrons. This suggests that energy arrives in quantal packets and that when an electron jumps out immediately it is because a quantal packet of sufficient energy happened to arrive right away. The suggestion is that light is transmitted by photons, and the wave is simply a probability distribution over the arrival time of photons. It is useful to remember here that light exhibits interference properties in other experiments, so we cannot adopt the corpuscular hypothesis for light as a general theory.

Let's look more closely at interference. If a gun repeatedly fires bullets through a hole in a suitable screen, the pattern on the screen will look roughly as illustrated in figure 1.

The smooth distribution illustrated on the screen and shown also as a distribution of hits on the right is both what is intuitively expected and what is observed when *solid particles* of some kind are fired through a narrow target area onto a screen. Historically, however, this observation has confronted a number of awkward experiments. For example, it has been known for a long time that, if light is shown through a *sufficiently* small hole, interference rings such as those shown in figure 2 are produced.

Interference rings are characteristic of wave phenomena. A pattern of

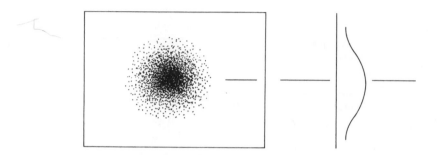

Figure 1

Figure 2

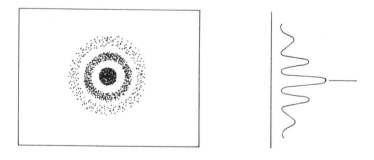

interference similar to that shown would be obtained by wave phenomena since wave energies may either cancel out or be reinforcing, and this accounts for the interference pattern. Light has always been somewhat of a puzzle for the wave / particle dichotomy since some experiments indicate wave properties for light and others (particularly QT observations made in connection with the photoelectric effect) indicate that there are particles (photons) of light. Most classical experiments are satisfactorily explained invoking a wave explanation. Similarly, most classical experiments involving electrons are satisfactorily explained invoking electrons as particles. In 1927 Davisson and Germer of the Bell Telephone Company discovered that the diffraction pattern of an electron beam shot through a crystal grating was that which fit the wave hypothesis proposed by DeBroglie in 1924. The wave hypothesis thus seemed to be corroborated by the results of this experiment.

The wave character of electrons associated with the special properties of QT is usually discussed in connection with idealized experiments such as the famous two-slit experiment illustrated in figure 3.

Let the source emit particles (electrons or photons) one at a time. Each time the screen is hit by a particle, replace the screen with a new one.[5] In the end, consider the distribution of hits on the screen as the composite distribution obtained by summing the hits on the developed single screens. If the source emits particles, we would expect (classically) that the particle travels either through slit$_1$ or through slit$_2$. The composite distribution should therefore be that which we would get if we closed slit$_1$ for half the time, and then opened slit$_1$ and closed slit$_2$ for the other half of the time on the assumption that path orientation from the source was random. This is not what happens. The distribution patterns for 100 hits with both slits open is not the same as the summed patterns for 50 hits with slit$_1$ open and slit$_2$ closed and 50 hits with slit$_2$ open and slit$_1$ closed. Some conclusion that electrons are not simply classical particles seems forced on us by this result. If electrons were particles and an electron happened to go through slit$_1$, it should not have mattered to it whether slit$_2$ was open or closed.

In the face of the two-slit experiment, what are we to do? There are at least four possibilities:

(A) We can say that an electron (or photon) has associated with it both a wave and a particle. The wave (pilot wave) explores the slits (hence the interference pattern), and the particle happens to go through one slit or the other with a probability determined by the pilot wave. (DeBroglie view.)

(B) We can say that the electron is neither a wave nor a particle but something else which shows wave-like or particle-like behavior in

Source   Sheet   Screen

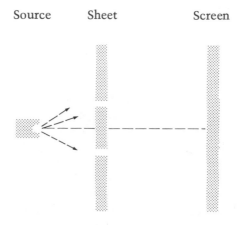

Figure 3   Openings in sheet represent slit₁ (*top*) and slit₂ (*bottom*).

Figure 4   Distribution   Distribution
                           for 100 hits,   for 100 hits,
                           both slits open   50 with slit₁
                                                     open and 50
                                                     with slit₂ open

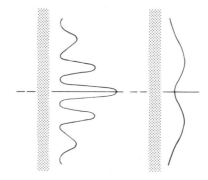

different situations. Thus, we could say that the electron leaves the source and arrives at the screen in a particle-like style but passes through the slits and takes a subsequent direction determined by its wave-like style. This view gives up the classical conception of state and may require some change in the classical conception of causality. (For all its apparent logical crudity and incipient operationalism, this is the majority view.)

(C) We can say that the electron is always a particle and the experiment comes out the way that it does because the probability distribution is determined by the experimental setup and consequent propensities. (Popper and Landé hold this view.)

(D) We could try to accept the wave hypothesis only and argue that the particle as shown in experimental situations is merely a singularity in some wave.

Alternatives (A) and (D) are usually dismissed by a single line of argument. (View (A), incidentally, can be formulated so as to be a hidden-variable theory.) The reason why (A) and (D) may seem to be appealing is that *wave* is ambiguous. There are, as in Maxwell's theory of electromagnetism and in the theory of sound, *physical* waves. The waves discussed in the QT theoretical formalism are not in physical space, however, but in Hilbert space, a mathematical function space whose dimensionality precludes a physical interpretation. This is easily seen also from the fact that wave amplitudes in Hilbert space can be complex numbers and hence can have no physical realization. In addition, the behavior of the waves is very strange on any assumption that they are physical. For example, the position wave of a particle may be spread out over a large area. As a result of a position measurement (say, catching the particle on a screen), the position of the particle may come to be known with great accuracy. The result is that the wave changes its structure very rapidly (and physically inexplicably because of the speed of change) as a result of the measurement from a nonlocalized to a sharply localized phenomenon. By way of looking ahead, the rapid change is not inexplicable if we treat the change as a change in our knowledge or in subjective probabilities for locating the particle. This is why the waves are usually treated as a measure of our chances of obtaining certain experimental results, that is, as a subjective measure of experimental outcome, and not as physical phenomena. Views (A) and (D) have not had adherents so much by way of overcoming this difficulty as they have by retreat into these positions by reaction to difficulties with other views. On all views, some theory of the waves of the QT formalism is required that has not yet been worked out satisfactorily in detail.

Now let's look at (B). The primary philosophical proponents of (B) in the recent philosophical literature have been Hanson and Feyerabend.[6] Briefly, the key objection to (B) is that its operational or positivistic character loses touch with scientific realism. The rebuttal to this objection is that (B) is forced on one by scrutiny of all of the experimental facts and that it can be regarded as doing the same sort of job for quantum experimental phenomena that classical theory did for classical experimental phenomena. To work this out requires treating (1)–(6) as an unbalanced extrapolation from classical theories. Classical theories should be seen as a way of perceiving the significance of data that takes on explanatory depth as it becomes familiar and successful. Thus Hanson, for example, sees QT as similar to classical theories in providing this kind of preceptual understanding. Historical support is offered by alluding to the large number of physicists (as opposed to philosophers) who have found some version of view (B) illuminating with respect to quantum data.

Given what we have said, it seems obvious that classical physical systems and quantum physical systems will not be describable in terms of any unified theory. We would want to say (Correspondence Principle) that quantum physics should be equivalent to classical physics in its predictions in the large, that is, in describing physical relationships between macro-observables. But in general, adherents of view (B) do not regard classical and quantum relationships as reducible, either to the other, in spite of numerical agreement in the solution of various problems. Some quantum relationships will be unique, and our account of measuring apparatus used to observe them may have to remain irreducibly in the language of classical physics. Within quantum language there will be properties of quantum objects that are not reducible to functions of other properties and at the same time are not independent of them (The Complementarity Principle). These relationships will be quite unlike any known in classical physics. This is because to determine the value of a pair of properties related in this way may entail that an arbitrarily precise measurement of one will make the value of the related property indeterminate to an arbitrarily high degree. A classic case of such a pair of properties (in general, such pairs are called *conjugate* pairs) is that of position and momentum. Position and momentum are not (classically) independent in QT. If they were, it would not matter in which order we measured these properties with respect to a given system. But it does matter in that a position measurement destroys the significance of a momentum measurement for the same time and vice versa, so they are clearly not independent. They are also dependent in a sense. A given particle with position and momentum known to some reasonable degree of accuracy will be related to a later position and momentum determination in calculable ways. But they are not dependent in the classical sense of being functionally dependent. An arbitrarily precise knowledge of the value of one property at a time precludes an arbitrarily precise knowledge of the value of the other property at that time.

In the two-slit experiment, we might attempt to test the hypothesis that the electrons or photons were traveling through one slit or the other by checking through a measurement of position or momentum the slit through which the particle traveled. One might put a particle counter at each slit to determine whether a particle passed through that slit when a particle was emitted from the source. One might also put the sheet with the slits in it into a moving arrangement, so that if the particle glanced off one of the slits we could infer from the movement of the sheet as a result of momentum transfer which slit the particle had passed through. It is an important fact that no such experiment can succeed because either means of determining particle path destroys the QT interference pattern on the screen. According to QT theory, nature has (cunningly) made sure that we cannot determine the paths or momenta of postulated particles if we want to obtain the characteristic QT effects in the two -slit experiment.

Let us contrast view (B) and view (C) on this point. It should be noticed that (B) and (C) are in agreement that probabilities are functions of experimental arrangements. Both views can hold that if the experiment is performed twice, once with one slit open and once with one slit closed, the results are likely to differ. View (B) contends that the probabilities measure what we will find in the experiment and that this can differ from experimental setup to experimental setup. View (C) contends that the probabilities are propensities and measure something objective about the experimental setup. Given just the data, the pragmatic difference between the theories is slight. One could therefore argue that view (C) is preferable because of the way in which it can be integrated into a methodology which avoids problems of subjective probability.[7] View (C) can contend that the electrons or photons are always particles and avoid the usual objections to this because of its indeterministic features. One cannot be a determinist and believe that the electrons are photons or particles throughout their paths because this means that it would not matter if $slit_2$ were open or closed if the particle passes through $slit_1$; but the experimental data refute this suggestion decisively unless causality is given up altogether, and a determinist is unlikely to make such a move. Therefore if we simply consider the data of the two-slit experiment, either view (B) or view (C) could be interpreted to explain it. Popper's achievement in developing view (C) is that he has shown that the two-slit experimental data by themselves do not force us to accept some version of view (B).

There are still a few subtleties to be explored in connection with the two-slit experiment. According to the usual versions of view (B), there is a sharp distinction between classical physics and QT such that some objects need to be viewed as classical objects and others as QT objects. The major difference is that classical objects are in well-defined states while QT objects are often in states described as superpositions of various QT states. In order for measurement to be successful, a classical object must take on a well-defined state that results in a state for the QT object which may represent a very sudden discovery that one of the superposed states is the state that the object is now in. Measurement would not necessarily have a determinate outcome unless classical objects always had definite states, which QT objects do not. This is the reason why view (B) adherents do not see classical physics as reducible to QT, because reducibility would imply, along with the theory of measurement, that measurements might result in indeterminate data, which they manifestly do not. On this view, the QT object may not be in a definite state but may be in a superposition of states until measurement puts it into a definite state because of the coupling with a classical system during the operation of measurement. In the two-slit experiment, all of the apparatus including the sheet and the screen are regarded as classical objects, and only the particles traveling through the apparatus are taken as QT objects. The probability that a particle will appear at a given spot on the screen is inevitably a subjective measure of expectation because there is no way of explaining the inter-action between the state of the sheet and the probability either within classical physics or within QT. This forces adherents of view (B) to deny that the particle has a definite path as it passes through the apparatus in order to avoid the difficulty that if it had a definite path it would not matter to that path whether or not the other slit was open. This view retains a reasonable view about causality by giving up the idea that QT objects have definite even if unknown states while passing through the apparatus.

Popper's view is that QT replaces and corrects classical physics. There is an implicit whiff of reductionism here in that Popper is not willing to live with the uneasy joint acceptance of classical physics and QT as indepen-dently viable theories that view (B) utilizes to describe the two-slit experi-ment. According to Popper, the sheet with its slits and the screen are all QT objects. The total sheet with the slits is therefore an object with different space periodicities built into it, depending on whether or not the two slits are open. A particle interacting with the sheet can then be re-garded as a classical particle (interpreted in QT as having definite proper-ties) interacting in an indeterministic fashion with a very complicated sheet whose structure requires a QT description in order to explain the experimental results. Since the QT description of the sheet is different in the two experimental arrangements, the relative probabilities of the pro-pensity theory allow us to match observed values with QT derived values. Therefore, given just the distributions for the one-slit and two-slit situ-ations, we can explain them piecemeal using either view (B) or view (C).

Let us go back to our discussion of presuppositions (1)–(6) of classical physics given at the start of the chapter, which we repeat here for convenience:

(1) Classical objects are described by state vectors.
(2) Classical objects have precise properties which are represented by numbers in the state vectors for the objects.
(3) Theories take state vectors into state vectors (on certain assumptions).
(4) Good theories are deterministic.
(5) Arbitrarily precise measurements are (in principle) possible which reveal the values of the state vectors of a system of classical objects.
(6) Arbitrarily precise predictions are possible of the values of the state vectors of a system of classical objects.

We see that Popper has already argued that presuppositions (4)–(6) are *not* true of classical physics. Presupposition (4) must be abandoned since good theories may be deterministic or indeterministic. We accept rather the fact that, since classical physics itself is indeterministic, there is no reason to assume that all good theories are deterministic. This allows us to accept indeterminism in QT and its theory of measurement as natural and as representing no essential break with classical theory. Popper would also reject (5) and (6) for the reason that he rejects (4). His indeterminism means that the result of measurement is governed by methodological rules which must deal with the fact that no precision in current measurement can guarantee given precision in future measurement. Although Popper waives the problem of error in measurement during discussion of the problem of prediction, it is clear that his indeterminism forces the view that even in classical physics measurement cannot achieve arbitrarily precise results. Popper sees both indeterminism and realism as important features both of classical physics and QT. In QT there is no problem for Popper with realism. Popper postulates the existence of real particles with definite properties and must then suppose that the quantization of results involved in QT is a feature of the particles measured. In other words, Popper must hold that (contrary to the usual interpretation) a particle has definite position and momentum at all times and that the impossibility of simultaneously measuring both is part of the QT theory of measurement. Measurement may only give certain kinds of values because of the nature of the measuring apparatus; this does not preclude the measured particle having exact values at other times or unmeasured properties having exact values at the same time. Although Popper's indeterminism separates his views from those of Einstein and various "hidden variable" adherents, he can agree with such views about the definiteness of properties of QT particles when they are not measured. Since Popper views only (1)–(3) as true of classical physics, he can regard QT as a methodological extension of classical physics and as a replacement for it while minimizing the "revolutionary" nature of QT which would render its appearance inexplicable from the standpoint of normative methodology.

As long as we limit ourselves to such topics as the observed distributions in the two-slit experiment, and as long as we suppose that a satisfactory theory of measurement can be supplied, view (C) seems an attractive alternative to view (B) from a methodological point of view. It is not possible to argue in this book any of the complicated technical issues surrounding QT since we are primarily interested in explicating Popper's views. Popper's views on QT, although they are suggestive in the manner we have indicated, remain seriously incomplete at present by comparison to the detailed views expounded by various adherents of versions of view (B). No one denies that there are problems with the versions of view (B) extant, particularly with the theory of measurement to be associated with it, so that some development of Popper's view could ultimately be found to be satisfactory. All that can be done here is to indicate the kinds of objections to Popper's view that keep view (B) the majority alternative.

One objection is that the propensity interpretation has little to offer by way of explanation of *why*, when the second slit is opened in the sheet in the two-slit experiment, the distribution changes in the way that it does. We can, after all, work out a classical pinboard such that classical particles put through it will show a certain probability distribution in terms of where they are observed to leave the pinboard. These can be well estimated from the structure of the board. When the pinboard is changed, the probability distribution is changed. At this level of abstraction, there is an obvious parallel with the two-slit experiment. Change the sheet and you change the distribution. The point is that *the kind of change* is completely novel in QT and could never be estimated from a description of the experimental setup, although by now sufficient experience enables us to fit a probability distribution to the QT experimental arrangements. View (B) adherents argue from the intuitive strangeness of the QT experimental data to the notion that QT objects must be quite different from classical objects. As has been noted, this is partly a result of the methodological decision to accept classical descriptions of the apparatus—but Popper's view is not yet equipped with sufficient postulations about the forces underlying the propensities revealed in experimental data to connect particle realism and indeterminism with the extant features of the total range of QT data.[8] We have considered here only the two-slit experiment, but even here it is clear that the propensity theory seems to provide only an ad hoc fit that is logically *compatible* with the facts. Popper needs more physical theory to enable prediction (even if only retrospectively) of a wide range of observed QT data.

The difficulty suggested becomes more obvious if we turn to slightly different kinds of QT data. Electrons possess in QT a property known as "spin," connected historically to the idea that a magnetic pole has a definite orientation in space. A source of electrons passed through an appropriate field will leave the field with quantized spin, say either *up* or *down*. Let us assume that the source is such that the electrons to be passed through such a field have either randomly oriented spin or indefinite spin, that is, no determinate spin value. View (C), by analogy with classical physics, would take the option that the electrons entering the field had randomly oriented, but perfectly definite, spin. Now the problem to be developed is connected with the time required for spin orientation to change in response to the action of the magnetic field. On the supposition that spin orientation is changed as a result of some causal process, calculation suggests that the change in orientation from some of the postulated spin directions to *up* or *down* requires far more time than elapses in the electron's path through the magnetic field. Without going into more detail, it is experimental findings of this kind that have forced the apparently classically contradictory aspects of QT interpretation onto adherents of view (B). The magnetic field is regarded as causing a definite spin orientation to appear where no definite value had existed, just as the particle detector in the two-slit experiment causes a definite path location that would not exist in the absence of the detector. What is required from view (C) is detailed interpretation of such experimental results, the sort of experimental result which historically forced adherents of view (B) into seeming paradoxes almost against their will and certainly contrary to their original physical intuitions.[9] In short, view (C) has a perfectly adequate methodological interpretation. What it requires is more physical theory.

In summary, Popper's discussion of QT and his development of view (C) must again be seen as symptomatic of his willingness to confront severe difficulties with his methodological views. On the basis of certain partial analyses of QT experimental data, Popper has proposed an interpretation of QT that is logically compatible with the data and methodologically indentical with his interpretation of classical physics. This is a considerable achievement well worth further elaboration in an effort to see whether it can be made compatible with the total range of QT phenomena (perhaps after reinterpretation) that have been involved in the development of majority-view interpretations of QT.

In this chapter we have concentrated on Popper's discussions of quantum theory, partly because quantum theory poses so many prima facie problems for any view holding that there is a common methodology for classical and quantum physics and partly because quantum theory has played an important role in Popper's extant writings on physical theory. Popper has contributed to the literature on other physical problems, and several future discussions of relativity theory and other physical theories have been promised.[10] This chapter should indicate the nontrivial nature of Popper's methodological views in that the combination of realism, indeterminism, and falsifiability entails definite views on various physical problems. I have tried to indicate the sort of strategy available to Popperians for assimilating awkward physical theories and interpretations while retaining a credible relationship between physics and philosophical methodology.

NINE

Popper's Account of the Social Sciences

In this chapter we will come briefly to terms with two major books by Popper, *The Poverty of Historicism* and *The Open Society and Its Enemies,* as well as other Popperian comments on the themes introduced in these books. The two books mentioned constitute the bulk of Popper's criticisms of Plato, Hegel, and Marx (principally in *The Open Society*) and his criticism of a spectrum of possible Marxist and socialist views which Popper calls *historicism* (principally in *The Poverty of Historicism*). Popper's books have not lacked for critics who have argued that Popper has misrepresented Plato, Hegel, and Marx in *The Open Society* and that his version of historicism is so tendentious that it does not represent views held by any actual Marxist or socialist theoretican. There is no point in attempting to assess Popper's accuracy in describing the views of other authors in a chapter such as this. It is also simply not possible here to relate Popper's views to staples of current social theory such as functionalism in view of the fact that a survey of social theory would outrun the confines of this chapter, and perhaps of this book. Popper has not, in any event, been a major figure in theoretical debates about social theory, no matter how useful some of this ideas might be to such debates. As we will see at the end of the chapter, this is perhaps due to his failure to discuss specific issues in the social sciences which social theorists themselves regard as important. This is in contrast to Popper's discussion of important physical experiments in his methodological discussion of physical theory. Popper's influence seems to have been felt most directly through his teaching at the London School of Economics where he influenced many students who later took part in governmental planning. What can be usefully accomplished here is to briefly outline Popper's views for those who are interested in social theory and who may wish to take Popper's views into account.

One major theme in Popperian social theory is that the methodological account provided by his philosophy of science should apply without alteration to the theories of the social sciences. As is well known, many theorists have argued that the subject matter of the social sciences is different from the subject matter of the physical sciences because human beings (due to free will, unconscious motivation, or societal influences with no analogies to physical forces) are not theoretically similar to physical objects. Popper refuses to see any distinction in the relative unpredictability involved in the social sciences since he has argued that even classical physical systems are indeterministic. Those who have posited separate methodologies have been seen by Popper as accepting a positivistic account of physical science and then finding themselves needing a different methodology for the social sciences, principally because they have failed to notice the inadequacies of their original account of physical science. Any need to posit a separate methodology for the social sciences can be circumvented, in Popper's view, by developing a correct nonpositivistic and indeterministic methodology for the physical sciences.

When Popperian methodology is applied to the social theories of the literature, it generally turns out that they fail to be clearly falsifiable under specifiable conditions. On this basis, Popper rejects all versions of large-scale Marxist and socialist social theories. Popper finds such theorists to suppose that their theories *must* be true, and hence they violate reasonable methodological prescription by refusing to discuss possible refutation. What is left after these criticisms does not amount to a large-scale Popperian social theory. Popper argues rather that societies which exist are clearly viable and should restrict their operations to the application of scientific knowledge in piecemeal social engineering, alleviating human misery and suffering by the application of established scientific knowledge. This advice may seem to have an odd sound. Popper the revolutionary in physical theory seems Popper the conservative in social theory—and this fact requires some explanation. Its appearance, however, suggests that a fissure may exist between physical and social theory that Popper has not noted. The refutation of social theories through the use of falsifiability could be simply misplaced. Perhaps the whole arena of social science that he enters is a metaphysical battlefield, and not a scientific congress, so that discussions of falsification are misplaced and merely confirm the obvious, at least in this stage of human knowledge about social systems.[1] By Popper's own theoretical admission, this would not make social science unimportant, but it would mean that some form of criticism other than the test of falsifiability is the appropriate tool of analysis.

Popper also has his own normative social theory, a form of liberal democracy, which consists in an attempt to argue that the concept of the Open Society provides a suitable ideal for all social systems. What seems to have happened here is that Popper has taken the structure (as he sees it) of the society of physicists as an exemplary structure for any society. The society of physicists adapts to new knowledge, solves problems that arise in connection with existing theories, and so forth. This provides the model for a society. Criticism should be welcomed and encouraged with the society, new ideas tested and then possibly utilized, and authoritarian and traditional elements minimized. Unfortunately, Popperian generalization from physicists to general societal structures proceeds to a defense of liberal democracy as the best form of human government without a careful investigation of whether there are conditions attached to scientific debate and progress which cannot meaningfully be met in practice by larger, more heterogeneous societies. On this topic Popper approaches vacuity, stating blithely that all societies should be regarded as problem-solving organizations and assessed in terms of their abilities to deal with problems, without any detailed consideration of what constitute social problems and what solutions to such problems are pertinent to our understanding of larger societies.

In defending liberal democracy, Popper is undertaking defense of a position not entirely analogous to positions that he has defended in connection with physical theory. Proponents of the standard version of quantum theory have been perhaps too smug. Their theories are, in practice, often presented as though they could not be falsified because they were manifestly true. In attempting to find other versions of physical theory, Popperian criticism can have the effect of improving standard physical theory even if it doesn't result in a fitter alternative theory. But in defending liberal democracy, Popper suggests that Marxist and socialist theoreticians are committed to historicist views which prevent their working out reasonable and falsifiable versions of their social theories in the future. To put it bluntly, Popper treats versions of these theories as though they had an essence which, if circumvented, would result in some version of liberal democratic theory if acceptable.[2] His methodological prescriptions thus have a higher prescriptive order in social science than in physical science.

The major interest in Popper's views on the social sciences is that he is one of the few philosophers of science to have explicitly argued a methodological scheme designed to have normative impact on both the physical and the social sciences. In the context of general methodological discussion, this attempt is an interesting venture, but it is nonetheless possible to avoid Popper's social prescriptions as binding while retaining the

sound insights of his methodology for physical theory. A Marxist or socialist might well respond to Popper by arguing either that social science is an
important form of metaphysics or that a scientific Marxism or socialism is
possible which is methodologically at least as sound as the theory of a
scientific liberal democracy.[3] For one thing, Popper has primarily argued
for liberal democracy and piecemeal social engineering by attacking Marxism and socialism. (We can ignore fascism here because its authoritarian
elements are so obviously in conflict with Popperian methodology.) Without offering a positive theory of liberal democracy fitting the situational
facts of large modern countries while remaining consistent with his methodology, Popper has not demonstrated that a suitable theory of liberal
democracy is actually viable.

I   The Methodology of the Social Sciences

As we have seen, Popper originally developed falsifiability as a line of
demarcation for physical science with the explicit intention of excluding
Marxism and psychoanalytic theory along with astrology. Current astrology surely deserves to be excluded, and Popper's remarks are apt. Historically, however, it might be noted that astrology began on a scientific
note.[4] Early astrologers, noting obvious correlations between such things
as climate and weather and human conditions, hence between the position of the sun and moon and human conditions, jumped to the bold
conjecture that there were correlations to be discovered between the positions of all the heavenly bodies and human conditions. It simply turned
out that the connections are few and quite loose, so that astrology could
never develop into an area of scientific knowledge by extrapolation from
its humble beginnings. Marxism and psychoanalytic theory are something
else. They have been proposed recently in human history, and they have
made an enormous contribution primarily because *they have fundamentally changed the way we think about human behavior.* Particular
forms of both theories have singled out phenomena that cry for explanation even if these particular forms of the theories are defective. As yet, they
have not developed into fully scientific disciplines, and perhaps they never
will in terms of Popper's line of demarcation. But it seems a fundamental
error to make the major assessment of their worth the rather negative
judgment that neither is currently a (Popperian) scientific discipline.
Given the general epistemological association of human knowledge to
scientific knowledge in Popper, this is to elevate sterile quantitative sociological analyses to a higher degree of epistemic importance than either of
two epoch-making systems of ideas.

In debates about the methodology of the social sciences, Popper has
often been accused of being a positivist by social philosophers convinced

that the methodology of the social sciences is distinct from the methodology of the physical sciences. Obviously, Popper bristles at the charge, and in a sense correctly. What these philosophers seem to have picked up, however, is not the technical difference between nonjustificationist and justificationist epistemology and why Popper is not technically a positivist but the fact that Popper along with the positivists assumes that facts can be gathered in the social sciences much in the same way that they are gathered in the physical sciences. A crucial case here is whether an intelligent and educated person can know what he is doing in any situation and whether he can articulate this knowledge (say, on a questionnaire) in response to clear questions. The Popperian and positivist attitude is that he *can* know what he is doing and that he *can* articulate this knowledge with sufficient effort. From this perspective Marxism and psychoanalytic theory are alike in that they view human action as motivated and as to be explained by forces, economic or psychic, typically beyond the understanding of the individual who is acting.

As an example, let us consider a cluster of concepts related to that of lying. Typically, physical systems not involving predictors cannot choose how to react to experimental situations. No problem of false data arises except with respect to incompetent experimental design or error in observation. In the study of human beings, however, the situation is quite different. Our attempts to gain knowledge can be frustrated by deliberate lying or unwitting deception on the part of the human agents involved. On Popperian and positivist grounds, lying always involves a conscious decision to tell something that the agent knows is not the truth. An honest and cooperative agent could always give correct data. In Marxist theory, an honest agent may give totally false data because his perception of his situation and the alternatives confronting him is determined by a class status and interest that he may not be consciously aware of. Further, it will do no good to ask him to ignore his class status and interests, because this makes no sense—he cannot help being, so to speak, who he is. In psychoanalytic theory, an honest agent may give totally false data because of repressed motivations and feelings which the agent does not consciously recognize even though they determine his responses. Further, it will do no good to ask him to focus on his repressed, unconscious states of mind because these are inaccessible to him without expert therapeutic help. In Marxist theory, the notion of what constitutes the objective state of affairs must be determined by an expert individual who can see the direction of the class struggle in a society. In psychoanalytic theory, the total state of an individual can be determined, if at all, only by an expert who can decipher the unconscious by reading off from events a significance that the individual cannot find without this expert assistance.

Popper is quite right to point to the conflicting claims of various Marxist schools of interpretation and various psychoanalytic theorists as evidence that these clusters of ideas are not objectively falsiflable. Given the same events, there can be conflicting Marxian or psychoanalytic explanations which cannot be differentiated because they refer to explaining concepts the existence of which in the events cannot be (at least at present) independently corroborated by experimental test.[5] All of this is quite compatible with the idea that these are metaphysical theories looking for scientific status. Popper's animadversions seem to be based on the idea that these theories can never achieve scientific status because they are theories about world 2 events (and hence would never be falsifiable in any form) and because they seem to involve an illicit form of determinism.

Interestingly enough, psychoanalytic theory receives minimal treatment (along with astrology) in Popper's published discussions. Indeed, Popper takes Marx to be a useful ally in the fight against psychologism (as represented in psychoanalytic theory), and he sees his problem with respect to the two theories to be primarily that of rebutting Marxist economic historicism rather than that of arguing against psychologism. Marxism and Popperianism can take the following kind of example to be a refutation of psychologism:

> And this remark gives us an opportunity to formulate the *main task of the theoretical social sciences. It is to trace the unintended social repercussions of intentional human actions.* I may give a simple example. If a man wishes urgently to buy a house in a certain district, we can safely assume that he does not wish to raise the market price of houses in that district. But the very fact that he appears on the market as a buyer will tend to raise market prices. And analogous remarks hold for the seller.[6]

What this quotation shows quite convincingly is that a person's psychological state as reflected in his intentional action cannot explain the social consequences of his action. Popperian (and Marxist) analysis suggests that a theorist should describe the objective consequences of objective acts in a given situation. Why the acts are done is not important. That act (or those acts) which has the best objective consequences is the rational act in the situation. Psychological states simply drop out. Actually, what such examples show is that psychologism *by itself* is an insufficient mode of explanation in the social sciences, not that psychological states are not important or that they are not important as *part* of the explanation in discussing social actions or social change. At this point, however, we will accept the insufficiency of psychologism and return to Popper's critique of Marx.

We will primarily consider Popperian criticisms of Marxist theory here, although Popper intends these criticisms to apply also to any form of the sociology of knowledge which is related to Marxist theory in holding that knowledge is determined at least partly by a societal structure that an individual embedded therein cannot adequately grasp. Popper's views about Marxist methodology are contained in his blanket condemnation of historicism. The views that Popper calls historicist seem to be all of the opinions he is opposed to in social theory, and he has created as the historicist doctrine an unattractive set of ideas that probably no one has ever held. Real historicists seem to have held some of these opinions but to have relaxed others.[7] It is therefore an easy criticism of Popper's attack on Marxist thought and on historicism in general to argue that no one worth considering has ever held the ideal type of historicist position that Popper develops in detail. We will consider here major historicist views related to Marxist theory that Popper has explicitly attacked without developing in this context the whole range of historicist opinions mentioned in *The Poverty of Historicism*.

Historicists have typically argued that the laws of social science are not universal in the obvious logical sense. They apply only to specific societies or human beings in the context of specific social situations. Human beings in different societies are in unique situations that are extremely difficult to compare. Historicists see prediction, therefore, as related to descriptions of societies which are unique and which require special insight to develop. They do not suppose that there are general laws of history to which boundary conditions can be attached to provide predictions for any given society. The role of societal laws in social science is thus not analogous to the role of physical laws in physical theory. Historicists have also typically held that societies and social institutions are not reducible in analysis to sets of individual human beings and their relationships. This is related, for example, to the Marxist view that societal structure has an impact on individual behavior that cannot be understood (typically) by the individual engaged in the behavior. The net effect of these historicist views is to produce descriptions of societies and histories which are insulated from falsification. Evidence from other societies is not relevant to a given society and its description. Evidence about the way men act in other societies is not relevant to a given description of a utopian society. It is then possible to describe theoretically a perfect society and argue that any apparently countervailing facts from present societies about the possibility of such a society do not count because the societies are different and so are the men in them. Each society may have a unique essence not reducible to facts about the individuals which comprise it and their actions; otherwise, comparison would be theoretically possible. Because of this, historicists typically have strong emotional ties to some form of utopianism.

The historicist study of societies is thus historical rather than scientific.

Historicists attempt to protect the future of the society from the course of its history. Since rational discussion of the possibilities of various changes through comparison to other societal structures is not possible, the historicist attempts only to determine what direction the society under scrutiny will in fact take. This is usually done simply through some form of intuitive understanding. Historicists often hold that the direction of the development of societal history is a necessary consequence of the structure of the society, as Marxists have held that capitalist societies must destroy themselves due to internal contradiction. Against this view of historical necessity, Popper may bring his arguments in refutation of determinism. Historicists may hold that long-range forecasts of the future of a society are the staple of a study of a society, whether the future is determined by societal structure or not. To this Popper will again reply that the general failure of determinism makes long-range forecasting impossible.

In addition to general arguments against Marxism as a form of historicism, Popper reserves some special comments for Marxist prediction. Popper argues that the Marxian sweep of history, in being determined by class structure based on economic factors alone, relies on a biased and misleading conception of the motivations for human action. This is, of course, a common criticism of Marxism that seems perfectly legitimate. It is unfortunate from this perspective that we do not have a more penetrating Popperian analysis, for example, of Max Weber's similar objection to the causal significance of economic motivation based on historical examples such as Weber's thesis about the motivational underpinnings of modern capitalism and the resultant voluminous discussion.[8] As we will see, Popper's own conception of an Open Society requires a conception of uniform human goals, so that an explicit account of the range of human motivational factors is required on Popperian grounds. Popper also argues against specific Marxist predictions, either that they were wrong or that they could have been made within a social theoretical perspective not based on historicist principles.

Popper is opposed to the twin strains of utopianism and totalitarianism that he finds in Marxist thought. Totalitarianism, even where it is employed as a means of achieving a better (classless) society, implies that knowledge is obtainable by some that can be used along with power to coerce others into a path they might not choose to follow. It is quite clear that scientific knowledge has been used in our time in this totalitarian fashion, but Popper suggests in many passages that he finds this equally reprehensible. In both cases, social or scientific totalitarianism stifles the open criticism which must underlie decision making in the Open Society. Utopianism is picking a plan in advance and then attempting to actualize it, usually through totalitarian change. Popper's objection here is the familiar one that the plan must change in the course of actualizing it, so that utopianism makes a kind of prediction about the future which cannot be realized. It is somewhat surprising that Popper makes no mention of the fact that Marxist planners have argued precisely over the nature of utopianism in this sense, and even if Marxist planning has been historicist in practice, this dimension of the theoretical debate is easily formulable in Marxist terms.

There are several difficulties with attacking Marxism on the basis of the failure of its specific predictions. One difficulty is that it is perfectly acceptable for scientific theories to be revised in the light of failures of prediction, and hence Marxism is not so much refuted by specific failures as it is shown to require some revision. Failure of prediction is consequently a refutation only of Marxist views which argue that mistakes are not possible in the correct application of Marxist views. Some Marxists have indeed argued that Marxism is like the Second Law of Thermodynamics, falsifiable but unfalsified.[9] These Marxists are forced to argue that what has been predicted by Marxian analysis and has not happened has simply not happened yet. In many cases, Marxist predictions are vague just on this score. They outline a development but do not or cannot provide a timetable for the development in real time. Thus there is no time at which failure of prediction constitutes refutation, and the theory is being treated as unfalsifiable. Popperians may well argue that more specific Marxist predictions are either impossible or are a desideratum in a revised theory, but Marxists could well agree with this. The development of history does not require totally accurate temporal prediction. Many Marxists have, of course, been vain about their ability to predict the course of history, as have many non-Marxists. This vanity does not seem an *essential* feature of Marxism any more than it does of rival views of human history. Indeed, many modern Marxists have condemned utopianism in the Marxist sense on essentially Popperian grounds, arguing that only general Marxist goals to be achieved in a society can be set in advance, the detail being established in the course of realizing them. What is required for an objective assessment of Marxism is some sort of detailed comparative study of Marxist and non-Marxist predictions about various societies. There can be no doubt even in the absence of such studies that the sort of prediction and analysis introduced by Marx and Marxists has proved valuable even to non-Marxists as a basis for understanding the social and economic dynamics of modern societies.

This leads to a difficulty of even greater scope. If one dismisses Marxism on the grounds that its predictive abilities are weak, as Popper does because of his emphasis on falsifiability, one tends to overlook the importance of the Marxian reorientation of our thinking about man in society. The crucial modern notion of alienation was developed by Marx and Marxists, and it seems a necessary concept to use in understanding psychological phenomena surrounding workers in an advanced industrial society. Even if one is not a Marxist, the phenomena singled out originally through the use of the notion of alienation require an explanation. Through the use of such concepts, Marxism seems to have made our understanding of societal structures much more sophisticated, even if we are not bound to the conceptual scheme within which they were introduced. Alienation is one example of a central Marxist concept which makes no appearance either in *The Poverty of Historicism* or in *The Open Society and Its Enemies.* Any analysis of Marxism that fails to come to grips with concepts like that of alienation seems clearly to have been grappling with a distorted image of the view to be discussed, an image revealing only those aspects of Marxism similar or dissimilar to current scientific theories.

To historicist doctrines, Popper opposes what he calls methodological individualism and situational logic. Methodological individualism is the view that facts about a society can always be explained by a suitable series of individual human actions. There is a noticeable lack of argument for methodological individualism in Popper. It might be supposed that Popper has simply transferred his physical science conception that physical systems can be analyzed into particles and their relationships, to a social science view that social systems can be analyzed into individual human beings and their relationships. In this case, objections to the physical science view can easily be made into objections to the social science view. One might suppose that any direct argument for methodological individualism should await a comparative study of social institutions done from the viewpoint of methodological individualism and from various historicist perspectives, to see which was more revealing and whether the more revealing could in fact express every important explanation contained in the framework of rival methodologies. The only direct argument for methodological individualism that Popper hints at is an argument that historicist conceptions cannot explain change in social institutions. A functionalist or historicist analysis of a social institution may explain why people act as they do so long as they continue to act that way. It cannot explain what happens when a societal institution is changed, according to Popper, because *individuals must change institutions by their actions;* institutions cannot change themselves. In addition, the historicist view that institutions control human behavior cannot explain what will happen when two institutions or two societies come into conflict:

> Not only does the construction of institutions involve important personal decisions, but the functioning of even the best institutions . . . will always depend, to a considerable degree, on the persons involved. Institutions are like fortresses. They must be well designed *and* manned.[10]

Methodological individualism holds that institutions are created by human decision and changed by the same method.

Both methodological individualism and historicist institutionalism may be partly right in the sense that institutions may cause actions which change institutions which cause actions, and so forth. Popper has drawn the lines of arguments in such a fashion that this prima facie reasonable view must be classed as historicist unless the functioning of institutions can be explained in terms of individual decisions so that institutions need never be given explanatory primitive status. But there is a problem for Popper here related to his use of world 3 in combating subjectivism. It is worth noticing that Popper's claims about world 3 as being independent of individual decision are quite like historicist claims about the existence and role of societal institutions. World 3 structures determine human actions but are not reducible to them. A world 3 structure, once established, will have coercive consequences for human thought. Thus Popper's relatively recent introduction of world 3 structures to help the objectivity of his methodology is in potential conflict with his early social theory. Popper would presumably see a difference between historicist institutions and world 3 structures, perhaps that in his conception of world 3 structures two human beings may come to have the same objective knowledge about some structure they are interested in, while in the historicist conception of institutions the influence of the institution may be through unconscious motivation in such a fashion that explicit common knowledge about the institution is not possible while the institution retains its motivating force. It is not at all clear that such a distinction can be drawn in a fashion that will allow Popper to retain methodological individualism *and* his account of world 3 structures, while eliminating all need to postulate societal institutional structures as explanatory primitives.

Popperian social theory is perhaps best revised in the light of this situation by agreeing that reduction of institutional coercion is in many cases not reducible to individual human acts, thus extending remarks made by Popper against reduction in the physical sciences to the social sciences, and simply admitting that some institutions and world 3 structures are basic and irreducible primitives for an explanation of contemporary human society. It could then be argued that changes in social institutions are typically indeterministic and that the actions of individuals may influence such changes. Utilizing Popper's criterion of reality, if we kick a world 3 structure, it may kick back. A conjectured change may result, for example, in contradiction. Now, individuals may kick social structures with no effect, or they may kick social structures which change as a result. The objective change will not necessarily be the intended change. We know that Popper wishes to hold this view about the effects of human actions. To do so, he must hold that world 3 structures have an independent existence and that changes in world 3 structures cannot be explained totally by individual kicks, or without individual kicks, but must be a complicated relationship between inertia in the structure and well-timed individual kicks. If methodological individualism cannot be retained in explaining change in world 3 structures, it can probably not be retained in explaining change in societal structures. Historicism about societal structures is thus refuted if and only if it must be associated with determinism of development.

As another example, consider a natural language like English. It seems difficult to deny that it is a world 3 structure and also difficult to deny that it is a societal artifact. A change in English may or may not occur as a result of an individual attempt to change it. If an individual proposes a change fitting a sufficiently general need which also conforms to the syntactical and semantical inertial features of the language, the language may change as a result. On the other hand, an individual cannot change the language just because he wants to do so, and teams of official grammarians have been unable to prevent various developments in linguistic evolution.[11] To understand linguistic phenomena, we need to develop an account of languages as structures not reducible to particular instances of the use of the language, structures which are objective but not perfectly understood by their users. Compare this situation to changes in agreed etiquette in a social group. Similar remarks apply. A felicitous kick may result in a change and a reputation as an innovator for the kicker, whereas an infelicitous kick may only cause the kicker to be considered a boor with no alteration in the social institution. It seems to me that an analysis of social change must rest on some such connection between relatively independent social structures changing indeterministically in response to individual human acts. This conception is not inconsistent with the Popperian outlook provided that social structures and institutions can be successfully analyzed from the standpoint of methodological individualism. This seems unlikely to me, and the revised Popperianism mentioned above more promising, but any Popperian attempt to retain pure methodological individualism is required to produce successful analyses of world 3 structures and social structures from the standpoint of methodological individualism, without taking structural descriptions as primitive. To this point in time, such a program remains at best a desideratum.

Let us now return to the relevance of situational logic for the social sciences. Popper's remarks about situational logic are brief and sketchy, and some reconstruction and guesswork are required. The basic thrust behind situational logic is the suggestion that methodological individualism can be carried out and explanations of individual actions given without reference to untestable psychological states.[12] Situational logic is normative in that it is designed to explain what action is most rational in a situation. A person may take some irrational action due to his irrational preference structure. Suppose an agent is confronted with some sort of decision. Situational logic supposes that a full description of the situation in which the decision is to be made plus a rationality principle will yield an appropriate normative action as the most rational (or a most rational) action to choose in the circumstances. Lapses from this action will be perceived in the theory as failure of information or lack of rationality. This is not much different from assuming that classical decision theory can explain rational action. Given that a businessman wants to maximize profits and that various permissible actions confronting him yield certain rates of profit, the rational businessman will choose that action (or from those actions) maximizing profit. Situational logic holds that there are universal laws about human behavior such that they will apply to particular situations when the situation is described fully and an assumption is made about rationality. It is usually assumed that an agent will act so as to maximize long-range pleasure under some suitable description, where pleasure may be represented in the situation by a utility function giving the agent's rational preferences. At first glance, situational logic may seem to provide a way of relativizing the rationality of human actions to concrete situations, much as the propensity theory of probability relativizes probabilities to experimental situations. It speaks once again to the overall harmony of Popper's methodological prescriptions.

There is at least one great difficulty with the concept of situational logic. The difficulty is that relativizing to a situation does not explain what action is actually rational in the situation unless one may postulate that all human beings have the same ends (avoidance of misery and maximization of comfort, and so on) that can be combined with full information about a situation to indicate which available action is maximal. In the background lurks the idea that a situation in one culture and a seemingly similar situation in another culture, as well as all pairs of cross-cultural situations no matter how seemingly different, can receive description in a common language. This is to assume that human beings, as rational agents, are potentially interchangeable. But why should this assumption be made rather than the Marxist assumption or the psychoanalytic assumption that human beings in different cultural circumstances may be in totally different and incomparable situations because of unknown cultural factors or unconscious beliefs? Situational logic is a mere slogan until useful situational analyses have actually been provided and reasonable evidence adduced for various cross-cultural comparisons. Otherwise, situational logic can handle clashes of cultures no better than some form of historicist institutional determinism.

Two poles involved in much current social science research which are somewhat independent of issues of historicism are a kind of cultural relativism and some form of scientific objectivism. Cultural relativists argue that the significance of any act is unique to the culture in which it is performed and that, consequently, cross-cultural comparisons or evaluations cannot meaningfully be made. A historicist, as we have seen, is most likely to accept some version of this view, but a nonhistoricist might also choose to adopt it. Scientific objectivists argue that scientific knowledge is the most comprehensive form of human knowledge and that it can be used as a touchstone to evaluate rationality in all cultures. Both positions have severe drawbacks. Relativism cannot handle the fact that at least some people have been able to become indistinguishably native in two (or several) cultures and that they have found that some cross-cultural evaluations can be made even if back-and-forth translation of individual situations is not always possible. Relativism also cannot handle the fact that struggles between cultures and simple cultural evolution both imply that some objective assessment of cultures is being made. In practice, the functional descriptions typical of relativism describe societies which could seemingly work perfectly in theory, but they overlook the fact that old practices die out and new ones are introduced in response to challenges to the adequacy of current practices. Once again, an uncertain future forces some sort of evolutionary adaptation, and functional descriptions cannot give a coherent account of such change and its direction by simply examining "time slices." Although unbridled relativism is surely wrong, scientific objectivism seems in equal difficulties because of its inability to produce valid general laws for social science. It is possible that cultural understanding does depend on some notion of *verstehen*, that is, the understanding produced by absorbing a culture through living in it. This is what is true in relativism. At the same time, one may come to (objectively) understand several cultures and to make valid cross-cultural comparisons. This is what is true about scientific objectivism. However the *verstehen* process may be such that it cannot be forced and takes, let us say, a minimum of three or four years. The shortness of human life coupled with the variety of human cultures would then doom any given social theorist to a partial understanding of the range of human society. Objectivists would not want to accept this as a theoretical limitation because there is nothing comparable to it in physics, where information obtained in one time and place may be freely extrapolated to other times and places, in a meaningful even if not a truth-preserving fashion. Physical theory postulates that many classes of physical entities are the same in the sense that any two entities belonging to the class will have the same physical properties no matter where they are found. On the other hand, social theories do not usually postulate that all human beings are alike from the standpoint of social theory.[13] The primary exception is precisely the battery of assumptions lying behind methodological individualism in conjunction with situational logic. In any event, there is not the data available to support such a postulation as there is in physical theory. Popper's attack on relativism leaves the possibility of a theoretically limited objectivism as described above entirely open—even if it clashes with his own assumption of methodological individualism and situational logic.

Popper has produced a list of sociological laws which he contends illustrate the essential similarity of physical and social science laws.[14] These laws are all too vague or nearly tautologous to provide interesting explanations and predictions about situations even where boundary conditions can be imagined filled in. Consider this one:

> You cannot, in an industrial society, organize consumers' pressure groups as effectively as you can organize certain producers' pressure groups.[15]

Of course consumers have fewer common interests and are harder to organize, but how does this correspond to a physical law? Are there counterexamples? What about cases like the disappearance of the Corvair in the United States automobile industry after Ralph Nader's sustained attack on automobile safety, a disappearance presumably not desired by the manufacturer?[16] We could avoid this as a counterexample by arguing that the United States is not a relevant industrial society, that Nader did not organize a consumer group, that he or his group had no real effect, or that even if he or his group had an effect it was outweighed by effects caused by some producer's group. All of these moves seem implausible and ad hoc and are likely to produce trouble elsewhere in any total effort to save Popper's extended budget of sociological laws. It seems that the cited law amounts to no more than the vague tendencies deplored in a historicist context. One more example:

> You cannot make a revolution without causing a reaction.[17]

It is hard to interpret this as empirically significant for any explanatory context. Since no specification of connection between *kind* of revolution and (more importantly) *kind* of reaction is stated, the putative "law" seems of no real value. Popper's examples of social science laws hardly seem to offer a convincing *illustration* of methodological unity between the physical and the social sciences.

Summarizing Popper's position on the methodology of the social sciences, it is easy to see that he has extended his general conception of scientific methodology to social theories. In most cases, large-scale social theories turn out not to be falsifiable and are hence not scientific. Science in social theory is reduced to the use of scientific (falsifiable) theories in "piecemeal" planning. This work of Popper's was largely produced early in his career. It is part of this work that methodological individualism is an important aspect of social theory, but Popper has by now caused severe difficulties for his social theory by introducing the concept of world 3. World 3 structures are objective structures not under the control of human beings, much as societies and social structures (institutions) are in historical theories. In offering arguments against various historicist positions, Popper has neither refuted historicism nor established the correctness of methodological individualism and situational logic. The future will undoubtedly provide social theories relying on an indeterministic theory of societies based on a typology of social structures and an accompanying psychology that will be methodologically somewhere between the historicism that Popper has attacked and the stark consequences of Popper's assimilation of the physical and social sciences.

II The Open Society

Popper's attitude about social change is based on what he openly recognizes to be a preference for reason as opposed to violence. This preference is *technically irrational* because one cannot prove that violence is wrong. At times Popper suggests that his preference can be partly justified by the fact that violence causes more pain to people and avoidance of pain is consequently desirable. This suggestion needs considerable further discussion in that, if the goals of a revolution can be met, a revolutionary may plausibly argue that less pain will be caused *overall* (including future generations) by a successful revolution than by moderation in changing a social structure. If the social structure dominates or causes pain to members of some other social structures and a revolution would relax this situation, less pain might result from the revolution if we consider all of the social structures involved. A revolutionary is not committed to the view foisted on him (or her), by Popper, namely, that pain and violence are desirable but perhaps only to an argument that they are necessary in certain circumstances. Any argument from pain to prescription of an action would have to be made contextual and would depend on particular circumstances. There seems to be no argument from pain to a general conclusion that violence should always be avoided.

The preference for reason over violence brings us to what appears to be a contradiction: while Popper's theory of scientific growth urges a series of intellectual revolutions, his theory of social growth advocates piecemeal moderate social engineering and planning.[18] How are these views to be reconciled? For one thing, this juxtaposition of views revives the observation that the evolutionary metaphor runs deep in Popperian epistemology, but it indicates a facet of this metaphor that has not so far appeared in our discussion. Popper's evolutionary metaphor must have many of the features of the neo-Darwinian interpretation of evolutionary theory which views large-scale changes as being the result of the accumulation of many small mutations and adaptations over a long period of time. There is a general problem for evolutionary theory of explaining, not small genotypic and phenotypic variations, but the origins of vast differences such as those exhibited by the various phyla. The orthodox view is that these changes occurred as the result of many small changes accumulating over time. The minority view is that "hopeful monsters" have occasionally appeared which have represented sudden large breaks in the development of plant and animal life. Popper must clearly favor the majority view. In physical theorizing, *revolutionary* advances in theories urged by Popper should be seen in a perspective in which rhetoric has colored his statement in order to make sufficient impact. *New* theoretical conjectures are sought, but ones which are intelligible given the state of physical theory. We have seen reasons of another kind earlier for supposing that Popperian boldness must be tempered by the existing standards in a field. A major problem for the minority interpretation of evolutionary theory is that it is hard to see how "hopeful monsters" can backcross with older forms in order to have offspring, and the joint probability of simultaneous "hopeful monster" mates being produced by mutation seems negligible. The argument for the majority interpretation is simply that too great a change in an organism is likely to be lethal or to render the organism incapable of reproduction. A similar point is urged by Popper with respect to societies. Living societies have a viable structure as given by the fact of their history and present existence. Improvement in current social structure can obviously be undertaken by trying small changes from which the society can recover if they have an adverse effect. A revolutionary change could easily prove so destructive that the chance of recovering might be eliminated. An argument for the rationality of piecemeal social engineering can be abstracted in this way from evolutionary theory, and some such argument seems to underlie Popper's dicta about conservative social experimentation.

Why do we search for lethal circumstances for scientific theories according to the falsifiability criterion but not search for them in social structure? Here we must remember the Popperian notion of acceptance. The acceptance of theories as most highly corroborated may have very little impact on practical affairs in typical cases because of the filtering impact of common-sense theories. For example, the development of molecular biology has had very little impact on farming because the rules followed by farmers are too robust to be easily changed in the event of theoretical revolutions in biological theory. The relative isolation of theoretical knowledge examined in world 3 structures means that new theories can be adopted freely and tested severely with the expectation that their early falsification will not destroy the scientists who accepted the theory or the

society in which they live. An institutional analysis of the relative isolation of theoretical scientific knowledge from practical concerns is required to explain how a form of social conservatism can be held consistently with a form of theoretical radicalism. It should be obvious from this
sketch that such an analysis is possible and can explain how the Popperian
paradox involving physical and social theories can be resolved. This analysis remains rather implicit in Popper's writings, but it must seemingly
be invoked to find consistency in his social methodology.

Popper describes liberal democracy as the best form of social structure,
and we need to examine the discussion on which this opinion is based. A
society (in general) could be viewed as a problem-solving organization, and
Popper chooses this basic orientation to all societies. General remarks
about problem solving in the sciences then become relevant to a discussion of problem solving in society. Forms of authoritarianism must be
rejected because in society, as in science, the best conjectures may come
from anywhere and free discussion is required to sift the total range of
conjectures. A society with maximum adaptability must therefore have
free communication among all of its members. Some form of democracy
therefore seems forced on us by theory in order to satisfy the desire to have
a society respond with maximal adaptability (not maximal speed) to problem situations. Popper sees the community of scientists in any area as
engaging ideally in the free discussion characteristic of a liberal democracy, and he transfers this normative structure to his conception of a good
society. It is clear that Popper could be criticized for his view of the
scientific community as a liberal democracy, as by employing Kuhnian
ideas about its structure, but we will not linger over this approach to
criticism. Popper's normative picture of an Open Society might be valuable even if he were to be found wrong in his descriptive remarks about the
scientific community.

Even if Popper's view of the relatively open nature of the society of
physicists is correct, there are considerable problems with transferring
that structure to the theory of large social bodies. As has been mentioned
elsewhere, the sheer size of a modern state in many cases prevents an easy
dispersal of relevant information. A given person has too many interests
and concerns to perhaps be able to spend sufficient time to reach a rational
decision on many issues, and in a situation where majority will prevails, a
majority of people must be sold on a given idea before it can be adopted.
The sheer size of a society may mean that it can easily absorb an idea for
change, and that a local and small-scale experiment, no matter how positive in consequences, will be lost in the total societal picture.[19] By contrast, major physicists know one another and can have a useful preliminary assessment of the likely importance of each other's work. In a large
society, drastic revolutionary change may be required to effect a change in

direction as a result of the inertia of the society and the difficulty in sharing and assessing ideas between total strangers. Nothing in Popper's methodology concerning the physical sciences prevents an extension to a social theory in which a knowledgeable and benevolent authority, alert to possible positions and arguments producing actions beneficial to the society, applies scientific information to improve the society governed by piecemeal social planning. The authoritarianism implicit in this version of what might be considered a socialist theory is repugnant to Popper, and questions about the selection and assessment of the authority may be difficult, but Popper's conception of a liberal democracy is not demonstrably superior, because it has not been shown that criticism can be sustained at the right level in a large and heterogeneous society. Important social improvements may fail to be established because they cannot be explained in such a fashion that, for example, sufficient voters will accept them as having important long-range social benefits by comparison to, and overriding, short-term personal advantages. We have reached a familiar and pressing knot in social ideology.

Popper has characterized liberal democratic theory in a series of theses, among which the following are especially important.[20] The first thesis regards the state as a necessary evil which should be no stronger than required to maintain democratic structure. Socialism differs primarily in Popper's view in extending state powers beyond this minimum. In practice, socialist and democratic theorists often differ, not in point of theoretical principle, but in what in fact constitutes maintenance of equal rights for individuals in a society and in whether the state institutions or private institutions should resolve such questions. Popper holds that state institutions may usefully prevent misery and suffering but that the advance of happiness is best served by private institutions.[21] The implied distinction between the alleviation of suffering and the increase of happiness is left unexplained. Returning to the positive characterization of liberal democracy, liberal democrats prefer that the state government be evaluated and changed without violence and that existing institutions be changed by modification rather than outright replacement. They also see the traditions of an existing society as providing the framework within which social equity is to be assessed, small piecemeal changes being undertaken if intuitions about equity sufficiently contradict tradition. Liberalism supposes that free and open discussion can gradually ferret out bias and find the objective assessments necessary as a secure base for social action.

The principles characterizing liberal democracy are vague enough that it is not clear how they are related to actual social structures. Popper has unequivocally stated that in the 1960s the major countries roughly in alliance with the United States as well as the United States constituted the best expressions of what he means by liberal democracy in the history of mankind (at least on this planet) and that these societies are presently in need mostly of minor institutional adjustment.[22] An evaluation of this assessment on Popper's part is therefore a potential way to criticize his liberal democratic theory. It would be possible, for example, to accept the theory of liberal democracy as correct but argue that it is so poorly instanced in any known modern social structure that all such social structures are at least one revolution away from achieving expression of the theory. Some Marxists would argue in this fashion, and it is clear that this defense of the theory, while rejecting any current embodiment of it, is a retreat into metaphysics. The problem arises partly because of an insufficient discussion in Popper as to what is to constitute a majority decision in a society that should be translated into social action. Popper is well aware that majority decisions can be anonymous and irresponsible forms of authoritarianism, but no *test* for such abuses has been supplied in Popperian theory. If one sees the United States as dominated by some form of military-industrial complex that overrides what would be the free expression of citizens' preferences, then Popper's assessment of current institutions will seem basically wrong even on his own theory.

Is liberal democracy an attractive normative ideal for a society of peers who are capable of mutual communication, as in scientific societies? One may hold that it is but argue that this situation is not met or cannot be met in practice for large societies, so that Popper's liberal democracy is hopelessly normative, offering little or no guidance for actual political and social practice. To take a Popperian example, to what extent are the citizens of the United States a group of peers who can achieve mutual free discussion? The size of the society alone probably precludes the kind of reasonable free discussion required in the theory of liberal democracy. Further, if Marxists are right, an open agreement freely arrived at after discussion (without even worrying about time consumed in the discussion) could be totally disastrous for the society because the nature of the class distinctions in a country like the United States precludes an objective assessment on the part of the individuals of what is in their own best interest or mutual interest. Economic exploitation may have simply induced a false consciousness as to what the situation is on the part of those who are in it. A Marxist could agree that there are many relative freedoms in the United States but hold that relevant economic freedom is more narrowly circumscribed and economic exploitation developed more fully in the United States than it has been or could be at other times and places. One could extrapolate from Hiroshima, Vietnam, various manifestations of racism, sexism, and so forth, a powerful assessment that the United States is not in any satisfactory objective sense a good society or a society that can be made good by piecemeal changes. To mention these arguments is not to endorse them, but they have been advanced so frequently that some rebuttal is demanded. Popper has not and, I think, cannot rebut this line of criticism simply by attacking general historicist doctrines which may be presupposed in typical expressions of this viewpoint.

The trouble with all attempts to fit the theory of liberal democracy or the concept of the Open Society to current social facts is that the theory is a metaphysical construct with no real empirical bite. We can imagine the society of a modern country like the United States as very much better or as very much worse. If one feels that it could be made *very* much better, one may hold that revolution is a reasonable means of achieving that better state in the near future. If one feels that the revolutionists' utopias could not be realized because the nature of man precludes the utopia persisting without corruption tending back toward the starting point, one will regard revolution as unreasonable and gradual change as a more desirable way of relieving misery. There seems to be no way to satisfactorily compare these rival intuitions on rational grounds. Our experience with large modern nations is simply too limited to permit reasonable extrapolation to possible cases. Nor will a comparative evaluation of the United States and other modern nations be of help. A Russian or Chinese apologist could admit greater contemporary tyranny and restriction of freedoms in his country but argue that it is a necessary condition on the path toward a new consciousness and a new human outlook in a better society. Differing conjectures here cannot receive significant corroboration from the facts when the facts seem so varied to people of diverse viewpoints, and the normative call to open discussion may be futile when leaders are in fact bent on annihilating one another.

This brings us to the seemingly deepest reason why the theory of liberal democracy, so eminently suitable for various groups of relatively small size, is not easily shown to be a suitable normative theory for larger social groups. Where there is unanimity of purpose and relative consensus on the merits of accomplishing that purpose, liberal democracy is an intuitively satisfactory form of decision making. As is well known in political theory, when consensus breaks down, democratic forms of decision making may either break down or result in intuitively unsound decisions with respect to individual preferences.[23] In large societies, various subgroups may well have divergent ends which need to be evaluated and perhaps ranked if the society is to make coherent decisions. Popper's normative theory can only suggest that these differences be resolved by sufficient debate. It seems almost too obvious to suggest that groups operating at cross-purposes may not be able to rationally resolve their disagreements by debate. Moral evaluations of conflicting aims may be important, and the notion of human suffering may be so diversely interpreted that no reasonable methodological decision about the reduction of suffering caused by a given policy can be reached. In these matters, psychologism, while not a sufficient explanation of human action, seems to be required to explain how people evaluate the success or failure of policies. If person A and person B both receive more goods as a result of a policy than they would have under the status quo, it might seem that since both A and B are better off (objectively) they should both rationally prefer the policy. But if, in the status quo, person A is relatively disadvantaged compared to B and, although both gain, B gains more than A, A finds himself *relatively* more disadvantaged under the policy than under the status quo. Therefore if A seeks equality with B, he may rationally prefer the status quo to the policy. This is a very simple situation which may involve groups of people or even total societies and not just single persons. Evaluation of alternative policies thus seems to involve some psychological data and theories constructed over it, contrary to the intent of Popper's methodological dicta for the social sciences.

Historically, liberal democratic theory has been linked to some form of utilitarianism, as in John Stuart Mill, and the fact that utilitarianism has never been able to solve problems about relative utility has been a problem for democratic theory.[24] Popper has not escaped, and he has not even indicated that he is aware of this problem and has a solution for it. Popper's theory can be plausible if and only if alleviation of human suffering is an objective common test of social policies. This means that some reasonable agreement can always in principle be reached on the relative alleviation of human suffering produced by two different social policies. Therefore, Popper's theory is potentially confronted with all of the problems of the comparative alleviation of suffering that can be gained by analogy to the problems of comparative utility in utilitarian theory. In sum, although Popper has presented an interesting budget of objections to historicist social theories on methodological grounds, he has not solved the positive problem of connecting his social theory to particular social problems and their successful resolution.

In these final chapters criticisms of Popper's views on the social and physical sciences have given rise to the observation that a further elaboration of Popperian views is in many cases a desideratum. I hope this will not be misconstrued. It is always possible to criticize a philosopher (lazily) by saying that his views seem to be garbled but that perhaps further elaboration of them will make sense of the garble. Popper's views are not garble. Requested elaboration of them is based on the fact that he has proposed clear, potentially exciting, and rather plausible views about methodology with bite for the total range of special sciences. Popper's systematic treatment of such a wide range of topics is a philosophical achievement par excellence. The hope for elaboration is that discussion and revision will bring us closer to sophisticated theories accommodating more and more of the available data. That this is a clear hope and that measurable progress has already been made are sufficient monument to the magnitude of the achievement.

NOTES

One

1. In the interests of brevity, Sir Karl Raimund Popper will be referred to simply as *Popper* throughout the text. Popper's importance may be measured partly by the number of important scientists who have cited an intellectual debt. See references to such acknowledgments by Sir Peter Medawar, Jacques Monod, Sir John Eccles, Sir Hermann Bondi, and others in chapter 1 of [M2]. Articles discussing Popper's impact on the authors by Medawar, Eccles and J. Bronowski are found in [S6].

2. [P15], p. 81.

3. For a collection of source papers and bibliography, see [A12].

4. [R10]. As is well known, the first edition of this work (1910) is the classic exposition of what is now regarded as Standard Logic. *Standard Logic* is used in the text to refer to systems of sentential logic and predicate logic descending from the *Principia* system.

5. The assumption that all mathematical truth could be developed this way was laid to rest with Gödel's Incompleteness Theorem. For a brief account, see [K8], esp. pp. 712–724.

6. The problems associated with various forms of phenomenalism are relevant. It was pretty well established in the history of rationalism and empiricism that private observations alone cannot guarantee the objectivity of science and that disagreement about measurement threatens the incontrovertibility of a physicalist basis for science. A positivistic refusal to study history seems retrospectively to have been fatal. Because positivists were interested only in science, their analysis never dealt with questions, imperatives, or any sentences

181

other than putative declarative sentences. The legacy of this neglect must be passed over here.

7. This is an adaptation of a formulation due to Carl G. Hempel. See [S4], p. 133.

8. We will accept the convention of the literature that this is of the form of a scientific law because it is empirically significant and is not true because a crow is partly defined as a black bird. Popper draws a distinction between numerical (accidental) and universal generality that is similar to such distinctions drawn elsewhere. See [P27], [S18], and [S19] for a discussion of details. We will assume that our candidate generalizations are always universal. Also, no sharp distinction is intended in this book between laws, theories, hypotheses, etc., and we will treat them as species of universal generalizations of various theoretical importance in what follows. No important point will hinge on the exact manner in which these varieties of generalization might be separated. Context and syntax should remind the reader that all of these kinds of generalizations are typically under discussion. It would be too tiresome to repeat this in each individual case.

9. [P13], p. 37. Popper seems to have been the first to formally raise this objection against the positivist program.

10. See the survey and discussion in [S4].

11. Nonlogicians may find this obscure, but the explanation will be given in detail in any sound elementary logic text. "Some A's are not B's" means that *one or more* A's are not B's, while "The A is not a B" or "Some A is not a B" suggests that there is a single A which is not a B. Clearly the former is the general denial of "All A's are B's." If there are *no* A's, modern logic treats "All A's are B's" as true for reasons of theoretical convenience that are not important from the standpoint of this discussion.

12. The terminology and the following discussion is heavily indebeted to Imre Lakatos' important papers, [L1] and [L2].

13. [P15], p. 258.

Two

1. [P15], chapter 5, "The Aim of Science," pp. 191–205. Not every quotation from Popper will support this simple statement. After this early paper (reprinted in [P15]), Popper sometimes speaks as though verisimilitude is the aim of science, but the purpose of verisimilitude is connected with having sound explanations, so that explanatory power (properly understood) can remain a valid summary of Popper's views. See the discussion of verisimilitude in chapter 5 below.

2. As we will discover below, this position is complicated by the necessity in Popper's late philosophy to draw a distinction between *falsified* and *rejected* theories. Strictly, scientific explanations should not contain laws, theories, data, or whatever which have been *rejected* by scientists. Falsified but not rejected statements are sometimes used when nonfalsified alternatives are not well corroborated. Popper's discussion of the deductive model does not have the same connotations as the discussion does in some other philosophers. A *logically possible* counterexample to the deductive link in an explanation which is not scientifically plausible is sufficient to cause many logicians to

reject an explanation because the argument it offers is logically invalid. Scientists do not (in practice) apply this rigorous standard—but reject explanations only when a scientifically plausible counterexample is available. Popper tends to trust scientific intuition rather than formalism in these matters.

3. [P7], pp. 33–39. Popper's charges against astrology and psychoanalytic theory will be discussed in chapter 9 along with his more extensive examination of Marxism.

4. See [G3], p. 176.

5. This is Popper's early view. As we will see below, falsifiers now may include incompatible *theories*. Cf. [P11], pp. 18, 19.

6. [P13], pp. 100, 101. Basic statements may sound like the simple observation statements of positivism, but basic statements can, for example, be about *theoretical* individuals as simple observation statements cannot.

7. [P13], p. 109.

8. [P9], and Carnap's reply on pp. 877–881 of [S7].

9. See [P7], chap. 9, pp. 201–214. Popper holds that Standard (two-valued) Logic should be used for criticism of theories because it is the strongest critical tool; see [P15], pp. 304–307. Weaker logics, such as intuitionist and many-valued logics, may be used to exposit theories. When a theory can be developed within a weaker logic, the development constitutes an interesting technical achievement in Popper's view. Thus, although Popper usually uses Standard Logic as a tool of criticism, he is sympathetic to the development of alternative logical calculi.

10. See the comment on p. 92 of [L5].

11. [H5], p. 52.

12. [P11], p. 988.

13. See the discussion in [P1], p. 328.

14. [B6], [B7], [W3], and [W4] are relevant; see also [A10].

15. These forms of rationalism are discussed in [P17], vol. 2, pp. 228–240, where Popper accepts a version of critical rationalism on the basis of a moral argument. It is not clear whether Popper had considered Comprehensively Critical Rationalism at this point.

16. [A9]. Agassi's article is a brilliant examination of themes closely related to Popperian epistemology.

17. See [P11], pp. 32–35.

18. [P11], p. 984.

19. See remark by J. O. Wisdom on pp. 65–66 of [L5]. Wisdom's example, "There are continuous values for energy," is incompatible with quantum theory. Popper replies on p. 92 of [L5] that on pp. 86–87 of [P13] he says that a falsifying hypothesis is required for falsification; but the contextual implication of the passage in [P13] is that the falsifying hypothesis will be an observational regularity.

20. [K17]. Some rough familiarity with the views expressed here by Kuhn will be assumed, although Kuhn's views will be discussed in some detail below.

21. [B11], esp. p. 41.

22. See the remark by H. Feigl on p. 48 of [B21].

23. [P15], pp. 34–35.

24. [L1] and [L2].
25. See [H9] for a collection of relevant papers.
26. See [Z1] and comments in [F5], [M11], and [S3].
27. [Z1] and [L8], for example.

Three

1. Idealism in quantum theory is another matter. Bad philosophical arguments *are* involved in its defense, but a Popperian realistic interpretation involves some problems in interpreting various experimental results. See the discussion in chapter 8.
2. [P15], pp. 60–64.
3. [P15], pp. 39–44.
4. See discussion in chapter 9.
5. [Q1]. There is important discussion by Quine in [D2] in response to various papers on his views about indeterminacy.
6. See [L4], pp. 56, 57.
7. This is developed by Kuhn in items cited in the bibliography. Extensive discussion of the relationship between Kuhn and Popper is to be found in [L4].
8. See [W9].
9. See articles by Feyerabend cited in the bibliography.
10. See remarks by Kuhn in [K17].
11. See remarks by Kuhn in [S20], pp. 206, 246, 247. Kuhn mentions Bohm's quantum theory in this connection.
12. [S20], p. 473.
13. [L4], pp. 222–225.
14. [B10].
15. For example, [B12], pp. 3–22, discusses a similar kind of distinction.
16. [A3]. A more extensive discussion of these ideas is in preparation.

Four

1. [K10]. Most books on probability theory now present at least one axiomatic treatment of probability; see [L14] for an example. It should be observed that notation is at the discretion of the author. For example, the order of the argument places of conditional probabilities is reversed in some books from that in others.
2. Strictly speaking, this is *not* a requirement of the probability calculus, but the epistemological considerations relevant to applications of the calculus in confirmation theory have caused this assignment of 0 to laws to be widely accepted. Popper and Carnap agree on this. But see [H15].
3. The original editions of Popper's and Kolmogoroff's books appeared within a year of each other.
4. See [F7] for a useful survey of modern systems.
5. [P13], p. 319.
6. See [K13] and the literature cited therein.

7. [P13], p. 353 n., cites this as (35′). See the related discussion in [P13], p. 331.

8. [M18]. Earlier work by von Mises and others dating back to the twenties is explicitly discussed by Popper in [P13].

9. The following discussion of collectives is heavily indebted to [C10].

10. [C10]. An explicit proof is not given by Church in this article, but one based on mathematical induction is easily supplied.

11. [C10]. Related restrictions have been proposed by other authors, notably A. Wald. See [M4] and [M5].

12. This objection, along with other interesting criticisms of the notion of a collective, is to be found in [V5].

13. See [M4] for discussion.

14. For Popper's objection, see [P13], p. 171 n. Reichenbach's repair will be found on p. 147 of [R5].

15. Popper's footnote on p. 175 of [P13] suggests the claim, "If a sequence is absolutely free (in my sense) it is normal (in Reichenbach's)," which is correct. The remark in the footnote attributed to Reichenbach means that both freedom from aftereffect (in Reichenbach's sense) and invariance under regular divisions are required to define normal sequences.

16. See [P13], app. iv, pp. 292–295. An effective construction of an admissible number can also be found in [C9].

17. [L15] and [S8].

18. See [P11], p. 79.

19. [P22] and [P23].

20. For examples, see [H1], [L13], and [M9].

21. Popper's major attacks on subjectivism, such as [P21], do not deal with modern subjectivism or personalism as represented in such works as [D6] and [S2].

22. For an elementary account, see [A2], pp. 83–103.

23. Carnap seems to be the chief target. See also a related point in [A11] and the following discussion.

24. [P20], p. 27.

25. See [P22] for examples.

26. It's hard to see how this differs from current versions of subjectivistic or personalistic theories. Notice that a probability conjecture is now falsifiable even though it may not be sufficiently tested (because only one trial is observed) to falsify it (if it would be falsified) on the basis of our methodological rules.

27. [S13].

28. See [M3] and [F9].

29. As there are minor differences between Fisher and Wald, say, in the treatment of specific problems, it should be noted that Popper's methodological remarks are not specific enough to resolve detailed disputes about statistical inference. This isn't required by Popper's program since he is willing to accept the results of a resolution of objectivist disputes.

30. See criticisms in [A1]. A detailed extension of Popper's probability observations to a theory of probability with an attached notion of the falsifiability of probability statements may be found in [G5]. See criticisms in [R4] and [S16]. As Popper has not publicly approved this work, it would be tendentious to discuss

it here. It should be noted, however that to find a suitable notion of falsifiability Gillies is forced to *restrict* the scope of applications of his theory more than most objectivists would find satisfactory.

31. [H5], p. 50.
32. See [P13], pp. 33, 34.

Five

1. [P11], p. 119.
2. Tarski's contributions are explained by Popper in [P15], pp. 319–340. The notion of the logical content of a statement is closely related to the notion of a probability measure over a language. Probability measures over languages will be discussed at the start of chapter 6.
3. This depends on the notion of *content.* Probability and content are placed in an inverse relationship so that high a priori probability is the same as low a priori content. A tautology of probability 1 has content 0. Since it is well known that consistent probability and content measures can be assigned to languages, it is not necessary here to give details. See, however, [P15], pp. 333–335, and also [K5].
4. There is a slight problem about the set of logical truths and falsehoods in a language. They may be taken as conceptually removed from the contents, or included. Popper vacillates on this matter, but any consistent way of handling it does not affect the force of the criticisms of verisimilitude to be offered.
5. See [P15], pp. 52, 53. Given our earlier remarks, it is not clear that Newton's and Einstein's theories are competitors in the way that Popper suggests.
6. See [H7], [M15], and [T1].
7. This proof is essentially the same as that given in [T1].
8. This criticism is expressed, for example, in (W2). It seems to me a commonplace blanket criticism of Popper's methodology.
9. [P15], p. 13, and the discussion on pp. 18–21.
10. [P15], p. 20.
11. See [P11], p. 82, and p. 175, n. 243.
12. [P13], p. 400. $P(x,y)$ is the conditional probability of x given y.
13. An important general discussion can be found in [K5].
14. See [P13], app. *ix, pp. 387–419. There seems to be a typographic error in line -5 of [P13], p. 400, where "$P(x)$" should read "$P(\bar{x})$." Popper has apparently not published *proofs* that the desiderata are satisfied, but they may be constructed without too much difficulty. Except for desideratum (vii), simple examination of cases and substitution will suffice. Desideratum (vii) requires some elementary algebraic identities.
15. These sentences are from [G8].
16. See the discussion of "fine structure" of content and simplicity in [P13], pp. 373–386.
17. [P15], p. 20.
18. [P13], p. 418.
19. [B4], p. 15. See [B5] and [K3] for discussion.

20. The rule previously cited as given on p. 20 of [P15] does not appear to have been formulated at the time of Barker's book and the discussion of it in [B5] and [K3].
21. [S1], p. 26.
22. [P7], p. 218 n.
23. [L12] and [L13], esp. pp. 100–120.
24. Levi holds that Popper is forced to some such view. Salmon attributes the view to Popper without textual evidence. Levi and Salmon are wrong if I'm right that the technical discussion of corroboration has as its essential aim simply to show the coherence of Popper's methodological views.
25. [P15], p. 103.
26. This formula cannot be derived from the discussions in [P15] or [P7] of verisimilitude, since relative verisimilitude is not introduced in these technical contexts. It is rather a consequence of the remark at [P15], p. 103.
27. Popper seems originally to have regarded high corroboration as something that *should* have coercive effect on scientists' preferences and action. More recently, in [P15], he has softened this view considerably. See the interesting indirect evidence in [A7].
28. The history of both theories has been frequently recounted. See a discussion of Darwin's theory in [L10] and of relativity in [B15].
29. Another familiar example from scientific history. See [B16] for an informal discussion at the time. Since then, of course, the steady-state theory has encountered increasing difficulties. The point is simply that falsifying tests are not always easy to devise when one would like to have them.
30. Popper admits this in [P15], p. 186.
31. [H8] and [P29].

Six

1. There is a formal analogy between negation and set complementation, disjunction and set addition (union), and conjunction and set multiplication (intersection). Formulas about sets translate into formulas about sentences when notation is translated and vice versa, as in the classic isomorphism between certain Boolean algebras of sets and the propositional calculus. We may thus use such notations interchangeably. See [K13] for details.
2. See [H15]. There are some difficulties with quantification that are not relevant to this introductory discussion; see [K13] and [J6] for extended discussion. On Popper's view, the probability assigned to a general law is 0, but the law can be corroborated in spite of this. Carnap's intuitions are revealed in [C4], pp. 571–575.
3. See [C7]. What follows is largely exposition of major points in [C2] and [C3].
4. This result is the classic theorem of subjective probability theory. See [J4] for references and a careful philosophical discussion.
5. Carnap literally uses *regular* where others would use *strictly coherent*. For the results about coherence and strict coherence, see [S12], [L11], [K4], and [V3].
6. [C3], p. 15.
7. A treatment of the case for one dyadic predicate is promised in a later volume of the series of which [C7] is the first volume.

8. Some important information will appear in vol. 2 of the series of which [C7] is the first volume.

9. The major articles are collected in [P13], app. *ix, pp. 387–419. For a full discussion of these articles and the literature related to them, see [M10].

10. [P13], p. 391.

11. See [P13], pp. 389, 393. If $p(x,y) = p(x)$, it is not clear whether $\sim Co(x,y)$ holds. For simplicity of exposition, we take $\sim Co(x,y)$ to hold if $p(x,y) \leqslant p(x)$.

12. See [K6].

13. If we are sampling (with replacement) from a box of buttons some of which are amber and some of which are black, and if we repeatedly find amber buttons when we sample, the probability that the next button examined will be amber can become arbitrarily close to 1 if the number of examinations becomes high enough. The relevant mathematical formula to apply is Laplace's Rule of Succession, and an analogue of this rule in Carnap's system forms the basis of Popper's original note. See [P16].

14. [P14].

15. "Box$_i$" here stands for the *conjecture* that the offered box is Box$_i$.

16. [M13]; relevant discussion in [B20], [G6], [M1], [M12], [M16], and [R9].

17. [P6].

18. This point about induction is commonly accepted. Popper *and* Carnap attempt to avoid inductive *inference* as a result. For a completely different approach to systematic preference for propositions on evidence, see the notion of entrenchment in [G7].

19. [C5].

20. [C5], p. 253.

21. Deep problems are glossed over here. For example, one would want to be as sure as one could that the (shortest) interval selected was likely to contain the true value. For an extended discussion, see [H1].

22. I hope it need not require explanation that *acceptance* is to be given a Popperian reading.

23. See also [A4], pp. 144–145.

Seven

1. This point has been made with clarity and force by John Earman; see [E1] and [E2].

2 [P10], p. 124.

3. This fact about the so-called n-body problem is discussed in most elementary physics texts.

4. The literature on Turing machines is extensive. Two useful references are [M17] and [D4]. [D4] contains some interesting examples of Turing machine computation.

5. Has Alonzo Church ever made an error? See [M17], p. 108.

6. See [M17], pp. 146–152, and [D4], p. 70. The reader should note that some halting problems are , of course, solvable.

7. This follows either from the definition of a simple ordering or by an easy proof. See the discussion of orderings in [S21].

8. [R1]. Popper's views are developed most carefully in [P10] although [P15], chap. 6, pp. 206–255, is also relevant.

Eight

1. Earlier we called what we are calling here a *state vector* simply a state. The word vector emphasizes the definite numerical values associated with properties in classical physics. Obviously, we could use vectors in which intervals replaced definite numbers provided that we revised the accompanying theory. A word of historical caution is necessary. Not all classical theories are in fact developed using the notion of a state vector. For purposes of conceptual methodological simplicity, however, they could be developed in such a manner compatibly with what is being said here.
2. There is an extensive literature on hidden-variable theories. A basic discussion accessible to nonspecialists may be found in [B13]. See also articles by Bohm and Vigier in [K11]. More recent discussion of philosophical issues surrounding hidden-variable interpretations and bibliography will be found in [B9].
3. *Almost* interchangeable at worst. For the complexities, see the discussion by N. R. Hanson and E. L. Hill on pp. 401–428 of [F1].
4. The original proof is given in [N2]. More recent treatments and discussion can be found in [J3], [B14], [K9], and [G2]. Quite recent philosophical discussion of issues can be found also in [B9] and [C12], and a discussion of Popper's position in [S5].
5. The screen must be in a *fixed position* with respect to the sheet containing the slit or slits in order to obtain the interference effect.
6. For Hanson's views, see [H3] and [H4]; for Feyerabend's views, [F2].
7. Most scientists and philosophers who have accepted some version of the majority (Copenhagen) interpretation of QT have felt comfortable with the subjectivistic interpretation of probability associated with the physical theory. Popper, of course, cannot accept the physical interpretation because of the subjectivistic interpretation of probability that it seems to entail. See [P24], esp. pp. 7, 17, 18. This article is Popper's major statement on QT. For related views by another physicist, see [L6] and [L7].
8. For detailed criticism, see [F2] and [F4].
9. [F2] is especially important. See also [H14], esp. pp. 147–152.
10. For one important example, see [G11]. A book by Popper on physics is apparently in press, and an important unpublished manuscript on the theory of relativity may appear in this publication. See [M2], p. 108.

Nine

1. We find in Popper extensive discussion of the physical sciences (QT in particular) and of political theory but little discussion of other sciences which might have indicated some sort of methodological gradualism. There have been attempts to apply Popperian conceptions of methodology to various sciences by

persons other than Popper. For a notable example, see [J1]. For an interesting attempt to show that psychoanalytic theory is not scientific from a completely different perspective, see [C16].

2. Like Popper, I prefer to live in an area he identifies as that whose political system is a liberal democracy. The problem of the chapter is to discuss theory and theoretical justification for various positions, not to determine how we should feel about various instantiations of the theories. It is perhaps not a terminable debate to ask about the relative advantages of living under different systems, since such debates turn to predictions about the future course of events that are difficult to assess. Except for some remarks in the latter part of the chapter, Marxism and socialism are taken as *theories* of political (and economic) structure which are not necessarily distinct in particular forms. Marx himself is subject to various interpretations and is treated lightly by Popper for his humanitarian feelings even where Popper is attacking the theory of Marxism. Marxists are loosely identified as a collection of theorists influenced by Marx but taking definite historicist positions. Popper's phrase "liberal democracy" may not seem to suggest a suitable theory for the forms of representative government he cites as embodiments of the theory, and the total terminology of his attacks and their possible targets could itself be the subject of a large treatise. I have restricted myself in this chapter to a discussion at the approximate level of generality of Popper's books on the topic.

3. Democratic theory is well known to be precarious because of the general impossibility of rational argument for a democratic decision-making process under a wide variety of circumstances where the parties concerned have sharply differing preferences. In this connection the Arrow Paradox is a staple of discussion. See the introductory discussion in [D1] and the recent overview in [P2].

4. The scientific origins of astrology are clearly presented in [P30].

5. As is well known, Freud thought that a physiological account of psychoanalytic phenomena might one day be found.

6. [P7], p. 342. It would hardly be fair to criticize Popper for not having sound opinions on everything, but there is an aspect of social engineering that he seems to have overlooked. A number of unfortunate experiences with urban renewal projects has brought to light the fact that people may react negatively to relocations which improve their physical environment enormously. The reasons are obviously diverse and still somewhat mysterious, but they are expressed in terms of a felt loss of identity or importance in the new circumstances. I see no reason why allowing for human feeling of this kind in handling social problems cannot be made consistent with Popperian methodology insofar as measurable tests of these feelings can be developed. Popperian methodology has an unfortunate tendency to rule out the reactions of such people as irrational and to concern itself primarily with normative, rational modes of behavior. By overlooking the possible validity of measurements of people's feelings of identity in various circumstances, Popper seems to have overlooked a potentially valuable area connected with social engineering.

7. There is an excellent discussion in [D7].

8. [W6]. Weber argues that modern economic structures and related motivations can in some cases be traced back to religious structures and motivations that

are not in turn reducible to economic factors. This would be an obvious counterexample to any form of economic reductionism. Extensive discussion of this famous thesis is available, for example in [W14].

9. [C15], pp. 19, 20.
10. [P17], vol. 1, p. 126. Pagination varies with editions; this passage is excerpted from chap. 7, sec. 3.
11. This point is made succinctly and convincingly in [K12], pp. 42–65.
12. See [L8] for a useful discussion.
13. A discussion of the methodological relevance of this point will be found in [E3].
14. [P19], pp. 62, 63.
15. [P19], p. 62.
16. Folklore.
17. [P19], p. 62.
18. [P25], p. 255. This point is frequently made by Popper.
19. [G3], p. 172.
20. [P7], pp. 350–352.
21. [P7], p. 345.
22. [P7], p. 369.
23. See [D1] and [P2] for discussion.
24. Popper somewhat implausibly accuses John Stuart Mill of holism in [P7], pp. 21,22. He seems not to take seriously the historical links between utilitarianism and a defense of liberal democracy, partly because he assumes utilitarians wish usually to promote happiness while he seeks a position that advocates governmental reduction of misery only. For a full discussion of cross-personal utility evaluation, see [S10].

BIBLIOGRAPHY

[A1] Ackermann, Robert. "Inductive Simplicity," *Philosophy of Science* **28** (1961): 152–161.

[A2] Ackermann, Robert. *Nondeductive Inference.* London: Routledge, 1966.

[A3] Ackermann, Robert. *The Philosophy of Science.* New York: Pegasus (now Bobbs-Merrill), 1970.

[A4] Ackermann, Robert. "Some Problems of Inductive Logic," pp. 135–151 of [D3].

[A5] Agassi, J. "Corroboration vs. Induction," *The British Journal for the Philosophy of Science* **9** (1958): 311–317.

[A6] Agassi, J. "The Nature of Scientific Problems and Their Roots in Metaphysics," pp. 189–211 of [B21].

[A7] Agassi, J. "Popper on Learning from Experience." In Rescher, N., ed., American Philosophical Quarterly Monograph no. 3, pp. 162–170. *Studies in the Philosophy of Science.* Oxford: Blackwell's, 1969.

[A8] Agassi, J. "The Role of Corroboration in Popper's Methodology," *Australasian Journal of Philosophy* **39** (1961): 82–91.

[A9] Agassi, J. "Sensationalism," *Mind* **75** (1966): 1–24.

[A10] Agassi, J.; Jarvie, I. C.; and Settle, T. "The Grounds of Reason," *Philosophy* **44** (1971): 43–49.

[A11] Ayer, A. J. "The Conception of Probability as a Logical Relation," pp. 12–17 of [K11].

[A12] Ayer, A. J., ed. *Logical Positivism.* Glencoe: The Free Press, 1959.

[B1] Bar-Hillel, Y. "Comments on 'Degree of Confirmation' by Professor K. R. Popper," *The British Journal for the Philosophy of Science* **6** (1955): 155–157.

[B2]   Bar-Hillel, Y. "Further Comments on Probability and Confirmation: A Rejoinder to Professor Popper," *The British Journal for the Philosophy of Science* **7** (1956): 245–248.

[B3]   Bar-Hillel, Y. "On an Alleged Contradiction in Carnap's Theory of Inductive Logic," *Mind* **73** (1964): 265–267.

[B4]   Barker, S. F. *Induction and Hypothesis.* Ithaca: Cornell University Press, 1957.

[B5]   Bartley, W. W., III. "A Note on Barker's Discussion of Popper's Theory of Corroboration," *Philosophical Studies* **12** (1961): 5–10.

[B6]   Bartley, W. W., III. "Rationality versus the Theory of Rationality," pp. 3–31 of [B21].

[B7]   Bartley, W. W., III. *The Retreat to Commitment.* New York: Knopf, 1962.

[B8]   Bartley, W. W., III. "Theories of Demarcation between Science and Metaphysics," pp. 40–64 of [L5]. Discussion on pp. 64–119 by J. O. Wisdom, J. Gledymin, A. E. Musgrave, K. R. Popper, and a reply by Bartley.

[B9]   Bastin, Ted. *Quantum Theory and Beyond.* Cambridge: The University Press, 1971.

[B10]   Berlin, Brent, and Kay, P. *Basic Color Terms.* Berkeley: University of California Press, 1969.

[B11]   Bernays, Paul. "Reflections on Karl Popper's Epistemology," pp. 32–44 of [B21].

[B12]   Bidney, David. *Theoretical Anthropology.* New York: Columbia University Press, 1953.

[B13]   Bohm, David. *Causality and Chance in Modern Physics.* New York: Harper and Row, 1957.

[B14]   Bohm, David, and Bub, J. "A Refutation of the Proof by Jauch and Piron That Hidden Variables Can Be Excluded in Quantum Mechanics," *Reviews of Modern Physics* **38** (1966): 470–475.

[B15]   Bondi, H. *Assumption and Myth in Physical Theory.* Cambridge: The University Press, 1967.

[B16]   Bondi, H.; Bonner, W. B.; Lyttleton, R. A.; and Whitrow, G. J. *Rival Theories of Cosmology.* London: Oxford, 1960.

[B17]   Bonnor, W. B.; Bondi, H.; Lyttleton, R. A.; and Whitrow, G. J. See [B16].

[B18]   Bub, Jeffrey. Review of [B22], *Philosophy of Science* **35** (1968): 425–429.

[B19]   Bub, Jeffrey, and Bohm, D. See [B14].

[B20]   Bub, Jeffrey, and Radner, M. "Miller's Paradox of Information," *The British Journal for the Philosophy of Science* **19** (1968): 63–67.

[B21]   Bunge, Mario, ed. *The Critical Approach to Science and Philosophy.* Essays in Honor of Karl Popper. Glencoe: The Free Press, 1964.

[B22]   Bunge, Mario, ed. *Quantum Theory and Reality.* Berlin: Springer-Verlag, 1967.

[C1]   Campbell, Donald T. "Evolutionary Epistemology," pp. 413–463 of [S6].

[C2]   Carnap, Rudolph. "A Basic System of Inductive Logic, Part I," pp. 33–165 of [C7].

[C3]   Carnap, Rudolf. "Inductive Logic and Rational Decisions," pp. 5–31 of [C7].

[C4]   Carnap, Rudolf. *The Logical Foundations of Probability.* Chicago: University of Chicago Press, 1950.

[C5]   Carnap, Rudolf. "Probability and Content Measure," pp. 248–260 of [F6].

[C6]   Carnap, Rudolf. "Remarks on Popper's Note on Content and Degree of Confirmation," *The British Journal for the Philosophy of Science* 7 (1956): 243, 244.

[C7]   Carnap, Rudolf, and Jeffrey, R. C., eds. *Studies in Inductive Logic and Probability*, vol. 1. Berkeley: University of California Press, 1971.

[C8]   Chalmers, A. F. "On Learning from Our Mistakes," *The British Journal for the Philosophy of Science* 24 (1973): 164–173.

[C9]   Champernowne, D. G. "The Construction of Decimals Normal in the Scale of Ten," *Journal of the London Mathematical Society* 8 (1933): 254–260.

[C10] Church, Alonzo. "On the Concept of a Random Sequence," *Bulletin of the American Mathematical Society* 46 (1940): 130–135.

[C11] Colodny, Robert G., Ed. *Beyond the Edge of Certainty.* Englewood Cliffs: Prentice-Hall, 1965.

[C12] Colodny, Robert G., ed. *Paradigms and Paradoxes.* Pittsburgh: University of Pittsburgh Press, 1972.

[C13] Copeland, Arthur H. "Admissible Numbers in the Theory of Probability," *American Journal of Mathematics* 50 (1928): 535–552.

[C14] Copeland, Arthur H. "Point Set Theory Applied to the Random Selection of the Digits of an Admissible Number," *American Journal of Mathematics* 58 (1936): 181–192.

[C15] Cornforth, Maurice. *The Open Philosophy and the Open Society: A Reply to Dr. Karl Popper's Refutations of Marxism.* London: Lawrence and Wishart, 1968.

[C16] Cuddihy, John Murray. *The Ordeal of Civility.* New York: Basic Books, 1974.

[D1]   Dahl, Robert A. *A Preface to Democratic Theory.* Chicago: The University of Chicago Press, 1956.

[D2]   Davidson, Donald, and Hintikka, J., eds. *Words and Objections: Essays on the Work of W. V. Quine.* Dordrecht: Reidel, 1969.

[D3]   Davis, J. W.; Hockney, D. J.; and Wilson, W. K., eds. *Philosophical Logic.* Dordrecht: Reidel, 1969.

[D4]   Davis, Martin. *Computability and Unsolvability.* New York: McGraw-Hill, 1958.

[D5]   Dear, G. F. "Determinism in Classical Physics," *The British Journal for the Philosophy of Science* 11 (1960): 289–304.

[D6]   DeFinetti, Bruno. *Probability, Induction, and Statistics.* New York: Wiley, 1972.

[D7]   Donagan, Alan. "Popper's Examination of Historicism," pp. 905–924 of [S6].

[E1]   Earman, John. "Laplacian Determinism, or Is This Any Way to Run a Universe?," *The Journal of Philosophy* 68 (1971): 729–744.

[E2]   Earman, John. Continuation of [E1] (unpublished manuscript).

[E3]   Elsasser, Walter. *Atom and Organism*. Princeton: Princeton University Press, 1966.

[F1]   Feigl, H., and Maxwell, G., eds. *Current Issues in the Philosophy of Science*. New York: Holt, Rinehart, and Winston, 1961.

[F2]   Feyerabend, P. K. "On a Recent Critique of Complementarity," *Philosophy of Science*. **35** (1968): 309–331, and **36** (1969): 82–105.

[F3]   Feyerabend, P. K. "Problems of Empiricism," pp. 145–260 of [C11].

[F4]   Feyerabend, P. K. "Realism and Instrumentalism: Comments on the Logic of Factual Support," pp. 280–308 of [B21].

[F5]   Feyerabend, P. K. "Zahar on Einstein," *The British Journal for the Philosophy of Science* **25** (1974): 25–28.

[F6]   Feyerabend, P. K., and Maxwell G., eds. *Mind, Matter, and Method*. Minneapolis: University of Minnesota Press, 1966.

[F7]   Fine, Terrence L. *Theories of Probability*. New York: Academic Press, 1973.

[F8]   Fisher, R. A. *The Design of Experiments*, 7th ed. Edinburgh: Oliver and Boyd, 1960.

[F9]   Freiberger, W., and Grenander, U. *A Course in Computational Probability and Statistics*. New York: Springer-Verlag, 1971.

[F10]   Frisby, David. "The Popper-Adorno Controversy: The Methodological Dispute in German Sociology," *Philosophy of the Social Sciences* **2** (1972): 105–119.

[G1]   Gardiner, P. L. Review of [P19], *Philosophical Quarterly* **9** (1959): 172–180.

[G2]   Gardner, Michael. "Quantum-Theoretical Realism: Popper and Einstein vs. Kochen and Specker," *The British Journal for the Philosophy of Science* **23** (1972): 13–23.

[G3]   Gellner, Ernest. *Legitimation of Belief*. Cambridge: The University Press, 1974.

[G4]   Giedymin, Jerzy. "A Generalization of the Refutability Postulate," *Studia Logica* **10** (1960): 97–108.

[G5]   Gillies, D. A. *An Objective Theory of Probability*. London: Methuen, 1973.

[G6]   Good, I. J. "A Suggested Resolution of Miller's Paradox," *The British Journal for the Philosophy of Science* **21** (1970): 288, 289.

[G7]   Goodman, Nelson. *Fact, Fiction, and Forecast*, 2nd ed., rev. Indianapolis: Bobbs-Merrill, 1965.

[G8]   Goodman, Nelson. "Safety, Strength, Simplicity," *Philosophy of Science* **28** (1961): 150, 151.

[G9]   Grenander, U., and Freiberger, W. See [F9].

[G10]   Grünbaum, Adolf. "Can We Ascertain the Falsity of a Scientific Hypothesis?" In Grünbaum, A.; Bromberger, S.; and Nagel, E. *Observation and Theory in Science*, pp. 69–129. Baltimore: Johns Hopkins Press, 1971.

[G11]   Grünbaum, Adolf. "Popper's Views on the Arrow of Time," pp. 775–797 of [S6].

[H1]   Hacking, Ian. *Logic of Statistical Inference*. Cambridge: The University Press, 1965.

[H2] Hammerton, M. "Bayesian Statistics and Popper's Epistemology," *Mind* 77 (1968): 109–112.

[H3] Hanson, N. R. "The Copenhagen Interpretation of Quantum Theory," *American Journal of Physics* 27 (1959): 1–15.

[H4] Hanson, N. R. *Patterns of Discovery.* Cambridge: The University Press, 1958.

[H5] Harré, R. *The Philosophies of Science.* London: Oxford, 1972.

[H6] Harris, E. H. "Epicyclic Popperism," *The British Journal for the Philosophy of Science* 23 (1972): 207–245.

[H7] Harris, John. "Popper's Definition of Verisimilitude," *The British Journal for the Philosophy of Science* 25 (1974): 160–166.

[H8] Harsanyi, John C. "Popper's Improbability Criterion for the Choice of Scientific Hypotheses," *Philosophy* 35 (1960): 332–340.

[H9] Henkel, Ramon E., and Morrison, D. E., eds. *The Significance Test Controversy.* Chicago: Aldine, 1970.

[H10] Hintikka, J., and Davidson, D., eds. See [D2].

[H11] Hintikka, J., and Suppes, P., eds. *Aspects of Inductive Logic.* Amsterdam: North-Holland, 1966.

[H12] Hockney, D. J.; Davis, J. W.; and Wilson, W. K., eds. See [D3].

[H13] Hoering, Walter. "Indeterminism in Classical Physics," *The British Journal for the Philosophy of Science* 20 (1969): 247–255.

[H14] Hooker, Clifford A. "The Nature of Quantum Mechanical Reality," pp. 67–302 of [C12].

[H15] Howson, C. "Must the Logical Probability of Laws Be Zero?" *The British Journal for the Philosophy of Science* 24 (1973): 153–182.

[J1] Jarvie, I. C. *The Revolution in Anthropology.* Chicago: Regnery, 1967.

[J2] Jarvie, I. C.; Agassi, J.; and Settle, T. See [A10].

[J3] Jauch, J., and Piron, C. "Can Hidden Variables Be Excluded in Quantum Mechanics? *Helvetica Physica Acta* 36 (1967): 827–837.

[J4] Jeffrey, Richard C. *The Logic of Decision.* New York: McGraw-Hill, 1965.

[J5] Jeffrey, Richard C. "Popper on the Rule of Succession," *Mind* 73 (1964): 129.

[J6] Jeffrey, Richard C. "Probability Measure and Integrals," pp. 167–224 of [C7].

[J7] Jeffrey, Richard C., and Carnap, R., eds. See [C7].

[K1] Kaufmann, Walter A. "The Hegel Myth and Its Method," *Philosophical Review* 60 (1951): 459–486.

[K2] Kay, Paul, and Berlin, B. See [B10].

[K3] Keene, G. B. "Confirmation and Corroboration," *Mind* 70 (1961): 85–87.

[K4] Kemeny, John G. "Fair Bets and Inductive Probabilities," *Journal of Symbolic Logic* 20 (1955): 263–273.

[K5] Kemeny, John G. "A Logical Measure Function," *Journal of Symbolic Logic* 18 (1953): 289–308.

[K6] Kemeny, John G. Review of K. R. Popper's "Degree of Confirmation," *Journal of Symbolic Logic* 20 (1955): 304, 305.

[K7] Kino, A.; Myhill, J.; and Vesley, R. E., eds. *Intuitionism and Proof Theory.* Amsterdam: North-Holland, 1970.

[K8]   Kneale, William, and Kneale, Martha. *The Development of Logic.* Oxford: Clarendon Press, 1962.

[K9]   Kochen S., and Specker, E. "The Problem of Hidden Variables in Quantum Mechanics," *Journal of Mathematics and Mechanics* **17** (1967): 59–87.

[K10]   Kolmogoroff, A. N. *Foundations of the Theory of Probability,* 2nd ed. New York: Chelsea, 1956.

[K11]   Körner, S., ed. *Observation and Interpretation in the Philosophy of Physics.* New York: Dover Publications, 1957.

[K12]   Kovesi, Julius. *Moral Notions.* London: Routledge 1967.

[K13]   Krauss, Peter, and Scott, D. "Assigning Probabilities to Logical Formulas," pp. 219–264 of [H11].

[K14]   Kuhn, T. S. "Logic of Discovery or Psychology of Research?," pp. 798–819 of [S6], and pp. 1–24 of [L4].

[K15]   Kuhn, T. S. "Reflections on My Critics," pp. 231–278 of [L4].

[K16]   Kuhn, T. S. "Second Thoughts on Paradigms," pp. 459–482 of [S20].

[K17]   Kuhn, T. S. *The Structure of Scientific Revolutions,* 2nd ed., enlarged. Chicago: University of Chicago Press, 1970.

[L1]   Lakatos, Imre. "Falsification and the Methodology of Scientific Research Programs," pp. 91–196 of [L4].

[L2]   Lakatos, Imre. "Popper on Demarcation and Induction," pp. 241–273 of [S6].

[L3]   Lakatos, Imre. "Proofs and Refutations," *The British Journal for the Philosophy of Science* **14** (1963): 1–25, 120–139, 221–243, 296–342.

[L4]   Lakatos, Imre, and Musgrave, A., eds. *Criticism and the Growth of Knowledge.* Cambridge: The University Press, 1970.

[L5]   Lakatos, Imre, and Musgrave, A. eds. *Problems in the Philosophy of Science.* Amsterdam: North-Holland, 1968.

[L6]   Landé, Alfred. *From Dualism to Unity in Quantum Physics.* Cambridge: The University Press, 1960.

[L7]   Landé, Alfred. *New Foundations of Quantum Mechanics.* Cambridge: The University Press, 1965.

[L8]   Latsis, Spiro J. "Situational Determinism in Economics," *The British Journal for the Philosophy of Science* **23** (1972): 207–245.

[L9]   Leblanc, Hugues. "On So-called Degrees of Confirmation," *The British Journal for the Philosophy of Science* **10** (1959): 312–315.

[L10]   Lee, K. K. "Popper's Falsifiability and Darwin's Natural Selection," *Philosophy* **44** (1969): 291–302.

[L11]   Lehman, R. Sherman. "On Confirmation and Rational Betting," *Journal of Symbolic Logic* **20** (1955): 251–262.

[L12]   Levi, I. "Corroboration and Rules of Acceptance," *The British Journal for the Philosophy of Science* **13** (1963): 307–313.

[L13]   Levi, I. *Gambling with Truth.* New York: Knopf, 1967.

[L14]   Lindley, D. V. *Introduction to Probability and Statistics from a Bayesian Viewpoint,* vol. 1, *Probability.* Cambridge: The University Press, 1965.

[L15]   Loveland, Donald. "A New Interpretation of the von Mises Concept of a Random Sequence," *Zeitschrift für Mathematische Logik und Grundlagen der Mathematik* **12** (1966): 279–294.

[L16] Lyttleton, R. A.; Bondi, H.; Bonnor, W. B.; and Whitrow, G. J. See [B16].

[M1] Mackie, J. L. "Miller's So-called Paradox of Information," *The British Journal for the Philosophy of Science* **17** (1966): 144–147.

[M2] Magee, Bryan. *Popper.* Fontana Modern Masters Series, Frank Kermode, gen. ed. London: Fontana, 1973.

[M3] Martin-Löf, Per. "The Definition of Random Sequences," *Information and Control* **9** (1966): 602–619.

[M4] Martin-Löf, Per. "The Literature on von Mises' Kollektivs Revisited," *Theoria* **35** (1969): 12–37.

[M5] Martin-Löf, Per. "On the Notion of Randomness," pp. 73–78 of [K7].

[M6] Maxwell, G., and Feigl, H., eds. See [F1].

[M7] Maxwell, G., and Feyerabend, P. K., eds. See [F6].

[M8] Meehl, Paul. Three papers, "Psychological Determinism," "Nuisance Variables," and "Methodological Reflections," pp. 310–416 of [R3].

[M9] Mellor, D. H. *The Matter of Chance.* Cambridge: The University Press, 1971.

[M10] Michalos, Alex C. *The Popper-Carnap Controversy.* The Hague: Nijhoff, 1971.

[M11] Miller, Arthur I. "On Lorentz' Methodology," *The British Journal for the Philosophy of Science* **25** (1974): 29–45.

[M12] Miller, David. "On a So-called Paradox: A Reply to Professor J. L. Mackie," *The British Journal for the Philosophy of Science* **17** (1966): 147–149.

[M13] Miller, David. "On the Comparison of False Theories By Their Bases," *The British Journal for the Philosophy of Science* **25** (1974): 178–188.

[M14] Miller, David. "A Paradox of Information," *The British Journal for the Philosophy of Science* **17** (1966): 59–61.

[M15] Miller, David. "Popper's Qualitative Theory of Verisimilitude," *The British Journal for the Philosophy of Science* **25** (1974): 166–177.

[M16] Miller, David. "The Straight and Narrow Rule of Induction: A Reply to Dr. Bub and Mr. Radner," *The British Journal for the Philosophy of Science* **19** (1968): 145–157.

[M17] Minsky, Marvin. *Computation: Finite and Infinite Machines.* Englewood Cliffs: Prentice-Hall, 1967.

[M18] Mises, Richard von. *Probability, Statistics, and Truth.* Rev. English ed., based on 1951 definitive German ed. London: George Allen and Unwin, 1957.

[M19] Morrison, Denton E., and Henkel, R. E., eds. See [H9].

[M20] Musgrave, Alan. "Logical versus Historical Theories of Confirmation," *The British Journal for the Philosophy of Science* **25** (1974): 1–23.

[M21] Musgrave, Alan, and Lakatos, I., eds. See [L4].

[M22] Musgrave, Alan, and Lakatos, Imre, eds. See [L5].

[M23] Myhill, John; Kino, A.; and Vesley, R. E., eds. See [K7].

[N1] Nerlich, G. C., and Suchting, W. A. "Popper on Law and Natural Necessity," *The British Journal for the Philosophy of Science* **18** (1967): 233–235.

[N2] Neumann, John von. *Mathematische Grundlagen der Quantum Mechanik.*

Berlin: Springer, 1932. English trans. by H. P. Robertson, *Mathematical Foundations of Quantum Mechanics*. Princeton: Princeton University Press, 1951.

[N3]   Neyman, Jerzy. *First Course in Probability and Statistics*. New York: Holt, 1950.

[P1]   Passmore, J. A. "Popper's Account of Scientific Method," *Philosophy* **35** (1960): 326–331.

[P2]   Pattanaik, Prasanta. *Voting and Collective Choice*. Cambridge: The University Press, 1971.

[P3]   Piron, C., and Jauch, J. See [J3].

[P4]   Popper, Karl R. "Adequacy and Consistency: A Second Reply to Dr. Bar-Hillel," *The British Journal for the Philosophy of Science* **7** (1956): 249–256.

[P5]   Popper, Karl R. "Birkhoff and von Neumann's Interpretation of Quantum Mechanics," *Nature* **219** (1968): pp. 682–685.

[P6]   Popper, Karl R. "A Comment on Miller's New Paradox of Information," *The British Journal for the Philosophy of Science* **17** (1966): 61–69.

[P7]   Popper, Karl R. *Conjectures and Refutations: The Growth of Scientific Knowledge*. New York: Harper and Row, 1965.

[P8]   Popper, Karl R. " 'Content' and 'Degree of Confirmation': A Reply to Dr. Bar-Hillel," *The British Journal for the Philosophy of Science* **6** (1955): 157–163.

[P9]   Popper, Karl R. "The Demarcation between Science and Metaphysics," pp. 183–226 of [S7].

[P10] Popper, Karl R. "Indeterminism in Quantum Physics and in Classical Physics," *The British Journal for the Philosophy of Science* **1** (1950): 117–133, 173–195.

[P11] Popper, Karl R. "Intellectual Autobiography" (pp. 3–184) and "Replies to Critics" (pp. 961–1197) in [S6].

[P12] Popper, Karl R. "Die Logik der Sozialwissenschaften," *Kölner Zeitschrift für Soziologie und Sozialpsychologie* **14** (1962): 233–248.

[P13] Popper, Karl R. *The Logic of Scientific Discovery*. New York: Basic Books, 1959.

[P14] Popper, Karl R. "The Mysteries of Udolfo: A Reply to Professors Jeffrey and Bar-Hillel," *Mind* **76** (1967): 103–110.

[P15] Popper, Karl R. *Objective Knowledge*. Oxford: Clarendon Press, 1972.

[P16] Popper, Karl R. "On Carnap's Version of Laplace's Rule of Succession," *Mind* **71** (1962): 69–73.

[P17] Popper, Karl R. *The Open Society and Its Enemies*, 2 vols. New York: Harper and Row, 1962.

[P18] Popper, Karl R. "A Paradox of Zero Information," *The British Journal for the Philosophy of Science* **17** (1966): 141–143.

[P19] Popper, Karl R. *The Poverty of Historicism*, 3rd ed. New York: Harper and Row, 1961.

[P20] Popper, Karl R. "Probabilistic Independence and Corroboration by Empirical Tests," *The British Journal for the Philosophy of Science* **10** (1959): 315–318.

[P21] Popper, Karl R. "Probability Magic or Knowledge Out of Ignorance," *Dialectica* **11** (1957): 354–372.

[P22] Popper, Karl R. "The Propensity Interpretation of Probability," *The British Journal for the Philosophy of Science* **10** (1959): 25–42.

[P23] Popper, Karl R. "The Propensity Interpretation of the Calculus of Probability, and the Quantum Theory," pp. 65–70 of [K11].

[P24] Popper, Karl R. "Quantum Mechanics without 'The Observer,' " pp. 7–44 of [B22].

[P25] Popper, Karl R. "Reason or Revolution," *The European Journal of Sociology* **11** (1970): 252–262.

[P26] Popper, Karl R. "Reply to Professor Carnap," *The British Journal for the Philosophy of Science* **7** (1956): 244, 245.

[P27] Popper, Karl R. "A Revised Definition of Natural Necessity," *The British Journal for the Philosophy of Science* **18** (1967): 316–324.

[P28] Popper, Karl R. "A Theorem on Truth-Content," pp. 248–260 of [F6].

[P29] Post, H. R. "A Criticism of Popper's Theory of Simplicity," *The British Journal for the Philosophy of Science* **12** (1961): pp. 328–331.

[P30] Ptolemy. *Tetrabiblos.* Loeb Classical Library. Waddell, W. G., trans. Cambridge: Harvard University Press, 1948.

[Q1] Quine, W. V. O. "On the Reasons for Indeterminacy of Translation," *The Journal of Philosophy* **6** (1970): 178–183.

[R1] Radner, Michael. "Popper and Laplace," pp. 417–427 of [R3].

[R2] Radner, Michael, and Bub, J. See [B20].

[R3] Radner, Michael, and Winokur, S., eds. *Analyses of Theories and Methods of Physics and Psychology,* Minnesota Studies in the Philosophy of Science, vol. 4. Minneapolis: University of Minnesota Press, 1970.

[R4] Redhead, M. L. G. "On Neyman's Paradox and the Theory of Statistical Tests," *The British Journal for the Philosophy of Science* **25** (1974): 265–271.

[R5] Reichenbach, Hans. *The Theory of Probability,* 2nd ed. Berkeley: The University of California Press, 1949.

[R6] Rhees, Rush. *Without Answers.* New York: Schocken, 1969.

[R7] Robinson, G. S. "Popper's Verisimilitude," *Analysis* **31** (1971): 193–196.

[R8] Robinson, Richard. "Dr. Popper's Defense of Democracy," *Philosophical Review* **60** (1951): 487–507.

[R9] Rozeboom, William W. "New Mysteries for Old: The Transfiguration of Miller's Paradox," *The British Journal for the Philosophy of Science* **19** (1969): 345–358.

[R10] Russell, Bertrand, and Whitehead, A. N. *Principia Mathematica.* 2nd ed., vols. 1-3. Cambridge: The University Press, 1925–1927.

[R11] Ryle, Gilbert. Review of [P17], *Mind* **56** (1947): 167–172.

[S1] Salmon, Wesley. *The Foundations of Scientific Inference.* Pittsburgh: University of Pittsburgh Press, 1966.

[S2] Savage, Leonard J. *The Foundations of Statistics.* New York: Wiley, 1954.

[S3]   Schaffner, Kenneth F. "Einstein versus Lorentz: Research Programmes and the Logic of Theory Evaluation," *The British Journal for the Philosophy of Science* **25** (1974): 45–78.

[S4]   Scheffler, Israel. *The Anatomy of Inquiry.* New York: Knopf, 1963.

[S5]   Scheibe, Erhard. "Popper and Quantum Logic," *The British Journal for the Philosophy of Science* **25** (1974): 319–328.

[S6]   Schilpp, P. A., ed. *The Philosophy of Karl Popper.* Library of Living Philosophers, vol. 14. Lasalle: Open Court, 1974.

[S7]   Schilpp, P. A., ed. *The Philosophy of Rudolf Carnap.* Library of Living Philosophers, vol. 11. Lasalle: Open Court, 1963.

[S8]   Schnorr, C. P. "A Unified Approach to the Definition of Random Sequences," *Mathematical Systems Theory* **5** (1971): 246–258.

[S9]   Scott, Dana, and Krauss, P. "Assigning Probabilities to Logical Formulas," pp. 219–264 of [H11].

[S10]   Sen, Amartya K. *On Economic Inequality.* Oxford: Oxford University Press, 1973.

[S11]   Settle, Tom; Agassi, J.; and Jarvie, I. C. See [A10].

[S12]   Shimony, Abner. "Coherence and the Axioms of Confirmation," *Journal of Symbolic Logic* **20** (1955): 1–28.

[S13]   Sklar, Lawrence. "Is Probability a Dispositional Property?" *The Journal of Philosophy* **67** (1970): 355–366.

[S14]   Sneed, Joseph. Review of [B22], *Synthese* **18** (1968): 464–467.

[S15]   Specker, E., and Kochen, S. See [K9].

[S16]   Spielman, Stephen. "On the Infirmities of Gillies's Rule," *The British Journal for the Philosophy of Science* **25** (1974): 261–265.

[S17]   Stopes-Roe, Harry V. Review of papers by Achinstein, Bar-Hillel, Carnap, and Popper on confirmation, *Journal of Symbolic Logic* **33** (1968): 142–146.

[S18]   Suchting, W. A. "Popper's Revised Definition of Natural Necessity," *The British Journal for the Philosophy of Science* **20** (1969): 349–356.

[S19]   Suchting, W. A., and Nerlich, G. C. See [N1].

[S20]   Suppé, Frederick. *The Structure of Scientific Theories.* Urbana: University of Illinois Press, 1974.

[S21]   Suppes, Patrick. *Introduction to Logic.* Princeton: Van Nostrand, 1957.

[S22]   Suppes, Patrick. "Popper's Analysis of Probability in Quantum Mechanics," pp. 760–774 of [S6].

[S23]   Suppes, Patrick. "Probability Concepts in Quantum Mechanics," *Philosophy of Science* **28** (1961): 378–389.

[S24]   Suppes, Patrick, and Hintikka, J., eds. See [H11].

[S25]   Swinburne, R. G. "Popper's Account of Acceptability," *Australasian Journal of Philosophy* **49** (1971): 167–176.

[T1]   Tichý, Pavel. "On Popper's Definitions of Verisimilitude," *The British Journal for the Philosophy of Science* **25** (1974): 155–160.

[V1]   Vesley, R. E.; Kino, A.; and Myhill, J., eds. See [K7].

[V2]   Vetter, Herman. "Inductivism and Falsificationism Reconcilable," *Synthese* **23** (1971): 226–233.

[V3]   Vickers, John. "Remarks on Coherence and Subjective Probability," *Philosophy of Science* **32** (1965): 32–38.

[V4]   Vigier, J. P. "The Concept of Probability in the Frame of the Probabilistic and the Causal Interpretation of Quantum Mechanics," pp. 71–77 of [K11].

[V5]   Ville, J. *etude critique de la notion de collectif.* Paris: Gauthier-Villars, 1939.

[W1]   Wald, A. *Statistical Decision Functions.* New York: Wiley, 1950.

[W2]   Warnock, G. J. Review of [P13], *Mind* **69** (1960): 99–101.

[W3]   Watkins, J. W. N. "CCR: A Refutation," *Philosophy* **46** (1971): 56–61.

[W4]   Watkins, J. W. N. "Comprehensively Critical Rationalism," *Philosophy* **44** (1969): 57–62.

[W5]   Watkins, J. W. N. "When Are Statements Empirical?" *The British Journal for the Philosophy of Science* **10** (1959): 287–308.

[W6]   Weber, Max. *The Protestant Ethic and the Spirit of Capitalism.* New York: Scribner's, 1958.

[W7]   Whitehead, A. N., and Russell, B. See [R10].

[W8]   Whitrow, G. J.; Bondi, H.; Bonnor, W. B.; and Lyttleton, R. A. See [B16].

[W9]   Williams, L. Pearce. "Normal Science, Scientific Revolutions and the History of Science," pp. 49, 50 of [L4].

[W10]   Wilson, W. K.; Davis, J. W.; and Hockney, D. J., eds. See [D3].

[W11]   Winch, Peter. "Popper and Scientific Method in the Social Sciences," pp. 889–904 of [S6].

[W12]   Winokur, Stephen, and Radner, M., eds. See [R3].

[W13]   Wisdom, J. O. "Some Overlooked Aspects of Popper's Contributions to Philosophy, Logic, and Scientific Method," pp. 116–124 of [B21].

[W14]   Wrong, Dennis, ed. *Max Weber.* Englewood Cliffs: Prentice-Hall, 1970.

[Z1]   Zahar, Elie. "Why Did Einstein's Programme Supersede Lorentz's?" *The British Journal for the Philosophy of Science* **24** (1973): 95–123, 223–262.

AUTHOR INDEX

SUBJECT INDEX